GCSE COMMERCE

A.G. HALL
Formerly Principal of Redbridge Technical College, Ilford, Essex

Additional material by
Sylvia Bowes
Keswick School, Cumbria

Editing and research by
Peggy Downs
Redbridge Technical College

HEINEMANN EDUCATIONAL

Heinemann Educational Books Ltd
Halley Court, Jordan Hill, Oxford OX2 8EJ

OXFORD   LONDON   EDINBURGH
MELBOURNE   SYDNEY   AUCKLAND
SINGAPORE   MADRID   ATHENS
IBADAN   NAIROBI   GABORONE   HARARE
KINGSTON   PORTSMOUTH (NH)

ISBN 0 435 45551 6

© A. G. Hall 1989

First published 1989

British Library Cataloguing in Publication Data
Hall, A. G.
  GCSE Commerce
  1. Commerce
  I. Title
  380.1

  ISBN 0–435–45551–6

Designed and produced by Gecko Limited, Bicester, Oxon

Printed and bound in Great Britain by Butler and Tanner Ltd, Frome and London

Preface

GCSE Commerce has been written primarily to cover the syllabus prescribed for GCSE Commerce, but also includes much of the work necessary for an understanding of GCSE Business Studies. The book can also be used with students preparing for BTEC First Diploma in Business Studies and various RSA, PEI and CPVE courses. The text departs from the usual descriptive analysis of commercial institutions and accepts the concept that all the students involved should be able to demonstrate what they know, understand and can do.

The book is arranged in self-contained double-page spreads to allow flexibility in use. Each spread provides activities within an individual topic, suggestions for *things to do* and *questions* on the text. Additional study materials can be obtained from the addresses given under the heading: *Sources of information*. The whole text is designed to challenge the full ability range of students preparing for GCSE examinations.

For ease of reference, the term 'Britain' is generally used, although in most cases this can be taken as meaning Great Britain and Northern Ireland, or the United Kingdom.

I must thank my secretary Jean Argent for her unstinting assistance in the preparation of *GCSE Commerce*.

Note to teachers

In order to reduce the increasing volume of correspondence, it is suggested that where students are asked to write away for information, leaflets, etc., only one letter should be sent on behalf of each class or group. This will greatly ease administration costs and assist the companies and/or individuals concerned to meet the many requests for project materials. Teachers may wish to select the best letter from those written by each student as an exercise, and then countersign it on the group's behalf. Alternatively, a letter could be compiled as a group exercise in class, again being signed by the teacher before dispatch.

Acknowledgements

The author and publisher would like to thank the following for permission to reproduce copyright material/illustrations: Abbey National (Fig. 9.14); Access (Joint Credit Card Company) (Fig. 3.6); Advertising Standards Authority (Fig. 6.1); Allied-Lyons (logo); Amstrad (Fig. 17.16); Baltic Exchange (Fig. 11.5); Bank of England (Fig. 9.18); Banking Education Service (Fig. 9.16); Banking Information Service (Figs 10.2, 16.8, 16.9) and National Westminster Bank (Figs. 9.5–9.9); Barnaby's Picture Library (Figs 4.2, 4.3, 4.10, 17.1); BAT Industries (logo); Batchelor's Foods (Fig. 4.4c); Body Shop (Fig. 17.15); Booker Cash & Carry (Figs 3.4, 3.5); Beecham Bovril Brands (Fig. 18.13b); Britax-Excelsior (Fig. 6.3); British Coal (Figs 7.2, 7.3); British Petroleum (Figs 8.1, 8.2); British Rail (Figs 13.1, 13.2); British Railways Board (Figs 13.3, 18.11); British Telecom (Fig. 1.7); British Waterways Board Photo Library (Figs 13.10, 13.11); Brooke Bond Oxo (Fig. 18.13c); Builders Merchants Federation (logo); Cadbury Schweppes (logo); Camera Press Ltd (Fig. 18.10); Christie's (Fig. 2.4); City of Bristol Publication Office (Fig. 5.8); Commercial Union (logo); Commission for the European Communities (Figs 16.1, 16.2); Consumers' Association (Fig. 15.4); Co-operative Retail Society (Fig. 7.4); Courtaulds (logo); *Daily Telegraph* (Figs 9.18, 18.18); Department of Trade & Industry (Fig. 17.2); Eagle Star Insurance Company (Figs 18.6, 18.7); Essex County Council (Fig. 17.19); Evening Standard Company (Fig. 10.1); Mary Evans Picture Library (Fig. 13.13); *Financial Times* (Fig. 6.4); Freight Transport Association (Fig. 3.11); General Accident Fire & Life Assurance Corporation (Fig. 12.1); Girobank (Figs 5.10, 9.15); GUS Catalogue Order (Fig. 4.1); Jeremy Hartley/OXFAM (Fig. 17.3); HLCC (Fig. 15.1, logo); HM Treasury/COI (Fig. 17.18); ICI (logo); International Coffee Association (Fig. 3.2 left); Keystone Collection (Figs 1.1, 3.3, 4.9); Kimberley-Clark (Fig. 4.4a); Legal & General Assurance Society (Fig. 6.5); Lintas Advertising (Fig. 6.2); Lloyd's of London (Figs 12.3–12.5); London Docklands Development Corporation (Figs 17.8–17.14); London Metal Exchange (Fig. 11.4); London Transport (Fig. 13.5); MFI Furniture Centres (Fig. 4.9); Manpower Services Commission (Fig. 1.5); Marks & Spencer (Figs 4.6, 17.17); Mercury Communications (Figs 14.4, 14.5); Mersey Docks & Harbour Company (Fig. 13.12); Adrian Meredith Photography (Fig. 13.14); Miele Company (Fig. 15.2); Motor Agents Association (logo); National Gallery (Fig. 9.1); National Savings, Department of (Fig. 9.2); National Westminster Bank (Figs 5.5, 8.1, 8.2, 18.5); Nestle Company (Fig. 3.2 right); *Observer* (Fig. 1.3); Philips Components (Southampton) (Fig. 1.9); Post Office (Figs 14.1, 14.2); Procter & Gamble (Fig. 4.4b); RHM Foods (Fig. 18.13a); Radio, Electrical and Television Retailers' Association (logo); Rank Organisation (logo); Scottish Motor Trade Association (logo); Société Coopérative Agricole de Vinification (Fig. 7.5); Society of Master Shoe Repairers (logo); Society of Motor Manufacturers & Traders (logo); St Michael Financial Services (Fig. 4.5); The Stock Exchange (Figs 11.1–11.3); Storehouse (Fig. 5.11); Telefocus (Fig. 14.3); Tesco Stores (Fig. 4.9); A H Turner Finance (Fig. 10.7); United Dominions Trust (Fig. 10.6); Vehicle Builders & Repairers Association (logo).

Contents

Unit 1	**Goods and Services**	
1.1	The Interdependent World	6
1.2	Human Wants	8
1.3	Opportunity and Change	10
1.4	Technological Change	12
Unit 2	**Personal Finance**	
2.1	Wages and Salaries	14
2.2	Savings and Budgeting	16
2.3	Savings and Investment	18
2.4	Borrowing and Credit	20
Unit 3	**Distribution and Marketing**	
3.1	From Source to Consumption	22
3.2	Wholesale Outlets, Cash and Carry	24
3.3	Competition: Price and Non-Price	26
Unit 4	**Shops and Shopping**	
4.1	Itinerant Trading	28
4.2	Small-scale Retailing	30
4.3	Large-scale Retailing	32
4.4	Supermarkets, Hypermarkets and Discount Selling	34
4.5	Location of the Retail Trade	36
Unit 5	**Commercial Documents**	
5.1	Paper Transactions	38
5.2	Settling Debts	41
Unit 6	**Advertising**	
6.1	How Consumer Advertising Works	44
6.2	Brand Names and Image-Building	46
Unit 7	**Business Organisations**	
7.1	The Private Sector	48
7.2	The Public Sector	50
7.3	Co-operation and Co-ownership	52
7.4	Planned Economies and Market Economies	54
Unit 8	**Business Finance**	
8.1	Formation and Investment	56
8.2	Capital, Assets and Liabilities	58
8.3	Cash Flow, Stock, Profit and Turnover	60

Unit 9	**Money and Banking**	
9.1	Decisions about Spending and Saving	62
9.2	Banks and Bank Accounts	64
9.3	Other Banking Services	66
9.4	The Bankers' Clearing House	68
9.5	Building Societies and the Post Office	70
9.6	The Bank of England	72
Unit 10	**Credit**	
10.1	Merchant Bankers and the Money Markets	74
10.2	Finance Houses and Credit Agreements	77
Unit 11	**Share and Commodity Markets**	
11.1	Stocks and Shares	80
11.2	Commodity Markets and Chartering	82
Unit 12	**Insurance**	
12.1	Personal Risk	84
12.2	Business Insurance	87
12.3	Lloyd's of London	90
Unit 13	**Transport and Distribution**	
13.1	The Railway Network	92
13.2	Road Systems and Freight Ferries	95
13.3	Waterways, Shipping and Ports	98
13.4	Air Transport	102
Unit 14	**Communications**	
14.1	The Post Office	104
14.2	Telecommunications	107
Unit 15	**Consumer Protection**	
15.1	The Buying Public	110
15.2	Consumer Protection in Action	113
Unit 16	**International Trade**	
16.1	The European Community	116
16.2	Imports and Exports	118
16.3	The Balance of Trade	121
16.4	Documentation	123

Unit 17	**The Government and Economic Activity**	
17.1	'Great Britain Ltd'	126
17.2	National Policies	128
17.3	Enterprise Zones and Development Areas	130
17.4	Economic Intervention	134
17.5	Taxation and the Community Charge	136

Unit 18	**Assignments**	
18.1	Paying in at the Bank	138
18.2	Insuring Your Property	140
18.3	Buying a Motor Vehicle on Credit	142
18.4	How Will You Get to Work?	144
18.5	Doing Market Research	146
18.6	Using Graphics and Illustrations	148

Index 151

1 GOODS AND SERVICES

UNIT 1.1
The Interdependent World

The photograph of the Earth on this page was taken during one of the Apollo Moon landings (Fig. 1.1). From that distance the world looks a pretty insignificant place, but in 1988 some 5000 million people inhabited the Earth. All these people depend on the essentials, the basic things that the human race can extract or produce, such as food, clothing, shelter and water, before any consideration can be given to non-essentials, like motor cars, television sets, furniture, sports equipment and cosmetics.

Fig. 1.1 The Earth, home for 5,000 million people

The human race has been clever in adapting circumstances to meet its needs. Some nations have been more successful than others. The Western world – Western Europe, the United States of America, Canada – and Western-style countries like Japan and Australia enjoy a very high standard of living.

There are wide differences in income levels, even in Britain, but our life-style and standards offer far more comfort than those of the poor countries of Africa, Asia, Latin America and the Caribbean, whose economies provide few of the luxuries which we have come to regard as normal. But even the poorest nations are at least in the struggle for affluence, whereas a few groups still live as hunter-gatherers where the daily routine is centred around maintaining the bare essentials of existence. If the meagre crop fails, or the domestic animals contract disease, then starvation becomes a reality.

Living like Robinson Crusoe

You are stranded on an island, completely alone. You have the clothes you stand up in and your bare hands to work with. Food, clothing, warmth and shelter must be made from the things you have about you – fish from the sea, fruit from the trees, a hut from driftwood and palm leaves.

Eventually, you might learn to build a hut, to make fishing lines and bone hooks, and to make rough tools to cut and chop. All your time would be taken up just by *survival*; there would be little rest, and without the necessary skills the results you achieved would often be inadequate.

The specialist

Few of us ever have to undertake such a variety of activities. We live in a world of *specialists*, people who become very skilled in the occupation of their choice. Although to save money I might decide to paint my own house, I never do it quite as well as a skilled painter and decorator. Instead of painting my house myself, I write books, something I do reasonably well; then I use my earnings to pay a professional to do my decorating. By concentrating on those activities we both do well we achieve a pleasing result, the job is done more quickly, and we have time to enjoy some leisure.

Fig. 1.2 From Robinson Crusoe to computer

You may become a bank clerk, a shorthand-typist, a police officer or a civil servant. In none of these occupations will you build houses, grow food or make clothes; but in becoming a specialist you expect someone else to specialise in farming, building or clothes-making. As a result of specialisation, more and better-quality work is done than would have been achieved if you had undertaken all these tasks yourself. By raising the *level of economic activity,* living standards are improved, and everyone benefits as a result. These benefits take the form of a wider choice of goods to buy at a cheaper price and in greater quantities. The amount of time we spend at work is reduced, and we can take part in all kinds of leisure activities.

Interdependence

Economic activity (i.e. working for a living) has usually been organised on the basis of *developed ability*, people doing what they are best at. Although most village people in the Middle Ages were almost self-sufficient, there was always work for a skilled blacksmith or thatcher; in fact, many English family names come from a connection with a particular occupation.

Since the Industrial Revolution the use of power machinery has added mechanical skill to human ability. The use of machinery has done two things. It has reduced the demand for craft workers in some fields, while increasing the need for special ability in new occupations. For example, the motor car, by reducing our reliance on horse power, made the blacksmith almost redundant, but has produced a much greater demand for the special skills of the motor mechanic. New industries have emerged, such as television and aircraft manufacture, both of which demand a high level of skill in working with precision machinery. These industries are mostly located in towns, which rely on the greatly improved techniques of our farming industry. Town and country depend upon each other: the town needs the food produced by the farmer, and the farmer needs the skill of the agricultural engineer in the design of farming equipment.

International co-operation

However, any farmer in Britain who relied on growing peaches for a living would quickly go out of business. The British climate is not suited to this activity. Peaches grow naturally in warmer countries, and using such natural advantages these areas can produce better peaches at a much lower price.

Britian has few natural resources in the form of raw materials and imports tin from Bolivia, copper from Zambia and rubber from Malaysia. These countries and others import products like cars, refrigerators and television sets from those countries like Britain which specialise in turning *raw materials* into *finished goods.*

Individually, and as a nation, we specialise in providing goods and services. We know that the money we earn can be spent on similar activities carried on by every other nation in the world. Without this interdependence we would have to revert to our 'desert island' existence, and our lives would be much poorer as a result.

●THINGS TO DO

1 Working in pairs and using the reference section of your library, find out about the origins of the following surnames, all of which are associated with occupations. Make a table of your own like the one given, and write in your answers.

Surname	Origin and occupation
Sadler	
Pargeter	
Cooper	
Fletcher	
Skinner	
Taylor	
Forester	
Chandler	
Cutler	
Barber	
Weaver	
Fowler	
Reeve	
Tanner	
Miller	
Carpenter	
Tyler	
Wright	
Pardoner	
Farrier	
Abbot	

2 From Fig. 1.3 answer the following: (a) Most dictionaries give two definitions of a *billion:* (i) a million million, and (ii) a thousand million. Which definition is being used for this graph? (b) In what year did the world population reach 5 billion? (c) What was the world population in 1650, 1800 and 1950? (d) Why did the world population increase so fast after 1950?

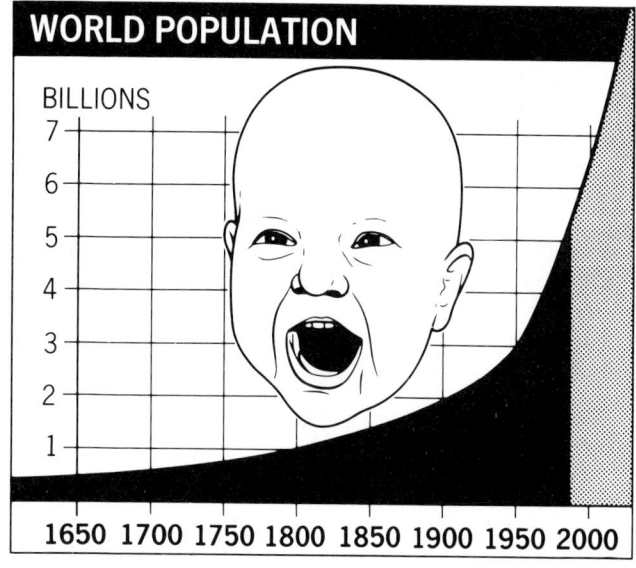

Fig. 1.3 World population

UNIT 1·2
Human Wants

Needs and wants

The human race needs water, food and shelter for survival; without them life is more-or-less impossible. As a hunter-gatherer, living in a hot climate, near a river, with animals to hunt and fruits on the trees, a person's wants are simple and easily satisfied. In Britain, things are not so simple although life may be more comfortable. Our water comes from a tap, purified and transported over many miles by water engineers. As well as what we grow ourselves, our food comes from the shop or supermarket, wrapped, tinned or in jars, produced in many countries by people employed in farming or food processing, and transported by other workers.

Shelter is also complicated; I live in a centrally heated building fitted with plumbing, gas, electricity and so on. When I go out, I shelter from the weather in warm clothing made by someone else, and I travel to work in motorised vehicles which are also comfortable and warm. In my non-working hours, I enjoy entertainments provided by still more people. From time to time I visit other countries, travelling long distances in just a few hours.

As a member of a tribe, our needs are few, simple, locally satisfied and inexpensive. As a member of a developed economy, our wants are many and satisfied by the efforts of many other people world-wide, all of which is expensive and complicated. *Needs* are essential for survival; *wants* are not so essential, but we expect and rely on them.

This book looks at the *satisfaction of wants* in a mature economic system, the life-style of those who live in it and the nature of specialist activity. It is human wants that create *demand,* and demand is satisfied by the extractive, manufacturing and service industries.

Supply and demand

My publishers are prepared to pay me to write this book in the belief that it will sell. Farmers grow food for a world market they never see or meet. A hairdresser opens a shop hoping to attract customers. We are all suppliers, all specialists, all hoping for a *reward*, when what we offer satisfies a demand.

I read a lot and buy many books and newspapers. Everybody eats, choosing the food they like. *Demand* in an economy means the way people choose to spend their money – the things they are prepared to pay for. We are all *consumers* making demands on the economy and paying for our wants with money, giving our suppliers their reward for the satisfaction of those wants.

What happens if there are too many hairdressers? What is the result of long years of drought? Who is going to read books when there is nothing to eat? We are used to a healthy demand being satisfied by a plentiful supply, but it is not always the case!

Agents of production

Houses don't build themselves; raw materials aren't mysteriously transported from one part of the country to another; money hidden under the bed benefits nobody; an idle workforce produces nothing. People take the initiative and make things happen: such people are called *entrepreneurs*, or *risk-takers*.

Production, business and trade all need *land* on which to operate. The owner of that land (with or without buildings) will receive *rent* for its use. *Capital* (i.e. money) is required to set up a business, and the provider of the capital will receive *interest* in return for a loan. Any economic activity also needs *labour*, people who will receive *wages* and *salaries* in return for their effort and skill.

So production or business activity needs *human factors* (labour and risk-taking) and *non-human factors* (land and capital). The risk-taker counts his or her *profits* when all the other factors have been paid their share.

Sectors of industry

All the agents of production are engaged in one or other of the following industries, grouped into three *sectors* or areas: primary, secondary and tertiary. Occupations are classified within those industries (see Fig. 1.4).

1. *The primary industries* – include fishing, farming, quarrying, mining, forestry, prospecting and hunting. These are the *extractive industries* and are 'primary' in that they represent the first link in the chain, producing raw materials for industry.

Fig. 1.4 Industries and occupations

2. *The secondary industries* – include manufacturing, processing, refining, assembly, blending (as with tea or whisky), construction and printing. These industries produce *finished goods* for consumption. Individual firms may specialise in one process (e.g. the production of car tyres) or they may combine a series of operations (e.g. the assembly of TV sets from parts made elsewhere).
3. *The tertiary industries* – (a) *commercial services*, such as banking, insurance, distribution, transport, finance, advertising and communications; (b) *personal services*, such as hairdressing, catering, decorating, public transport and leisure.

This book, though it will mention both primary and secondary industries will concentrate on commercial services within the tertiary sector.

In Britain, during the Agricultural Revolution (1750–1800) people moved from primary tasks on the land to secondary industries in the towns and cities associated with the Industrial Revolution (1780–1820) and the development of manufactured goods. Following the Second World War (1939–1945) automation, computerisation and the use of robotics have reduced the need for labour (i.e. people to do the job) but have increased the level of wealth. In turn, a more wealthy community increases its demand for both commercial and personal services; so many workers no longer needed in the secondary industries are, following retraining, moving to employment within the tertiary or service sector.

All occupations can be classified as belonging to the primary, secondary or tertiary sector. The British government officially lists about 30 000 occupations, stating the approximate number of people in each classification and the percentage this figure represents of the total number employed.

Specialisation: the key to prosperity

As we have seen, a developed economy like that of Britain demands a network of interdependent specialists: this is the key to prosperity. It is also essential that Britain does not waste its time doing something which other countries do better or more cheaply, but concentrates on those things it does best.

With the introduction of machinery and computerisation, fewer *units of labour* (people) are needed in the extractive and manufacturing industries generally. Highly trained specialists + production-line techniques = a reduction in demand for labour *in those industries*.

A specialist economy increases output, reduces overheads (costs) and produces a highly paid workforce. A highly paid workforce has money to spend on luxuries, like holidays, entertainment and personal services generally.

●THINGS TO DO

1 Copy and complete the following table:

Agent of production	Reward
Land	
Labour	
Capital	
Risk-taking	

2 Copy out the table below. Classify the occupations listed by putting a tick in the appropriate column. Discuss any differences within your group.

Occupation	Primary	Secondary	Tertiary Commercial	Personal
Bank manager				
Fishmonger				
Blacksmith				
Storekeeper				
School meals cook				
Landscape gardener				
Mushroom grower				
Footballer				
Carpet layer				
Lumberjack				
Factory hand				
Bricklayer				
Wigmaker				
Trawler skipper				
Tailor/cutter				
Oil rig roustabout				
Baker/pastry cook				
Disc jockey				

UNIT 1.3
Opportunity and Change

We live in a world of fast and constant change. In extreme cases goods are virtually out of date before they reach the consumer. An example of this is the market in computers, where every new model outdates and outperforms a system only just installed. Motor-car manufacturers constantly produce new models, changing trim and improving performance, making older models out of date. Clothes are sometimes discarded as unfashionable after only a few weeks or months.

Industrial change

During the 1920s and 1930s Britain's staple industries (the basis of the country's economy) were coal, iron and steel, shipbuilding and cloth-making. For historical reasons, much of this heavy industry was located in the North of England. There were new and growing industries: radio in the South-East, and the new motor-car industry was emerging at Dagenham, Essex and Oxford.

Since 1945 Britain has lost much of its manufacturing base to countries abroad. The wool and cotton trades have virtually disappeared from Yorkshire and Lancashire. There is world-wide over-production of coal, iron and steel. Shipbuilding has suffered fierce competition from the Far East (mainly Japan). The assembly of radios and televisions is now concentrated in countries like Taiwan and Korea, while the 'white goods' industry (washers and refrigerators) is dominated by Italy and West Germany.

Britain has maintained a strong position in commercial services (e.g. banking and insurance) through the City of London. We have a flourishing computer software trade, and our aircraft design and fabrication are in a healthy state. The motor-car industry, following a difficult period in the 1960s and 1970s is now recovering. Japanese firms are moving to Britain in order to trade in the European Community (see Unit 16). Britain now tends to concentrate on the *high-tech.* industries (e.g. computerised systems, laser technology, medical research and armaments); but we still have large and profitable multinational corporations like British Petroleum (BP) and Imperial Chemical Industries (ICI).

Occupational change

We have said that fewer people are now employed in the extractive and manufacturing industries in Britain. At the same time, more people are working in the commercial services, especially the distributive trades. Many former crafts have either been *de-skilled* (i.e. broken down into repetitive processes which can be learned quickly) or taken over entirely by computerised assembly lines. The specialist workforce which remains is highly skilled and has undergone long periods of training.

Manual work in industry has largely disappeared. The hard graft is now done by precision machinery, designed to dig, mix, strip and relay at speeds never achieved by the use of muscle power. Remember that canals, railways and roads were once dug and levelled with picks and shovels!

Equal opportunities

The really big occupational change is in the number of women now employed, both full-time and part-time: 40 per cent of our workforce. Ten million jobs are now done by women. Until quite recently unskilled jobs for women, outside offices, were limited to processing, assembling and packing within light manufacturing industries (like biscuits and clothing), or working as shop assistants. This insistence that certain occupations were for women only, and that others were reserved for men, kept women mostly in junior and poorly paid jobs.

We have not totally removed these artificial barriers, but the equal opportunities movement and resulting Acts of Parliament have opened up to women large areas of employment formerly regarded as reserved for men. We are no longer suprised by women bank managers or business chiefs. At the same time, more men have entered the traditionally 'female' professions of nursing and social work and now occupy senior positions in hospitals and social services.

A similar battle is developing around equal opportunities for ethnic minorities. There is growing awareness of the need to ensure a multi-racial society and to remove racial discrimination in the world of work. Ethnic-minority women and men find employment opportunities closed to them, especially in the more highly paid occupations. The ethnic minorities have more than their share of the lower paid jobs and of unemployment.

Location of industry

The *North-South divide* is a term used to illustrate the difference in employment opportunities between the prosperous south of England and the rest of Britain, from Birmingham northwards. The gradual decline of Britain's manufacturing base has led to the North having much higher levels of unemployment than the South.

Traditional heavy industries like iron and steel, coal-mining, textiles and shipbuilding are all confined to Wales, the North of England, Scotland and Northern Ireland; and trade through the ports of Liverpool, Glasgow and Belfast has declined along with the industries they used to serve. Fishing, again a northern speciality, through Hull, Grimsby and Aberdeen, has been drawn away to the continent of Europe. The use of fish processing *factory ships* which do not use port facilities in Britain has harmed the British fishing industry.

By contrast, the lighter and newer industries like electronics and computing are concentrated in the South-East. London provides plenty of employment in the service industries, which themselves are growing as a result of the new industries. The southern ports of

Southampton and Dover gain from their closeness to Europe and the EC. Although Manchester has the fastest growing airport in Britain, Heathrow, Gatwick and London's third airport at Stansted will, because of their international status and closeness to the capital, always handle far more passengers and freight than all the other British airports combined.

In theory, because of the ease of transport and the speed of communications, industry could be located anywhere in Britain. The British government has over the years made great efforts to tempt new enterprises from the South to the North of Britain, but with surprisingly little success, despite offering financial inducements. This is even more surprising when you realise that the motor-car and truck industry in Britain is serviced by parts manufactured all over Western Europe, then transported long distances to central locations for assembly.

Multinational influences

Multinationals are the giant corporations (Ford, Coca-cola, Shell, ICI) which operate world-wide and move resources from one country to another to reduce costs and to maximise profits. These companies are so large that their international turnover is greater than the national income of smaller countries such as Portugal or New Zealand. Any *relocation policy* (e.g. getting employment back into the North) depends in part on the government's ability to persuade multinationals (vast employers of labour) to set up factories in areas most in need of new industries and new jobs.

With the possible exception of Japanese companies which have set up large establishments in the North-East and Wales, there has been little sustained overseas capital invested in the northern areas of Britain.

To some extent, multinational activity in North Sea oil and gas sparked a boom in the areas around the north-east coast of Scotland. While the reserves of oil and gas will last many more years, the peak of production has now passed, and further exploration in this area is unlikely.

●QUESTIONS

Using Fig. 1.5, answer the following questions:

1. Why, in your opinion, has employment in *food and drink* declined while it is increasing in *hotels and catering*?
2. (a) Which of those avenues of employment shown as having increased lie in the tertiary sector?
   (b) Which avenues of employment shown as having decreased lie in the secondary (or manufacturing) sector? (c) Explain the lack of extractive industries in the London area.
3. What explanation(s) can you give for the decrease in employment opportunities in *transport*?

●THINGS TO DO

Fig 1.6 shows two office workers on the telephone.
1. What do you think might be the occupation of each?
2. How do you feel each will announce him-/herself on the phone?
3. If they are speaking to each other, what do you think the conversation is about?
4. Who is asking for information and who will take the final decision?

Fig. 1.6 Equal opportunities?

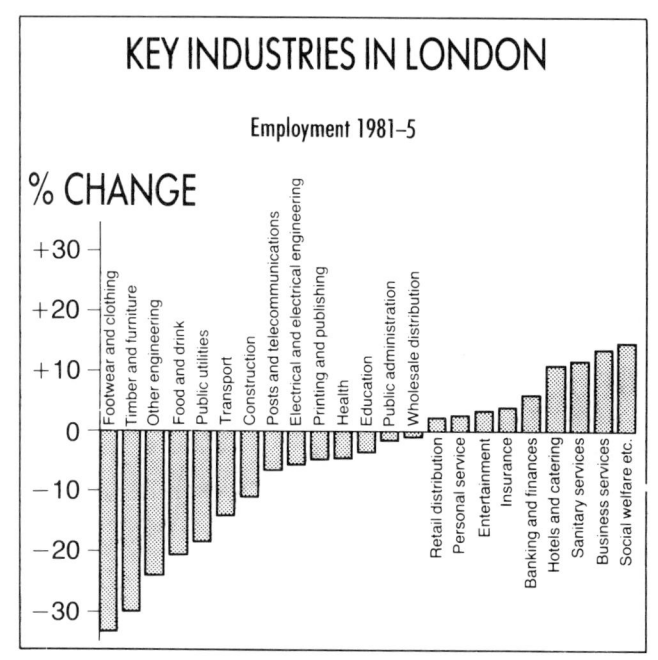

Fig. 1.5 Occupational change shown as a bar chart. The bars to the left of the chart show percentage decreases in employment; the bars to the right show percentage increases

Answer

Most people answering these questions will assume that the man is the boss and the woman is his secretary or a junior clerk working for him. Because of the lack of equal opportunities in the past, we tend to suppose that it is men who give instructions and take important decisions, while women have a less important role. But look at Fig. 1.6 again. There is no reason why the woman shouldn't be the boss.

UNIT 1.4
Technological Change

We have seen the kinds of change that affect the economy and people's occupations: industrial and occupational change, reorganisation (mainly involving the way in which people live, work and play) and legislation (new laws). There is another factor, *technological change*, the speed of which reshapes our standard of living, our working patterns and our contacts with the rest of the world. Technological change results from scientific research, the discovery of new techniques and the application of these techniques in industry and commerce.

Transport

One writer described the world as a *global village*, by which he meant that no part of the world is physically more than 24 hours' travelling time away. Concorde takes off from Heathrow and, because of the speed of the plane (3 hours 30 minutes to New York), 'races' the sun across the Atlantic, to arrive (by the clock) before it left Britain. It is possible to go to the USA for a conference and be back home on the same day. Distance is now no problem.

Trains can be made to run at over 200 miles per hour and will soon do so. This will make Glasgow to London a journey of two hours. Oil tankers are now so large that you could organise a game of football on the deck with ease. Space travel is nothing new but space stations are now used for advanced scientific experiments that could not be done on Earth because of the force of gravity.

Communications

We take for granted the ability to communicate by telephone with any part of the world merely by dialling a series of codes; this is also part of the global village idea. Connection is swift and conversation is untroubled by the distances involved. Yet international subscriber trunk dialling is relatively new, a recent technology which we now take for granted.

No one is suprised to see on the television tennis from Forest Hills, USA or a cricket match from Bombay in India. This again is a new technology: giant reflector satellites, hanging in space, bring news and sport from the other side of the globe. Industry and commerce also make use of these facilities to beam messages, documents and visual material to all parts of the world. By the use of television monitors a group of individuals, each in a different country, can conduct a conference as if they were meeting face to face. Such electronic facilities are not cheap, but they avoid the long delays involved in physically sending information or travelling by land, sea or air.

Cellular phones

We all know how business and domestic telephones are linked to a telephone exchange by underground wiring and overhead cables. Any conversation using this system is carried over these cables; speech is translated into a

Fig. 1.7 Cellular car phone

series of electrical impulses at one end and decoded by the handset at the other.

The cellular system, first fitted to cars, does not use wiring or cables. Instead it uses radio links to a cellular exchange. Car phones use the motor-car battery and can be carried in a briefcase; you can even hire a cellular telephone by the day or the week.

Telecommunication links by means of radio will in the end make all that wiring along the sides of roads and railways redundant. Fixed telephone points in the house or office will also become a thing of the past. Cellular networks rely on the miniaturisation of components (parts), microprocessing of a system using telephone exchange 'cells' and radio wavelengths rather than electrical impulses carried along cables.

So far, each country of the European Community has developed its own cellular system. The cellular telephone of one country will not work (or receive messages) in the rest. This problem is similar to that experienced with our different domestic electrical systems. You may have taken a hair dryer to France or even the USA, for example, and found: (a) the plug doesn't fit, and/or (b) the voltage is different. Such difficulties will only be solved by international co-operation.

Micro-electronics

The micro-chip is at the heart of technological change. A computer analyst will tell you that at present no computer can do more than it is programmed to do. But we are about to produce a family of computers which will be able to think for themselves, recognise mistakes and correct those mistakes. Computers can calculate at a fantastic speed, and this abililty can be used for a great many tasks.

Banks use computers to 'move' vast sums of money about every day. The technology already exists to transfer the cost of your groceries from your bank account to that

Fig. 1.8 Computers in daily use

of your grocer's merely by passing your credit card through a sensitised slot in the check-out till. A computerised check-out, already installed in many larger supermarkets, automatically reads the bar codes on each grocery item; the computer then tots up the bill and gives you an itemised receipt, storing information on the total sales of each item and automatically transferring that information to stock control records.

Automation

In industry, especially in assembly processes like car production, computers can be used to do the work automatically. They can be programmed to control the process of assembly like welding together a car body (called *robotics*), to ensure the delivery of parts and equipment to the points on the assembly line where they are needed, to test the finished product (e.g. television sets), to pin-point faults and to reject damaged parts. The carpet-weaving and knitwear industries are now almost entirely automated. Computer control will eventually extend to all manufacturing processes where repetitive work is a major part of production.

Miniaturisation

Scientific development within the electronics industry was speeded up by the various space programmes. Where the amount of room is limited, as in a spacecraft, smaller and smaller items of equipment are essential. Not so long ago a computer installation would have filled a large room; now equipment just as powerful will sit on the top of a desk.

Fig. 1.9 A microchip on the head of a daisy

The Sony Walkman, a masterpiece of electronic engineering, is as efficient as larger equipment which occupies shelf space at home. The electronic keyboard, now essential equipment for many pop groups, has the range and the versatility of the old cinema organs which would fill a large house (and the garage!).

Levels of employment

Technological advances have removed much of the muscular effort from the work people do; machinery and mechanical aids now supply much of the brute strength. As a result, job opportunities in engineering (particularly mechanical engineering) have declined, and the posts which remain demand a much higher standard of education and skills training. Automation and computerisation have produced very efficient manufacturing and extractive industries which are wealth producing.

With more money in our pockets to spend, the tertiary (service) industries have benefited, especially leisure and personal services. So job opportunities in areas like hotels and catering have expanded, and people spend far more money than before on clothes and cosmetics, furnishings, sports and entertainment. The retail trade has changed shape completely, with smaller shops giving way to supermarket/hypermarket selling, shopping malls and precincts. Increased private transport calls for more petrol-stations, car maintenance and repair services. The demand for foreign holidays increases the number of travel agents, providing work for the printers of brochures, aircraft cabin crews and baggage handlers. Increased prosperity starts with technological change.

●SOURCES OF INFORMATION

1 Any encyclopaedia, for a short account of the Industrial Revolution.
2 Newspaper or magazine articles on the electronic transfer of funds by financial institutions.
3 Any material on methods of transferring documents by the use of computers (fax).

●THINGS TO DO

1 With your local Careers Service, research the job opportunities which require 'high-tech' qualifications. Find out how you could obtain such qualifications.
2 Look through several daily newspapers, such as the *Daily Mail, Daily Express,* your local weekly papers and your local evening paper. See what technical qualifications are called for in jobs advertised.
3 Hold a group discussion on how computers have played so great a part in technological change.
4 The fourth quarter of the twentieth century (1975–99) is likely in the future to be called the Second Industrial Revolution. Do you think there is any comparison to be drawn between technological change today and the change experienced in the period of the first Industrial Revolution?

2 PERSONAL FINANCE

●UNIT 2.1
Wages and Salaries

Most people's income is obtained from employment, from which they receive either a wage or a salary. A salary is usually expressed as a figure for the year (e.g. £7500 per annum) which is paid in twelve equal instalments on a fixed date each month. A wage can be expressed as a fixed amount (e.g. £140 per week) or as a rate per hour (e.g. £3.50 per hour for a 38-hour week). Given the chance, which would you choose: £7500 p.a., £140 p.w. or £3.50 p.h., for a 38-hour week?

Income gross and net

The above figures indicate a *gross* wage or salary, that is, before stoppages or deductions have been made. Your *net* or take-home pay is calculated by deducting income tax, National Insurance contributions and other stoppages from the gross amount (see Fig. 2.1). What remains is your net pay.

Your wage packet, pay slip or salary slip gives details of your gross income, stoppages (and the reason for the stoppages), and the net amount actually paid to you (see Fig. 2.2).

Overtime

In some occupations there is the possibility of increasing your take-home pay by working overtime. All jobs have 'normal' hours (e.g. 9.00 am–5.00 pm or 38 hours per week) which are usually stated in your letter of appointment. These are the hours you are expected to work to earn the salary or wage that goes with the job. Overtime is time worked beyond your contracted hours, and such hours usually have a higher rate of pay. For example, if your hourly rate is £3.50 then your overtime rate might be £4.00. Overtime is not necessarily worked on a regular basis and must be agreed between you and your supervisor before it takes place.

Calculation of income on a pay slip

Fig. 2.2 shows a typical pay slip or wage packet for a week's work. A pay slip is a single sheet of paper which shows how much has been paid into your bank account or accompanies a cheque; a wage packet is an envelope which contains your wages in notes and coins.

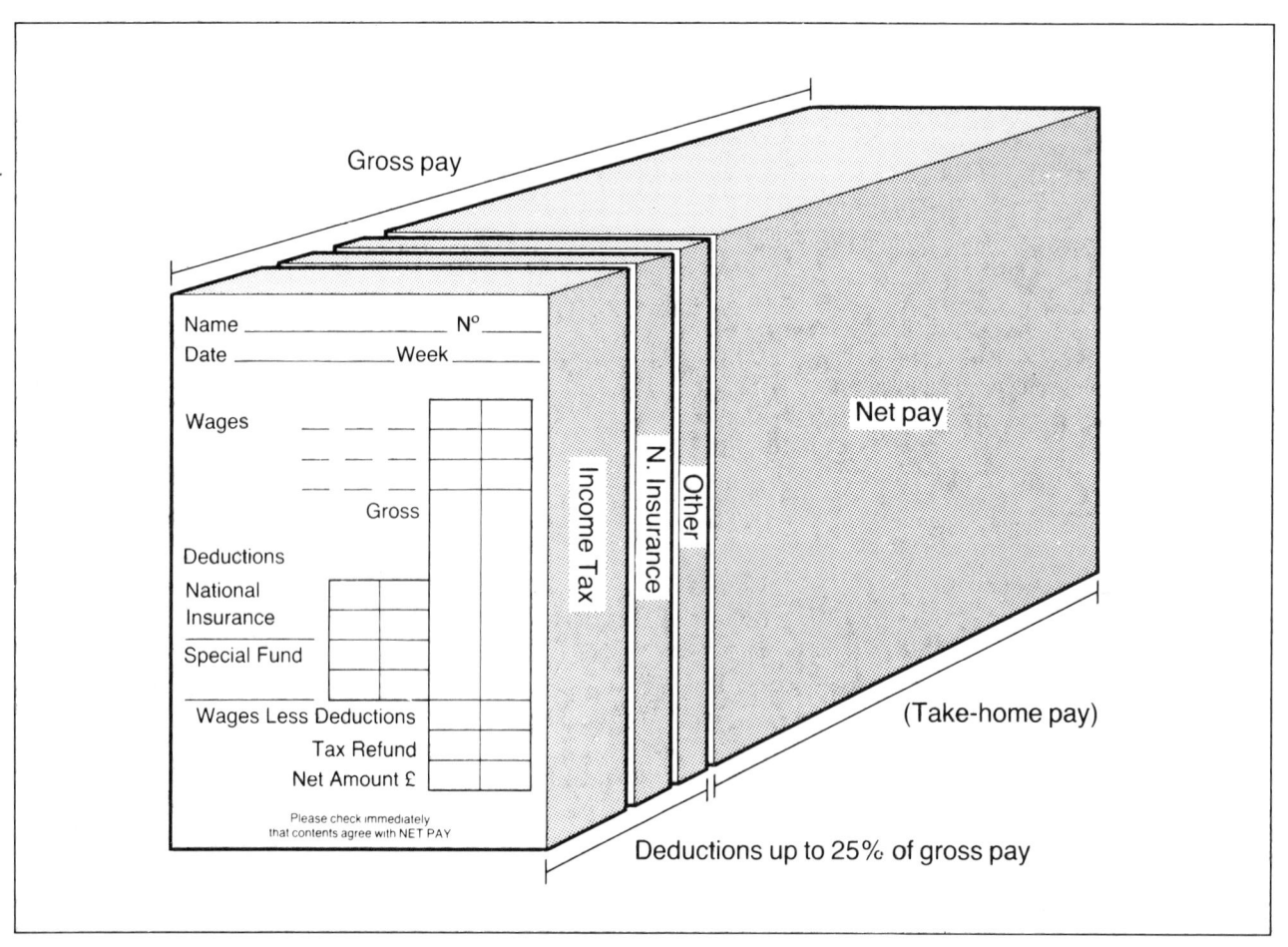

Fig. 2.1 Gross and net pay

Here is what the terms on the pay slip mean:

W/Beg = tax week (1 to 52)

Tax Code = determines income tax deductions

NI = National Insurance contributions

Pension = deduction for firm's pension fund

Union = deduction for trade union subscriptions

Name				Payroll number	
W/Beg:				Tax Code:	
Basic Pay		Overtime		Total Gross Pay	
Deductions					
NI	Tax	Pension	Union	Saving	Total Deductions
				Net Pay	
CRUNCHY BISCUITS LTD				£	

Fig. 2.2 A pay slip

National Insurance and income tax

A National Insurance contribution is made by all people who are employed or self-employed. A roughly equal contribution is paid by all employers for each employee on the payroll. The amount due is calculated according to the amount of gross pay – the more you earn, the greater is your National Insurance contribution and that of your employer.

For all employees, income tax is deducted on a *pay as you earn* (*PAYE*) basis. The amount due is calculated on gross pay by the application of a tax code issued to each employed person by the Inland Revenue. Your tax code tells you and your employer the amount you are allowed to earn *before* you start to pay income tax. Your employer is issued with tax tables from which he can calculate the amount due in income tax; the firm has to deduct this tax before your take-home pay is determined. Self-employed people (working for themselves) pay tax rather differently, in two instalments each financial year.

Both National Insurance contributions and income tax deductions go into the Treasury as government income. The money then provides services like education and health.

Payment of wages and salaries

There are three ways you can receive net or take-home pay:
1 in cash (notes and coin);
2 by cheque (which will have to be paid into a bank, Giro or building-society account);
3 paid directly into the account of your choice by arrangement with your employer.

Firms do not much like handling lots of pay packets containing cash, especially if they have to be moved from one branch to another. Equally, cheques are not always safe, because they are occasionally lost or stolen. Employers much prefer to pay your wage or salary direct into an account. No money changes hands, and the system is safe and reliable.

●SOURCES OF INFORMATION

1 Yellow Pages – Look up 'Trade unions' and contact them for details of membership and subscription rates.
2 Telephone directory – contact the Department of Employment for a brochure on National Insurance contributions.
3 Telephone directory – contact the Inland Revenue for brochure(s) on PAYE.
4 Your local library or Citizens' Advice Bureau should also have copies of the brochures mentioned in **2** and **3**.

●THINGS TO DO

1 Make a copy of Fig. 2.2 and enter the following details on the pay slip using your own name:

 (a) Payroll number: 76/4117
 (b) W/Beg: 48
 (c) Tax code: 300L
 (d) Basic pay: 38 hrs at £3.50 p.h.
 (e) Overtime: 8 hrs at £3.75 p.h.
 (f) NI: £2.75
 (g) Income tax: £16.40
 (h) Pension: £8.30
 (i) Union: 50p
 (j) Savings scheme: £10.00

2 Work out your total gross pay, total deductions and net pay, and enter them on your pay slip.
3 If Week 1 for tax purposes is the week containing 5 April, in what month will Week 48 fall in the tax year?
4 The taxes you are most likely to pay personally are: income tax, road tax on your car or motor cycle, value added tax (VAT: a tax, currently of 15 per cent, added to the cost of most goods and services you purchase), the television licence fee and the community charge or poll tax. Hold a group discussion as to the fairest method of taxation. What taxes would you abolish and why? What additional taxes would you consider and why?
5 Using advertisements in your local newspaper, research the various forms of employment offered. Are qualifications required? Is an age limit mentioned? Are there any 'fringe benefits' like luncheon vouchers? Is the job likely to be 'clean' or 'dirty'? Are unsocial hours (shift work, late-night duties or weekend working) involved? Is experience of similar employment required?
6 From your investigations in **5**, say which, if any, of these factors influence the levels of wages and salaries: (a) qualifications; (b) age; (c) 'dirty' and repetitive working; (d) unsocial hours; (e) experience; (f) fringe benefits ('perks'). Which of these factors is likely to influence *your* chances of obtaining employment?

UNIT 2·2
Savings and Budgeting

Parents, grandparents, friends and relatives often give small amounts of money to be 'put away' for a new baby. When we are older and understand the value of money, we may have a piggy bank, a few Premium Bonds or savings certificates or even a larger amount of money on deposit at a local bank, earning interest. Later we may decide to save some of our weekly pocket money or part of what we earn from a paper round or weekend job. The urge to save is strong in all of us, especially if the money is intended for a holiday or a much wanted possession like a new CD unit. Few people can save regularly just for the sake of it. We all need the feeling that by saving now we will enjoy something better in the future.

Savings advice

You can save money through banks, the Post Office, building societies, government schemes and in many other ways. These agencies compete to look after our savings, advertising their services in newspapers, on posters and television. Young savers are much sought after, being offered gifts and special terms when they open an account. As we shall see, some forms of saving involve risks, but the advertisers rarely draw attention to this aspect.

Budgeting and financial planning

Before you can start saving, some financial calculations are necessary:

1. What is your total spendable income each month? (Remember, from your gross wages or salary will be deducted income tax, National Insurance contributions, etc.)
2. What bills (often called *outgoings*) will have to be met during the month? (Remember travelling expenses, meals, entertainment, etc.)
3. Taking one from the other, the amount remaining is available for some form of saving. Note that some bills (like the TV licence, dry-cleaning and shoe repairs) do not appear every month. Is it possible to include an estimate of 'big' bills over the year and to calculate a monthly cost? This average amount should be included in your calculations.

A *budget* (see Fig. 2.3) is a sensible method of keeping control of your income so that all *outgoings* (the bills you have to pay) can be met, you don't overspend, and a little is left over for your savings account. A business man or woman would call this *financial planning*.

A savings policy

Successful saving depends upon sensible budgeting. You need to control your weekly or monthly *expenditure* (spending) so that income exceeds outgoings. What is left can be saved. Week by week and month by month, regular savings accumulate, with interest, to meet the cost of that exciting holiday or new CD unit.

How to save with interest

All your savings can be kept in a cash-box in your bedroom. You run the risk of burglary, you may not be able to resist 'borrowing' a pound or two ('just until the weekend') and, under the bed, your savings do not attract interest. *Interest* is the reward received when you deposit your savings with, say, a bank, which will then lend your money to other people, charging interest on the loan at about 15 per cent (i.e. a charge of £15 for every £100 borrowed for twelve months). The bank will pay you maybe 7 per cent (i.e. £7 a year for every £100 you have on deposit over twelve months). The difference is the bank's profit, from which it pays wages, rent, light, rates, etc. In section 2.3 we will discuss *investment*, a process where the interest your savings earn can be much greater than that offered by a bank. Unfortunately, as interest increases, so does the risk. In other words, some people are prepared to risk losing all their savings to attract a high rate of interest.

Where to save with interest

Most 'small' savers will not wish to take any risks and will be satisfied with an average rate of interest. For these people *deposit accounts* are available at the banks, at building societies, at the Post Office, at co-operative stores (see Unit 7, section 7.3) and with Friendly Societies. We will concentrate on the first three.

Deposit accounts or *savings accounts* can be opened at a bank, with a building society or at Post Office branches, with as little as £1. A building society and the Post Office issue a savings book in which they record all deposits (payments into your account), and all withdrawls; accumulated (totalled-up) interest is added to the balance either once or twice a year. Banks issue a *paying-in book* which records all payments into your account; *you* are expected to keep a record of withdrawals. At regular intervals, usually monthly, the bank sends you a printed statement, showing all in-payments, all withdrawals and added interest. On some deposit accounts, especially with building societies, a slightly higher rate of interest is paid if you are prepared to give longer notice of withdrawals (e.g. you agree to tell the branch 90 days before you take any money out).

Save as You Earn

Save as You Earn is a scheme by which you agree to save a fixed amount regularly each week or month. The amount is usually deducted from your wage or salary by your employer and placed in the deposit account of your choice. Because you are saving regularly, the bank or building society may be prepared to pay a slightly higher rate of interest for the use of your money.

The growth of your savings

How large will your savings grow? This will depend on a number of factors:

1. The amount you have on deposit.
2. The regularity of your savings.
3. The length of time your savings remain on deposit.
4. The rate of interest.
5. The risk involved.

● SOURCES OF INFORMATION

1. Yellow Pages – banks, building societies, co-operative societies, Friendly Societies, Post Office branches.
2. All the institutions given in **1** for leaflets and booklets.
3. Any branch of one of the major banks, for a student pack on banking and saving.

● THINGS TO DO

1. Split into groups to research the advantages of saving with all the institutions mentioned in 'Sources of Information' above. You will need to consider:
(a) How easy is it to open an account? (b) What rate of interest is offered? (c) Do I have to attend at one fixed place for paying in and withdrawing money or are there other places where I can do this? (d) How much *notice* (time in advance), if any, must I give before a withdrawal? (e) Are there any limits on the amount I can withdraw at any one time? (f) Can I only deposit cash? (g) If I withdraw, must it always be in cash? (h) What alternative form of payment is available? (i) Can two or more people have a joint account? If so, what arrangements can be made to prevent one individual cheating the rest? (j) Are cash point facilities available? (k) Am I allowed to overdraw? Report back to your class and discuss your findings.

2. Sandra shares a flat with four other people. Fig. 2.3 shows her weekly budget.

Weekly income (after deductions)	£78.60
Outgoings:	
Share of flat's rent, electricity etc.	£25.00
Share of grocery bills	£15.00
Clothes, repairs, etc. (average)	£10.00
Travelling expenses	£8.50
Entertainment	£20.00
	£78.50
Amount available for savings	£ Nil

Fig. 2.3 Sandra's budget

The five friends plan to go on holiday together in six months' time. The holiday costs £350 each with Sunshine Tours. (a) How much per week will Sandra have to save over the six months? (b) Discuss how she could adjust her budget to achieve the required savings. (c) How might Sandra be able to increase her weekly income? (d) In your view will there be any other expenses connected with the holiday; if so, what are they likely to be and how much more might Sandra need? (e) Adjust your calculations accordingly.

● UNIT 2.3
Savings and Investment

What is investment?

Another word for saving money or buying with it something likely to increase in value is *investment*. Investment as a form of saving involves: (a) a lump sum of fairly sizeable proportions; (b) a long-term arrangement; (c) the hope that your investment will increase in value; (d) a possible return in the form of interest or dividends; (e) a risk, sometimes a considerable one, that you will lose all your money or that your investment will *depreciate* (fall) in value.

Investment and risk

Investing money involves risk. You invest in something because you think the value of your investment will increase over time. We call this increase *appreciation* or *capital growth*. Some forms of investment involve more risk (that the value will go down instead of up) than others.

1. We hear people say, 'We decided to invest in a house', meaning that they considered buying a house better use of their money than renting one. If you purchase (buy), your house will appreciate (grow) in value; rent brings no long-term gain at all. Buying property is usually 'safe' (low in risk); its value rarely, if ever, falls.

2. You can invest in a picture by a well-known artist, in the hope that his or her paintings will become more and more popular, increasing in value over the years (see Fig. 2.4). If you are right, your gains are considerable. If you are wrong, your 'investment' could be worthless.

3. You may decide to invest by buying *shares* in companies such as British Telecom and British Airways. These shares offer both an annual *dividend* (see Unit 11, section 11.1) and the chance that they will increase in value if the companies do well. Of course there is always the risk that they could do badly, and the price you get when you sell may be less than you paid for them in the first place.

4. Some people may decide to invest their savings in a business of their own. Success will offer increasing profits, and a prosperous business can often be sold as a

Fig. 2.4 Paintings for investment

going concern. The amount received following such a sale will be far greater than the amount of the original investment. Some initially small businesses that have become very successful (e.g. the Body Shop, Tesco, McDonalds), earn huge returns for their founders. But not all businesses prosper. Even with a hard-working owner failure is possible, and the original investment may be totally lost. Many new firms are not successful and lose large amounts of money before disappearing completely.

5 'Angels' are people who invest money in plays or musicals such as those at many West End theatres in London. Such an investment is very risky, but successful shows (like *Cats*, *Phantom of the Opera* and *No Sex Please We're British*), which run for many years, provide a handsome profit for their 'angel' sponsors. Other shows which fail to attract audiences close down, and the sponsors lose their money.

Endowment policies

Endowment policies involve some of the characteristics of both saving and investment. Such policies, offered by insurance companies, invite people to save/invest an agreed sum each month over a stated period, which can be as long as 20 or 25 years. In its turn, the insurance company agrees to pay the policy-holder a lump sum at the end of that time or at earlier death. The capital sum involved could be as much as £100 000, to which might be added a yearly bonus calculated on the annual profits declared by the insurance company.

One disadvantage of an endowment policy is that your money is 'tied up' for a very long time. But, at the end of that time, the reward for your patience can be a large sum. This is useful for retirement, to pay off the amount of a loan outstanding on your house or, in the case of an unfortunate early death, to ensure that your family are not left unprovided for. The amounts received from various policy-holders are invested by the company in stocks and shares, government securities, property development (like new shopping centres) and other profit-making opportunities (like lending money to industry for expansion). The income received ensures that your investment is secure and that bonuses are added regularly which will increase the total value of your policy.

The importance of savings and investments

All business ventures need additional capital to grow and prosper. Some of this money is provided from within industry and commerce itself, which uses annual profits to purchase (say) new equipment. However, the vast quantity of new capital required each year is provided by the joint efforts of 'small' savers like you and me. All the relatively small sums of money which we save and invest through banks, building societies and insurance policies are brought together as loans to industrial and commercial organisations. These businesses borrow money from the savings and investment institutions to create new offices, to extend factories, to replace old and worn-out machinery, to build ships and to set up new industries in developing countries. The government collects small savings through the Post Office and other agencies, using the money to build new schools and hospitals, and to develop new industry.

Individually we gain by accumulating savings to use later, for example as a deposit on a new house. In the meantime, those savings are used to help firms to develop and succeed. Success provides new jobs and safeguards existing employment. The fruits of saving and investment are economic expansion and employment opportunities.

●SOURCES OF INFORMATION

1 The booklet called *Spending and Saving*, (Life Offices Association; Association of Scottish Life Offices) available from LOA/ASLO Information Centre, Buckingham House, 62–63 Queen Street, London EC4R 1AD.
2 Yellow Pages – contact insurance companies for details of endowment policies.
3 *Money in Focus*, from Save and Prosper, Freepost, Romford, Essex RM1 1BR.

●THINGS TO DO

1 Split up into four or five groups. Each group selects from Yellow Pages a well-known insurance company with a local office. One from each group then writes to or calls at the chosen office to ask for a brochure on endowment policies. Assuming your age next birthday to be 21, choose a 'with profits' policy worth £50 000 at maturity (i.e. after 20 years): (a) How much do you have to pay each month? (b) What are your total payments over: (i) one year, and (ii) 20 years? (c) Does the brochure suggest the total amount you might expect to receive after 20 years; if so, what is your 'profit'? (d) Contrast your findings with those from the other groups. Which appears to be the best offer?
2 Discuss the advantages of an endowment policy from the point of view of an investment for the future. From your reading of the brochure, what disadvantages are there in this form of regular saving?
3 In this section it has been suggested that a personal policy on *savings* has different characteristics from a personal policy on *investment*. In your view, is investment a sensible idea for a person under the age of, say, 20? Hold a class discussion on the topic.
4 Your aunt dies, leaving you 1000 shares in Amalgamated Goldfields Incorporated, which distributes a steady annual dividend of 7.8 pence per share after income tax has been paid. You can sell the shares for £1.25 cash. Calculate: (a) the annual income from the shares in the form of dividends; (b) the total you would receive if you sold the shares, minus £20 for the bank's costs; (c) the annual interest you would receive if you were to place the proceeds on deposit at a building society of your choice.
Discuss the advantages and disadvantages of: (a) retaining the shares; (b) selling the shares and opening a building society account with the proceeds.

UNIT 2.4
Borrowing and Credit

Most youngsters sometimes borrow a pound or two from Mum or Dad to keep themselves going until the weekend. In the adult world, provided you are 18, loans are available to you in quite large amounts. So, when we think about income (see sections 2.1 and 2.2), we can now add borrowing or credit facililties as a means of financing (paying for) our day-to-day spending.

Borrowing means being lent a lump sum, usually for a particular purpose (e.g. a new car or to refit the kitchen). The contract involves regular monthly repayments, over an agreed period. Interest is added to the sum borrowed (Fig. 2.6).

The term *credit facilities* can refer to a simple arrangement with the local dairy to have milk delivered daily and pay at the end of the week. Most credit transactions, however, involve a *hire purchase agreement*, where you 'buy' goods (like new furniture or a video recorder) and repay the money borrowed by instalments over a period like twelve months. A credit charge is added to the cost of the goods, and your total repayment includes both the cost of the goods and a credit charge. If you don't pay, the hire purchase company may well be able to repossess (take back) the goods.

The difference between saving and borrowing

Borrowing, by taking out a loan or arranging credit terms through a contract of hire purchase, allows you to have goods now and to pay back the money involved over a period of time. The weekly or monthly repayments are very like a *save as you earn* scheme, with the added benefit of enjoying the goods while actually 'saving' the money to pay for them. However, see Figs. 2.5 and 2.6.

You are considering the purchase of a television and video recorder, total cost £990. Fig 2.5 shows one method of funding the purchase, by allowing your deposit account balance to remain with the building society over one whole year: balance at the end of that year £990. Fig 2.6 shows the situation where you buy via a hire purchase contract, which requires twelve equal payments of £90.75 over one year; total cost of purchase, £1089. It would seem that the cost of enjoying the goods *now* (instead of waiting a year) is (£1089 – £900) = £189.

But, what if the goods in question had gone up in price by £200 during the year, and the purchase price becomes (£990 + £200) = £1190. Your total savings are still £990 i.e £200 short of the purchase price, and you cannot afford the goods in question; so in this case hire purchase would make more sense than trying to save the full amount first. But what would happen if the interest on the loan was 20 per cent and the goods only went up £100?

Hire purchase

An extremely popular method of credit purchase is the use of a hire purchase agreement. Most firms sellling goods like furniture, domestic equipment, cars and motor cycles will offer credit terms (see Unit 10, section 10.2).

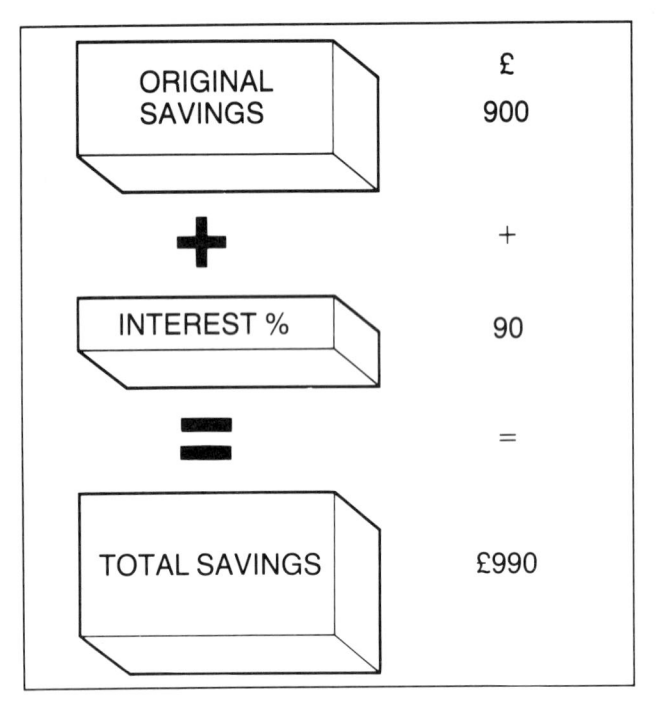

	£
ORIGINAL SAVINGS	900
+	+
INTEREST %	90
=	=
TOTAL SAVINGS	£990

Fig. 2.5 Saving

	£
LOAN	990
+	+
INTEREST %	99
=	=
TOTAL COST OF BORROWING	£1089

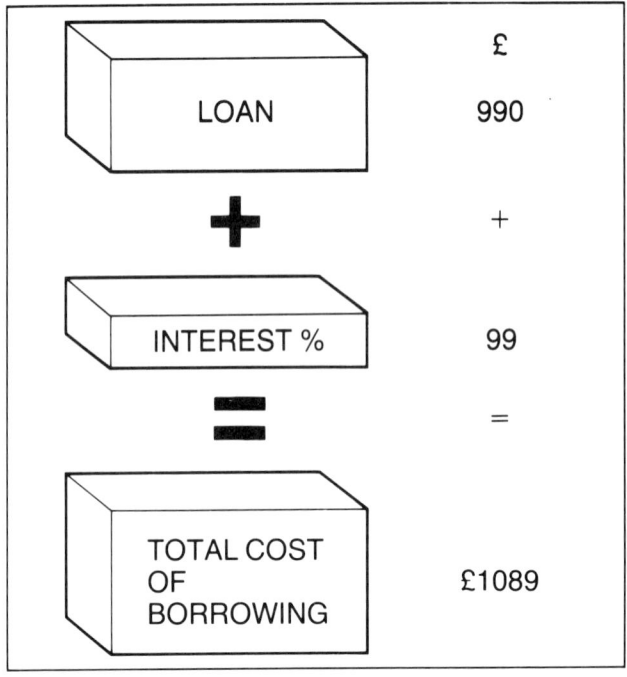

Fig. 2.6 Borrowing

Short-term borrowing: banks

A person might borrow money on a short-term basis: (a) to buy a car; (b) to buy new furniture or household equipment; (c) to redesign a kitchen or a bathroom; (d) to finance an expensive holiday. Most banks (including Giro) will agree a loan up to about £5000 without *security* (see below), provided they are satisfied that the customer is reliable and is able to meet the agreed repayments out of income (i.e normal wage or salary). Banks will also, by prior arrangement, allow certain customers to *overdraw* (spend more money than they have in their account) up to an agreed limit. This form of borrowing is expected to be for very short periods; a permanent overdraft is not encouraged. These loans and overdrafts are *short term;* banks expect repayment in less than three years.

Credit cards

Access and Visa Card (see Unit 5, section 5.2) allow people to buy goods up to an agreed limit. Once your limit is reached you cannot make any further purchases and you will be expected to repay a minimum sum (or more) each month. Any interest charged on the loan outstanding is likely to be in excess of that for a bank loan. There is no set period over which the loan must be repaid, and all kinds of goods may be purchased up to your personal limit. Credit card companies also allow cardholders to borrow cash, but at an extremely high rate of interest.

Charge cards

American Express and Diners Club issue charge cards to approved customers. Cardholders may charge the cost of any goods and services to their charge card account, and there is no limit to the credit facility offered. However, the outstanding balance must be repaid each month and an annual charge is made for the privilege of having such a card.

Long-term borrowing: mortgages

About the only kind of long-term borrowing to affect an individual will be the purchase of a house on mortgage. A mortgage is granted by a bank or a building society, often involving a large sum of money. The advance is calculated upon an individual's or a couple's combined annual income, up to the full value of the property. But 100 per cent mortgages are rare, and usually the prospective householder is expected to find a deposit of about 10 per cent of the purchase price. A mortgage will be granted for any period up to 25 years, repayments of *principal* (the amount borrowed) and interest being made each month over the whole period of the loan. Income tax relief is allowed on some of the interest charged.

Mortgages are often repaid before the date agreed, because people buy and sell houses regularly.

Security against loans

The main security for any short-term loan or credit arrangement is your promise to repay the sum borrowed plus interest charges. Unfortunately, some people get into financial difficulties, and the lender must then take action either to take back the goods or to make some arrangement through the law courts to recover the money outstanding. A court can order that an individual's personal possessions be sold and the money received paid to the lender. Courts can also instruct an employer to deduct an amount regularly from the borrower's wage or salary until the debt is repaid.

In cases of long-term borrowing and borrowing of large amounts, the lender will require some security other than the borrower's promise to repay. This is called *collateral security* and may consist of the deeds to the house mortgaged, share certificates, an endowment/insurance policy, or anything of value that can be sold to cover the debt if the borrower is unable to repay. In the case of a mortgage, the bank or building society will retain the deeds to the property (i.e. the certificates of ownership). Should the borrower default (fail to pay), the house will be sold and the occupier will have to leave.

●SOURCES OF INFORMATION

1. Any bank or building society, for a brochure on mortgage facilities.
2. A brochure on credit card facilities. Try any branch of the National Westminster or Barclays banks.
3. Almost any shop in the high street will help with details of hire purchase and may have a leaflet explaining their own scheme.

●THINGS TO DO

1. Hold a class discussion on the advantages and disadvantages of buying on credit. In your view:
   (a) What goods are best suited to credit purchase?
   (b) Would you buy food or petrol with a credit card?
2. Two friends, Pat and Alex, both in their early twenties, are thinking about buying a flat for joint occupation. Pat has a salary of £9500 p.a.; Alex earns £150 p.w. including overtime; both have been saving with a building society. Research the maximum amount they can expect to borrow from that building society towards the purchase of their flat. Will that be enough to purchase a two-bedroom flat in your area? How much will they be expected to find as a deposit?
3. John has a credit card with a credit limit of £250. He has reached that limit but is finding it difficult to pay even the miminum repayment required each month by the credit card company, which has now offered to increase his credit limit to £350. In your view, would John be wise to accept this offer? Offer him advice on any adjustment to his monthly budget which might allow him to reduce the amount outstanding on his card.

3 DISTRIBUTION AND MARKETING

●UNIT 3.1
From Source to Consumption

The journey that the goods we buy make from their original extraction and production, through manufacture and processing, warehousing, storage and transportation to the firms that supply us, the consumers, is called the *chain of distribution*.

The extractive industries

Everything we eat, use and consume started life as a raw material of one kind or another which was extracted from the earth we all live on. Some raw materials and food which Britain does not produce have to be imported from abroad.

The manufacturing and construction industries

We use raw materials to make goods for sale, or put together the results of manufacture in the construction of buildings, roads, railways, and harbours. Again, Britain does not manufacture all its wants; some are imported from abroad. The construction industries often import pre-fabricated parts, which are assembled on site (e.g. for oil rigs). Processed foodstuffs (cheese, canned foods, etc.) are also imported ready for sale.

Warehousing and storage

All goods are produced in anticipation of demand. They have to be stored until that demand materialises or the goods are ready for sale. For example:

1 Coal is produced continuously and has to be stored at the pit-head until required. Think also of gas and petrol.
2 Timber has to season and is stacked until ready for use, as are building materials generally.
3 Cereals and animal feed are stored in silos from which they are delivered to the baker, the brewer or the farmer.
4 Perishable foods (meat, vegetables and frozen foods) are kept in special cold stores to preserve freshness or to aid ripening (e.g. fruit and vegetables).
5 Wines and spirits are maintained in maturing vats until the day they can be bottled and dispatched for sale.
6 Warehousing is a major industry, storing goods in bulk until the time for distribution. For example, seasonal goods (cards, decorations and fireworks) are manufactured year round and stored until November and December. Similarly, the clothing trade is busy each spring producing next winter's fashions.

Most of the large firms selling goods to the public maintain their own warehouses, supplying their shops direct from the manufacturer. Smaller-scale retailers rely on private warehouses, most of which specialise in a particular trade (e.g. hairdressing), buying from the manufacturer, storing in bulk and 'breaking' that bulk into more easily manageable consignments for dispatch to their retailer customers.

Transport

Goods are constantly on the move by sea, air, road and rail (think also of pipelines for fuel and cables for electricity). An efficient transport industry is essential to serve the chain of distribution. Again, the larger companies maintain their own fleets, while private firms provide a service for the smaller trader. Later in the book (Unit 13) we will discuss each mode of transport separately.

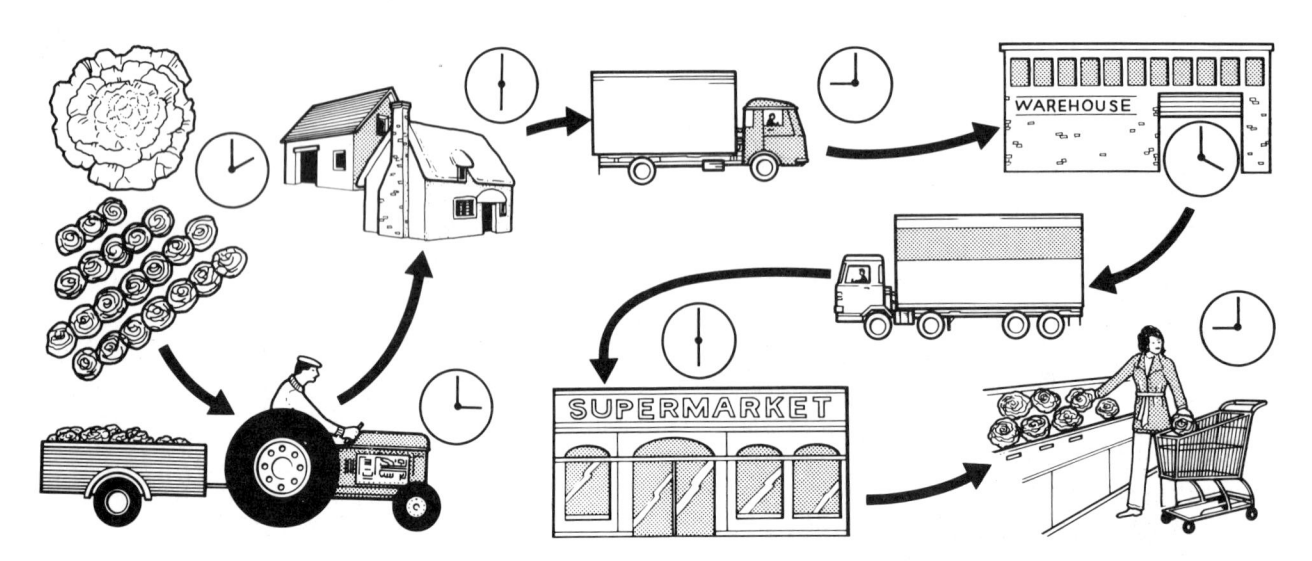

Fig. 3.1 Chain of distribution for fresh lettuce

The retail trade

The retail trade is the final link in the chain of distribution and is the point of contact with the general public, the consumer. The retail trade is supplied by the *wholesale trade* (see section 3.2). Besides shops, retail outlets include petrol stations, resturants, markets, door-to-door selling, exhibitions and trade fairs, market gardens, builders' merchants, DIY warehouses and direct selling via advertising.

People and businesses involved in extraction, manufacture, construction, warehousing and transport rely on the demands made by the consumer. The money paid by consumers for goods includes a reward to all individuals in the chain of distribution.

Commercial services

Banking, insurance, advertising and communications are associated with the chain of distribution. They offer essential services at each point of the chain while not being actually involved in moving goods to the point of sale. No part of that chain can exist alone; industry, distribution and commercial services are interlinked in a complicated pattern.

● SOURCES OF INFORMATION

1. Association of British Chambers of Commerce, 212 Shaftesbury Avenue, London WC2 8EW
2. Transport 2000, Public Transport Campaign, Walkden House, 10 Melton Street, London NW1 2EB
3. Retail Consortium, 1 New Oxford Street, London WC1A 1BA

● QUESTIONS

1. In your view, is it important that goods are moved from warehouses or storage as soon as possible? If so, why?
2. Commercial services are said to aid the chain of distribution. Explain, with examples, how warehousing helps the distribution of goods.
3. Why is transport essential to the extractive industries, the manufacturing/construction industries and the retail trade? How does the cost of the transport affect the final cost of a product?
4. What forms of transport exist other than road, rail, sea and air? What kinds of goods are carried?

● THINGS TO DO

1. Study Figs. 3.1 and 3.2. Describe those parts of the chain of distribution illustrated and fill in the gaps, if any.
2. Working in pairs, agree a well-known product with your teacher and, by research, illustrate the chain from extraction through production and sale to the consumer. Remember to include transport and warehousing/storage.
3. Research an extractive industry of your choice. What raw materials are involved? In what production processes will the raw materials be used?

Fig. 3.2 From coffee bean to coffee cup

UNIT 3.2
Wholesale Outlets, Cash and Carry

The wholesale trade

Wholesale outlets buy from manufacturers and producers and sell to retailers. Retailers visit wholesale traders to choose their stock, which the wholesaler is usually prepared to deliver. Credit is available to the retailer; this can be useful, allowing retailers to sell the goods before having to pay. Alternatively, a wholesale representative makes regular visits to the retailer and takes an order, which is usually delivered at an agreed time and date. The representative provides a list of available products with grades and prices, so that the retailer gets the quality required. Urgent orders can be placed by telephone.

Fig. 3.3 Smithfield Market, London

Wholesale markets

General wholesalers usually stock a variety of goods but tend to lean towards a particular section of the retail trade (like soft furnishings or clothing). There are, however, wholesale markets which are very specialised. London has two prime examples of these specialist markets: Smithfield Meat Market (supplying meat, poultry and game: see Fig. 3.3) and New Covent Garden Market at Nine Elms (supplying fruit, vegetables and flowers). These are open markets; anyone can visit, and the goods are displayed so the customers can see clearly what they are buying. You can't buy a pound of tomatoes at these markets, however – you must buy in bulk and take the goods away immediately. You either use your own transport or hire delivery from carriers who tout for trade, rather like taxi drivers.

In the case of the large London markets, produce is taken to the market each day by producers and growers from a wide area. It is then dispatched again to customers in the Midlands, the South and the West of England.

Produce markets

Some towns still hold traditional produce markets where animals and farm produce are auctioned. A similar process exists for the distribution of seafood at traditional fishing ports like Hull, Grimsby, Aberdeen and Great Yarmouth. Goods are displayed and sold to the highest bidder. When the produce has all been sold, the market closes for the day.

Cash and carry

The term *cash and carry* is self-explanatory. Goods are paid for when selected and then carried away by the purchaser. This is an alternative source of wholesale supply of increasing importance in the retail trade. Retailers are able to visit cash-and-carry suppliers to see and judge the produce (its quality and price) on offer. There are no credit terms, and delivery (if any) is extra.

Some wholesale cash-and-carry firms offer *own-brand* products at reduced prices (Fig. 3.4), providing retailers with a list showing the purchase price (to the retailer), the suggested selling price (to the consumer) and the profit margin for the retailer.

BIGGEST RANGE   BEST QUALITY   HIGHEST POR

BOOKER CASH & CARRY   *Family Choice — quite simply a good buy*

Fig. 3.4 Own-brand label, cash and carry

Buying from a wholesaler or cash-and-carry supplier

References are always required for retailers wishing to become a customer of the wholesaler. Customers of a cash-and-carry company must obtain a member's card (Fig. 3.5) and specify those people who are allowed to buy on behalf of the firm.

Doing without the wholesaler

Some manufacturers sell direct to the general public, by offering their manufactured goods from a factory shop, e.g. a shoe factory selling shoes, or Brentford Nylons (sheets, duvets and curtains). Some retailers buy in such large quantities that they buy direct from the manufacturer and do not deal with a wholesaler. Marks and Spencer buy from manufacturers who often produce goods solely for the St Michael brand.

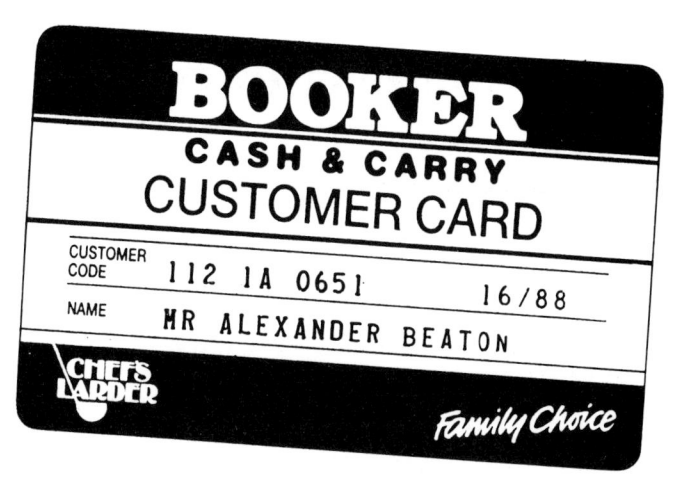

Fig. 3.5 Cash-and-carry member's card

●QUESTIONS

1. In what circumstances might a retailer prefer to buy from a traditional wholesaler rather than a cash-and-carry wholesaler? And what factors would influence the retailer in buying only from a cash-and-carry company?
2. Who would be likely to provide the necessary references before a retailer is accepted as a customer?
3. Why must a retailer carry a cash-and-carry member's card?
4. Why must retailers retain the receipts for all goods purchased?
5. What does the abbreviation *VAT* stand for? How is VAT on retail goods recorded at the point of sale?

●THINGS TO DO

1. Research your area to make a list of all manufacturers who sell direct to the general public by advertising in newspapers and magazines. State the advantages and disadvantages of buying direct from the manufacturer.
2. (a) Within your group choose different-sized organisations to evaluate (your choice will depend on your area), i.e. small retailer, large retailer, wholesaler, cash-and-carry supplier. In pairs, compile a short questionnaire to be sent to managers of such organisations to find out how their business works. You should include questions on staff recruitment, staff training, type of goods involved and how obtained, promotional offers and marketing.
   Compare your list of questions with those of others in your group: what has been included – or left out – in each list? After agreeing which questions are most important, compile a class questionnaire.
   (b) Write a polite letter to the manager of the organisation you have chosen, asking if he or she can spare the time to complete your questionnaire. Include a stamped addressed envelope for the reply. Each pair should then prepare a report to be given to the class.
3. Over a period of one month during your family shopping at a supermarket, write down the prices of products such as eggs, tomatoes, butter and washing powder each week. Make a note of any changes in price. Why do you think prices go up and down?
4. Research as many wholesalers' 'own brand' names as you can (e.g. Fig. 3.4). Compare the cost and quantity with well-known brand names and state which products you consider to be 'value for money'.

●SOURCES OF INFORMATION

1. Yellow Pages and your local telephone directory.
2. *The Grocer* Magazine, 5–7 Southwark Street, London SE1 1RQ
3. Smithfield Market, London EC1, and New Covent Garden, Nine Elms Market, London SW8

UNIT 3.3
Competition: Price and Non-Price

Pricing policies

A price for a product must be high enough to cover all the costs which the seller has met and yet be low enough to attract customers. Retailers sometimes reduce the price of one or more articles below the normal selling price just to attract customers into the store. The hope is that the customers will remain and spend enough to cover any loss on the reduced item(s). 'Today's special offer' is known as a *call-bird* or *loss leader*, a term usually used in food retailing, especially in supermarkets.

There are three main influences on pricing policies:

1 *The market factor* – attracting customers and achieving a high enough volume of sales to cover costs and make a profit.
2 *The image factor* – retaining satisfied customers and boosting sales.
3 *The competition factor* – maintaining a level of sales when in competition with other outlets.

Before prices are set, a business will assess the competition, the distance people may have to travel to shop with a competitor and the additional services offered by the competition.

For the small retailer, *Shaw's Guide to the Retailer*, published monthly, gives a review of retail prices over a wide range of products. It details price increases and reductions, without which the smaller retailer could experience a loss of sales (or a decline in profits) just by sticking to an out-of-date pricing policy.

In many outlets (especially those selling clothing and shoes) retail traders follow a policy of *sales promotion* by what seem to be enormous price reductions. In reality the goods are priced at cost just to move them from the shelves and rails, so that new stock can be introduced. Supermarkets often reduce the price of goods when 'sell-by' dates are approaching or when there is a special promotion of a new line which has to compete with existing *brand leaders* (i.e. the most successful brands; see Unit 6 on brands).

Generally traders charge 'what the market will bear', pricing at levels they think the customer is prepared to pay rather than shop around. Successful pricing requires detailed knowledge of competition in the area and much careful thought.

Non-pricing methods of competition

There is a limit to how much you can reduce prices. Supermarkets buy in huge quantities at very low prices and regularly undercut the competition in terms of special offers, range of goods and ease of shopping.

Smaller retailers need to compete using *non-pricing methods*. For example:

1 By remaining open 'all hours', Saturdays and Sundays included. If you offer a service, then you must be prepared to turn out when called. Plumbing jobs tend not to wait until Monday morning. The Sunday Trading Act restricts what can normally be sold on Sundays.
2 By maintaining a quality of service (with a smile) so that your customers rely upon a friendly and helpful attitude, time for a gossip, and offer of expert advice. Call back in ten minutes and it will be ready – what is called 'the personal touch'.
3 By keeping your goods or produce clean and fresh, well displayed and clearly priced.
4 By offering a delivery service, perhaps even collecting orders at the same time.
5 By replacing faulty goods readily and with an apology.
6 By maintaining welcoming premises, perhaps with a chair for elderly customers. Many shops now have music to encourage people to come inside.
7 By attractive window displays, frequently changed and tastefully arranged.
8 By knowing your regular customers by name and anticipating their requirements. (I prefer a cheerful newsvendor who has my correct paper ready when he sees me approaching.)
9 Above all, by doing *what* you promised *when* you promised it and not keeping customers waiting.

While low prices will always be attractive, the quality of service is equally important. Customers like to be treated as special, not ignored or kept waiting. The restaurant employing the world's best chef will prosper only if the food is properly presented in clean and comfortable premises by waiters who are helpful and friendly.

Exclusivity

To some extent the amount you can charge depends upon where and what you are selling. For example, you can sell a bottle of wine in a restaurant for two or three times its cost in an off-licence. You expect to pay more for a box of chocolates in an expensive store like Harrods than you would in the local supermarket; possibly the 'snob value' of the carrier bag is important. Is a suit with a Savile Row label really worth £800? Why are people prepared to pay so much more for a first-class rail ticket, especially on a Pullman train? Why will people *pay* to obtain an American Express charge card when they can have an ordinary Access card with ample credit limit *for nothing*? Do cut-glass tumblers really make your Coke taste better than if you use a straw straight from the can?

Here we have the third element in competition: *exclusivity* or 'snob value'. If you can convince the buying public that your goods are exclusive, if you can make them feel good, at ease or confident, or can provide a sense of superiority, then you can charge almost what you like – and get away with it!

Plastic money and credit trading

The practice of buying goods on credit is a necessity in some trades. Very few cars would be sold if everyone had to pay cash. So traders have to compete by offering credit terms or accepting credit cards. This is a form of non-price competition.

Retailers offer credit terms, either through a finance company (see Unit 10, section 10.2) or by making an arrangement with credit card companies (Access, Visa). The credit card holder presents a card, takes the goods and settles with the card company at the end of each month. The trader receives payment immediately, using the voucher signed by the customer rather like a cheque. The trader is charged with commission by the card company of 1 or 2 per cent on the value of the goods sold. This is really a reduction in the trader's selling price and reduces his profit. But credit-card purchasing is now so widely accepted that without the system suppliers would fail to attract many potential customers. A reduced profit is better than none at all, and the increase in *total* sales which results from the availability of credit facilities increases the *total* profit.

Cheques and cheque guarantee cards

Every trader is willing to accept cash, but most people prefer to pay by cheque, even at supermarket checkouts; large amounts of cash are easily lost or stolen. Cheque guarantee cards are some protection against fraud, but will only cover a single cheque up to £100 in value (at the time of writing). Even so, cheque fraud is widespread; traders must make a quick assessment of any customer who offers a cheque in payment or in part-payment. With a credit card the retailer can check on the customer by telephoning the credit-card company. This is impossible in the case of the cheque. However, competition is so fierce that a trader unwilling to accept cheques would lose a lot of business.

●SOURCES OF INFORMATION

1. Barclaycard Centre, Northampton, NN1 1SG
2. National Westminster Bank, plc, Access House, Southend-on-Sea, Essex SS99 9BB.
3. *Shaw's Guide to the Retailer*, Shaw's Price Guide Ltd, PO Box 32, Abingdon, Oxon OX14 3LJ
4. *Glass's Guide* to the Motor trade, Glass's Guide Service Ltd, Elgin House, St George's Avenue, Weybridge, Surrey KT13 OBX

●THINGS TO DO

1. Compare prices of the same brand of goods in a small shop and a large supermarket. If there is a difference in price – and you must compare like with like – how do you explain the ability of the local shop to charge more?
2. You are considering starting up in business as a stationer and tobacconist in your local shopping centre, by purchasing an existing outlet. What factors will you take into consideration in arriving at your decision? What problems are you likely to face? What other fast-selling lines could you add to existing stock?
3. *Passing trade* (i.e. potential customers passing the shop and deciding to enter and buy) is a real advantage to a trader and a potential boost to profits. Discuss the best sort of location to benefit from passing trade. Suggest how a retailer could take full advantage of passing trade. In your view, what types of retail outlet most enjoy the benefits of passing trade?
4. Using Fig. 3.6, research the problems associated with credit-card sales. What are the drawbacks and what are the advantages? What does *Obtain authorisation* mean?
5. What is a *loss leader*? What is involved and how does the retailer hope to benefit? What sort of goods are used as loss leaders? How do direct sales outlets employ loss-leader techniques?

Sales procedure for over the counter sales

1. Check that the card is acceptable
2. Imprint the Sales Voucher.
3. Complete the Sales Voucher.
4. Customer signs.
5. Check the signature and the Card.
6. Check Details are clear on all four copies.

Obtain authorisation at this stage if necessary

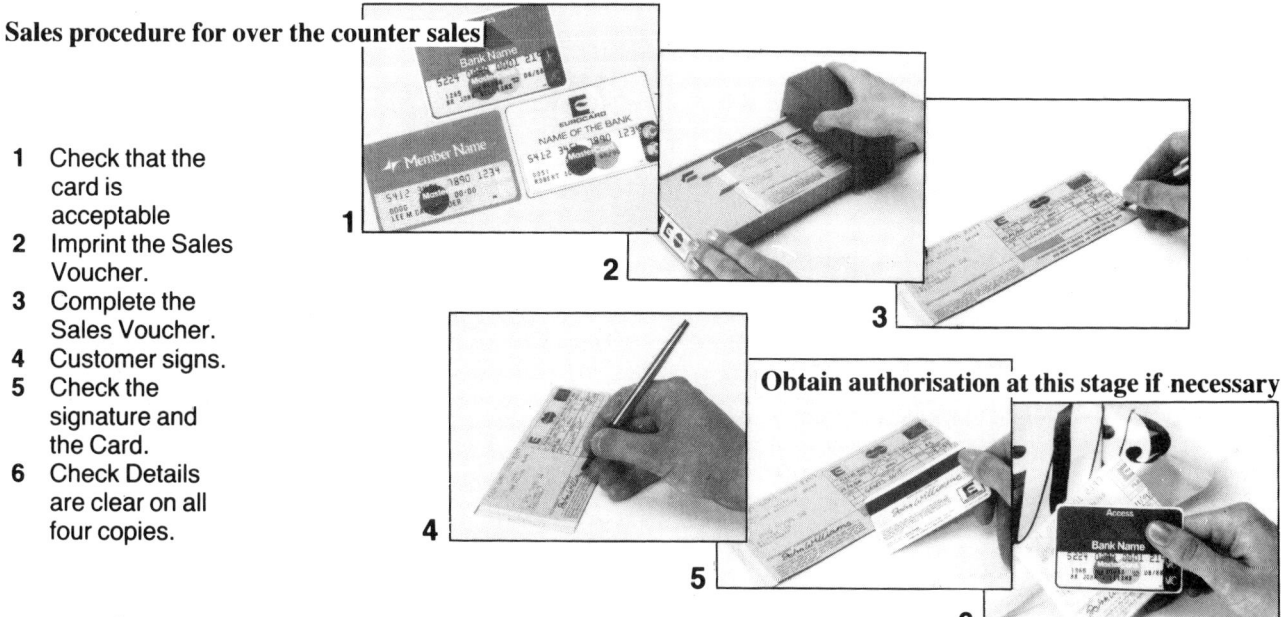

Fig. 3.6 Completing a credit-card sales voucher

4 SHOPS AND SHOPPING

UNIT 4.1
Itinerant Trading

The term *distributive trade* is used to describe any work involved in retailing. Plenty of selling is done by outlets other than shops. An *itinerant trader* literally means one who moves from place to place, but the term now includes unusual forms of retailing offering convenience to the public, which are available 'round the clock'. Let us look at some of these retail outlets.

Mail order

The press and television advertise mail-order goods, but the best known mail-order selling is by catalogue. There are a vast number of companies involved: Freeman's, John England, Kay, Choice, Trafford, etc. An agent is appointed, often a woman who wishes to earn extra money working from home. The agent places orders with the company on behalf of her customers and for this work she is usually paid 10 per cent commission. There is very little work involved apart from completing order forms (see Fig. 4.1), recording all payments made and taking cash to the bank. Cash can be sent with orders, but the attraction of mail order is to buy on credit terms: have the goods now and pay later by instalments.

Party selling

Party selling is usually operated by housewives who become agents and make contact with people who are prepared to hold a 'selling party' in their home. The hostess invites a number of people and usually provides refreshments. For this she receives a free gift, and the agent who visits the party gets a commission on all goods sold.

Direct selling

Increasingly, goods are offered for sale via advertisements, or by the issue of a brochure inserted in a magazine, pushed through your door as 'junk mail', or included with (say) credit card invoices. To buy, you complete an order form and pay by cheque or credit card for goods, or you agree to join a book or record club offering attractive discounts. Unfortunately, some of these outlets practise *inertia selling*, where goods you haven't ordered and don't want arrive on your doorstep.

●QUESTIONS

1. Why do you think people buy from a catalogue instead of visiting shops?
2. What questions would you need to ask an agent before ordering goods?
3. What problems might be associated with inertia selling?
4. List three advantages of party selling to (a) the agent and (b) the customer. Can you think of any disadvantages?

●THINGS TO DO

From a catalogue, choose ten items which you would like to purchase. Copy out and complete the order form (Fig. 4.1) correctly: total the cost of the order and calculate how much commission is due to the agent, assuming the rate of commission to be 10 per cent.

Fig. 4.1 Mail-order form

Fig. 4.2 Market shopping

Other outlets

Markets People selling from a market stall often visit a different market each day, others may have a shop but choose to sell from a market stall once or twice each week (Fig. 4.2).

Travelling shops This method of selling is less popular than it used to be but is nevertheless useful to people living in rural areas, who are not always close to shops.

Door-to-door A salesperson calls at every house in a particular area hoping to sell his or her product. Double glazing is one of the many products sold in this way.

Automatic vending machines Goods are sold from machines. Customers place coins in the slot and the goods are delivered. Vending machines are found in many public places, e.g. office buildings, stations and colleges.

Petrol stations Selling petrol is still a retail service. Some petrol is sold by an attendant filling the petrol tank, but customers often serve themselves and then go into the office/shop to pay (Fig. 4.3). Many petrol stations give away vouchers with petrol sales and this again can attract custom. (If you collect enough vouchers you can obtain free gifts, such as mugs, glasses, cassettes, cutlery, etc.)

Most petrol stations now have small shops on their premises. Goods offered include sweets, cigarettes, magazines, flowers, car accessories and seasonal goods.

●QUESTIONS

1 In your view, do open or street markets have any future? What service do they offer?
2 What does the shopping public expect from travelling shops? List the various types of customer most likely to benefit from travelling shops and the goods they are likely to need.
3 What is meant by the term *high-pressure selling*? With which forms of trading is this often associated? How can the public resist high-pressure selling?
4 What are the advantages and disadvantages of vending machines? Research the kind of products sold via vending machines.
5 Why do some people dislike self-service petrol stations? Explain the growth of retail selling at petrol stations.

●THINGS TO DO

1 Visit your local market and list the different types of stalls. Look for any duplicate stalls, i.e. two or more selling fruit and vegetables or dairy produce. Do prices vary from stall to stall? If so, by how much? Give reasons for any difference in price.
2 Write down six different items from a market stall, showing the price, and then visit a shop in town and compare the prices. Which is the cheapest place to shop? What about quality? Try to explain the reason for any differences.
3 Write a polite letter to your local council asking the price of renting a market stall. What would your takings have to be to make a reasonable profit after paying rent, travelling costs, etc.?
4 One member of each group in the class should write to one of five large companies asking if they offer a mail-order service (e.g. House of Fraser, Marks & Spencer, Debenhams). Compare: (a) the replies you receive, and (b) the services offered.
5 Consult the Citizens' Advice Bureau on the action to take if goods arrive which you haven't ordered and don't want.

Fig. 4.3 A self-service petrol station

●SOURCES OF INFORMATION

1 Yellow Pages and your local telephone directory
2 Local council offices
3 Esso Petroleum Ltd, Esso House, 94–8 Victoria Street, London SW1E 5JW
4 Marks & Spencer PLC, 47–67 Baker Street, London W1A 1DN
5 House of Fraser, 10 Buchanan Street, Glasgow G1 3LW

UNIT 4.2
Small-scale Retailing

Small shops are often run by families operating as sole traders or in partnership. They cannot compete with supermarket prices, since supermarkets buy stock in huge quantities. Shopkeepers know most of their customers, and shopping in a small shop can be a pleasant social activity; although prices may be higher, people often prefer the friendly and relaxed atmosphere. Many smaller shops now offer self-service shopping, which allows customers to examine prices before purchase. To help to combat supermarket prices many small shops now offer own-label goods, which can be sold much cheaper than the usual brand names.

Specialist outlets

Specialist outlets are another type of small shop usually run by families or by one person: such shops *specialise* in certain goods, e.g. butchers, bakers, shoe shops, wool shops, etc. The majority of these still operate a counter service and meet a local need.

Voluntary chains

Many individual retailers have found survival difficult and now operate within voluntary groups. There are many of these chains, e.g. Wavy Line, Mace and Spar. Voluntary groups allow the individual retailer to place orders with wholesalers servicing the chain. The wholesaler can then place large orders with manufacturers and obtain a worthwhile reduction in price. National advertising can be done by the group, which also advises on shop layout and may help with finance and with credit facilities.

Small retailers survive by joining a voluntary chain, but in some cases they may lose their independence, and have little say in advertising, shop layout or goods for sale.

Special offers

Certain products carry a *special offer* label (Fig. 4.4). These offers aim to attract higher sales, by encouraging customers to buy products they would perhaps not normally try, or to buy more of a particular product than they would otherwise do.

Fig. 4.4 Special offers attract higher sales

Franchising

Franchising is the term used when a person rents the right to trade in the name, product and method of selling that product. He or she is known as the *franchisee*; the owner of the franchise is known as the *franchisor*. Research ensures that setting up a particular business in a given area is likely to be a profitable venture. When agreement is reached the franchisee is given help in:

1. finding suitable premises;
2. ongoing training;
3. advertising;
4. supplying goods at competitive prices.

Franchising is becoming increasingly popular; some well-known names are the Body Shop, Benetton, Wimpy, Kentucky Fried Chicken, Tie Rack and Home Tune.

Anyone starting up in business needs capital, some knowledge of the trade they are about to enter, premises and a stock of materials. None of this is easy. Any new business, lacking an established reputation, will have difficulty in gaining and keeping a share of the market. A chance to run a business which has an established group of customers, which trades under a well-known name and whose products are widely advertised, tried, tested and in great demand, is an opportunity not to be missed.

Anyone who is accepted as a trainee by McDonalds, for instance, with the promise of a franchise in one of their shops, has a real chance of business success. However, franchisees are never completely their own master; the parent company will expect them to buy stock only from them, to sell only the range of products approved by them and to maintain the outlet according to their policies. One McDonalds looks pretty much the same as another, and the service offered is identical.

The profits from a franchise belong to the franchisee, but he or she is contracted to pay to the parent company a rental based on profit.

● SOURCES OF INFORMATION

1. British Franchise Association, Franchise Chambers, 75a Bell Street, Henley-on-Thames, Oxon RG9 2BD
2. Department of Industry (Small Firms Division), 123 Victoria Street, London SW1 6RB
3. Small Firms Centre, Business & Technology Centre, Bessemer Drive, Stevenage, Herts SG1 2DX, publishes leaflets advising about starting and running a small business
4. CoSIRA (Council for Small Industries in Rural Areas), 141 Castle Street, Salisbury, Wiltshire SP1 3TP
5. Your local Citizens' Advice Bureau
6. Yellow Pages and telephone directory

● QUESTIONS

1. Why is the small shop not able to sell most well-known brand-named goods at supermarket prices?
2. List the advantages and disadvantages of shopping in a small shop. What conclusions can you draw from your list?
3. What are the advantages of shopping in specialist shops?
4. What are the disadvantages to voluntary chains not offering well-known brand products for sale? How do they make up for this lack? What could be a disadvantage to voluntary chains offering well-known as well as own-brand products for sale?
5. Discuss as a group: (a) the advantages, and (b) the disadvantages of franchising. Draw up a wall chart showing franchise outlets in your area. Is there a pattern to the type of business offered as a franchise?

● THINGS TO DO

1. Go into a small shop and write down the prices of six different products. Then go to a supermarket and write down the prices of the same products. Calculate the total cost in each shop. Is the total cost different? By how much does each item differ? If the small shop is more expensive, why, in your view, might it still be cheaper to shop there?

2. Some products are labelled with a special offer, e.g. 8p or 10p 'off your next purchase'; others offer a free gift (Fig. 4.4). Discuss any disadvantages these vouchers may have for the small retailer. Research what happens to the vouchers once they have been exchanged for goods.

3. Imagine you are ready to open a retail business. Choose any product that appeals to you. (a) What are the first decisions you will take? (b) What will you need to consider when deciding whether to apply for a franchise or remain independent? (c) What influenced your choice of product and your decision about franchising?

4. Write to the British Franchise Association, asking for details on franchising and a list of franchisors. From the list, choose a franchise that is not already in your area. Research the amount of capital you would need to become a franchisee. In your opinion, do you think the product you have chosen would be a success in your area? Discuss your choice in class and say why you think the business might be successful.

5. Assume you are considering starting a small business in an Enterprise Zone (see Unit 17, section 17.3).
(a) Write to the Small Firms Division of the Department of Trade and Industry asking where these government-assisted areas are. (b) Write to CoSIRA (the Council for Small Industries in Rural Areas) asking about the kind of small business they want to encourage. (c) Go to your local Citizens Advice Bureau and ask for the names of agencies in your area offering help to people starting a small business.

Discuss your findings in class. What are the advantages of: (a) starting up in your own area, and (b) moving to an Enterprise Zone?

●UNIT 4.3
Large-scale Retailing

Chain stores

Chain (or multiple) stores have at least ten branches. Some are specialist chains, such as Halfords, W. H. Smith and Burton's. Variety chain stores sell a wide range of goods, e.g. Woolworths, Littlewoods and British Home Stores. Many sell goods carrying their own brand name, e.g. Marks & Spencer (St Michael), Littlewoods (Keynote) and Woolworths (Winfield).

Chain stores are controlled at their head office, where all major policy decisions are made by their centralised management. Store managers receive instructions from their head office concerning store layout, prices, decisions to move goods not selling to another branch and the number of staff to be employed.

Chain stores have a system of central purchase of stock. Buying decisions are made by *buyers* at the head office, which guarantees standards.

Chain stores are happy to exchange goods if they are accompanied by the original receipt. If a receipt is not available (perhaps the goods have been bought as a present), then a voucher (a credit note to be spent in the store) for the value of the goods may be given. The policy of offering gift vouchers has proved very popular especially at Christmas, as the recipient can use the voucher at his or her local branch of the store. Most stores operate their own charge card system which enables people to buy goods on credit (see Fig. 4.5).

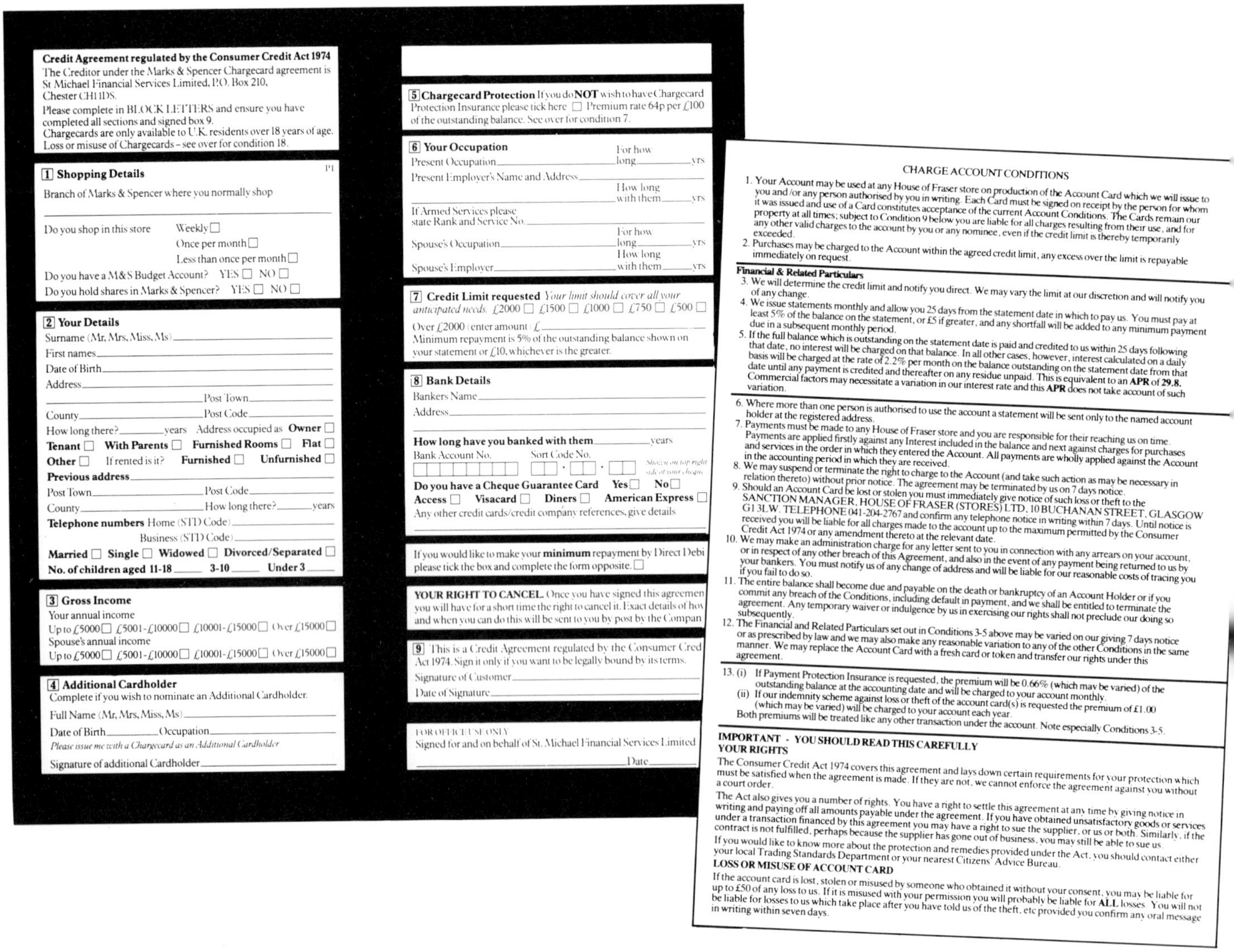

Credit Agreement regulated by the Consumer Credit Act 1974
The Creditor under the Marks & Spencer Chargecard agreement is St Michael Financial Services Limited, P.O. Box 210, Chester CH1 1DS.
Please complete in BLOCK LETTERS and ensure you have completed all sections and signed box 9.
Chargecards are only available to U.K. residents over 18 years of age.
Loss or misuse of Chargecards – see over for condition 18.

1 Shopping Details P1
Branch of Marks & Spencer where you normally shop ____
Do you shop in this store Weekly ☐ Once per month ☐ Less than once per month ☐
Do you have a M&S Budget Account? YES ☐ NO ☐
Do you hold shares in Marks & Spencer? YES ☐ NO ☐

2 Your Details
Surname (Mr, Mrs, Miss, Ms) ____
First names ____
Date of Birth ____
Address ____
____ Post Town ____
County ____ Post Code ____
How long there? ____ years Address occupied as **Owner** ☐
Tenant ☐ **With Parents** ☐ **Furnished Rooms** ☐ **Flat** ☐
Other ☐ If rented is it? **Furnished** ☐ **Unfurnished** ☐
Previous address ____
Post Town ____ Post Code ____
County ____ How long there? ____ years
Telephone numbers Home (STD Code) ____
Business (STD Code) ____
Married ☐ **Single** ☐ **Widowed** ☐ **Divorced/Separated** ☐
No. of children aged 11-18 ____ **3-10** ____ **Under 3** ____

3 Gross Income
Your annual income
Up to £5000 ☐ £5001-£10000 ☐ £10001-£15000 ☐ Over £15000 ☐
Spouse's annual income
Up to £5000 ☐ £5001-£10000 ☐ £10001-£15000 ☐ Over £15000 ☐

4 Additional Cardholder
Complete if you wish to nominate an Additional Cardholder.
Full Name (Mr, Mrs, Miss, Ms) ____
Date of Birth ____ Occupation ____
Please issue me with a Chargecard as an Additional Cardholder
Signature of additional Cardholder ____

5 Chargecard Protection If you do **NOT** wish to have Chargecard Protection Insurance please tick here ☐ Premium rate 64p per £100 of the outstanding balance. See over for condition 7.

6 Your Occupation
Present Occupation ____ For how long ____ yrs
Present Employer's Name and Address ____
____ How long with them ____ yrs
If Armed Services please state Rank and Service No. ____
Spouse's Occupation ____ For how long ____ yrs
Spouse's Employer ____ How long with them ____ yrs

7 Credit Limit requested *Your limit should cover all your anticipated needs.* £2000 ☐ £1500 ☐ £1000 ☐ £750 ☐ £500 ☐
Over £2000 (enter amount) £ ____
Minimum repayment is 5% of the outstanding balance shown on your statement or £10, whichever is the greater.

8 Bank Details
Bankers Name ____
Address ____
How long have you banked with them ____ years
Bank Account No. ☐☐☐☐☐☐☐☐ Sort Code No. ☐☐ · ☐☐ · ☐☐ *Shown on top right side of your cheque*
Do you have a Cheque Guarantee Card Yes ☐ **No** ☐
Access ☐ **Visacard** ☐ **Diners** ☐ **American Express** ☐
Any other credit cards/credit company references, give details ____

If you would like to make your **minimum** repayment by Direct Debi please tick the box and complete the form opposite. ☐

YOUR RIGHT TO CANCEL. Once you have signed this agreemen you will have for a short time the right to cancel it. Exact details of hov and when you can do this will be sent to you by post by the Compan

9 This is a Credit Agreement regulated by the Consumer Cred Act 1974. Sign it only if you want to be legally bound by its terms.
Signature of Customer ____
Date of Signature ____

FOR OFFICE USE ONLY
Signed for and on behalf of St. Michael Financial Services Limited
____ Date ____

CHARGE ACCOUNT CONDITIONS

1. Your Account may be used at any House of Fraser store on production of the Account Card which we will issue to you and/or any person authorised by you in writing. Each Card must be signed on receipt by the person for whom it was issued and use of a Card constitutes acceptance of the current Account Conditions. The Cards remain our property at all times; subject to Condition 9 below you are liable for all charges resulting from their use, and for any other valid charges to the account by you or any nominee, even if the credit limit is thereby temporarily exceeded.
2. Purchases may be charged to the Account within the agreed credit limit, any excess over the limit is repayable immediately on request.

Financial & Related Particulars

3. We will determine the credit limit and notify you direct. We may vary the limit at our discretion and will notify you of any change.
4. We issue statements monthly and allow you 25 days from the statement date in which to pay us. You must pay at least 5% of the balance on the statement, or £5 if greater, and any shortfall will be added to any minimum payment due in a subsequent monthly period.
5. If the full balance which is outstanding on the statement date is paid and credited to us within 25 days following that date, no interest will be charged on that balance. In all other cases, however, interest calculated on a daily basis will be charged at the rate of 2.2% per month on the balance outstanding on the statement date from that date until any payment is credited and thereafter on any residue unpaid. This is equivalent to an **APR** of **29.8.** Commercial factors may necessitate a variation in our interest rate and this **APR** does not take account of such variation.
6. Where more than one person is authorised to use the account a statement will be sent only to the named account holder at the registered address.
7. Payments must be made to any House of Fraser store and you are responsible for their reaching us on time. Payments are applied firstly against any Interest included in the balance and next against charges for purchases and services in the order in which they entered the Account. All payments are wholly applied against the Account in the accounting period in which they are received.
8. We may suspend or terminate the right to charge to the Account (and take such action as may be necessary in relation thereto) without prior notice. The agreement may be terminated by us on 7 days notice.
9. Should an Account Card be lost or stolen you must immediately give notice of such loss or theft to the SANCTION MANAGER, HOUSE OF FRASER (STORES) LTD, 10 BUCHANAN STREET, GLASGOW G1 3LW. TELEPHONE 041-204-2767 and confirm any telephone notice in writing within 7 days. Until notice is received you will be liable for all charges made to the account up to the maximum permitted by the Consumer Credit Act 1974 or any amendment thereto at the relevant date.
10. We may make an administration charge for any letter sent to you in connection with any arrears on your account, or in respect of any other breach of this Agreement, and also in the event of any payment being returned to us by your bankers. You must notify us of any change of address and will be liable for our reasonable costs of tracing you if you fail to do so.
11. The entire balance shall become due and payable on the death or bankruptcy of an Account Holder or if you commit any breach of the Conditions, including default in payment, and we shall be entitled to terminate the agreement. Any temporary waiver or indulgence by us in exercising our rights shall not preclude our doing so subsequently.
12. The Financial and Related Particulars set out in Conditions 3-5 above may be varied on our giving 7 days notice or as prescribed by law and we may also make any reasonable variation to any of the other Conditions in the same manner. We may replace the Account Card with a fresh card or token and transfer our rights under this agreement.
13. (i) If Payment Protection Insurance is requested, the premium will be 0.66% (which may be varied) of the outstanding balance at the accounting date and will be charged to your account monthly.
(ii) If our indemnity scheme against loss or theft of the account card(s) is requested the premium of £1.00 (which may be varied) will be charged to your account each year.
Both premiums will be treated like any other transaction under the account. Note especially Conditions 3-5.

IMPORTANT - YOU SHOULD READ THIS CAREFULLY
YOUR RIGHTS
The Consumer Credit Act 1974 covers this agreement and lays down certain requirements for your protection which must be satisfied when the agreement is made. If they are not, we cannot enforce the agreement against you without a court order.
The Act also gives you a number of rights. You have a right to settle this agreement at any time by giving notice in writing and paying off all amounts payable under the agreement. If you have obtained unsatisfactory goods or services under a transaction financed by this agreement you may have a right to sue the supplier, or us or both. Similarly, if the contract is not fulfilled, perhaps because the supplier has gone out of business, you may still be able to sue us.
If you would like to know more about the protection and remedies provided under the Act, you should contact either your local Trading Standards Department or your nearest Citizens' Advice Bureau.
LOSS OR MISUSE OF ACCOUNT CARD
If the account card is lost, stolen or misused by someone who obtained it without your consent, you may be liable for up to £50 of any loss to us. If it is misused with your permission you will probably be liable for **ALL** losses. You will not be liable for losses to us which take place after you have told us of the theft, etc provided you confirm any oral message in writing within seven days.

Fig. 4.5 A chargecard application form

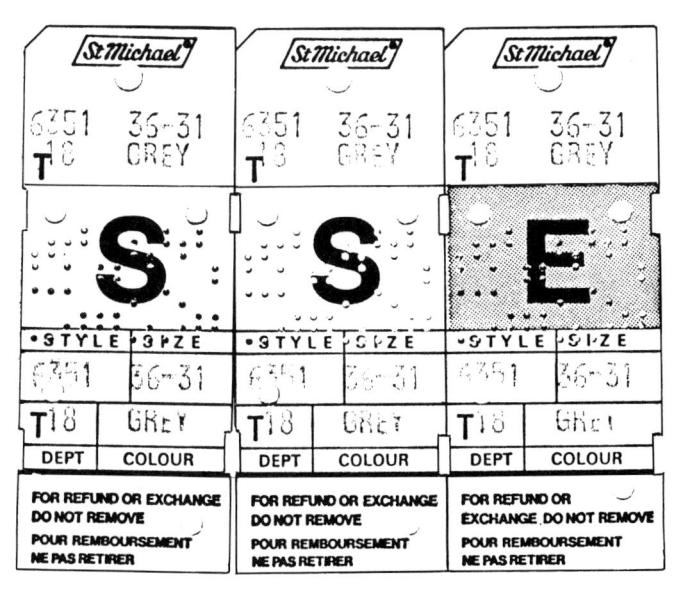

Fig. 4.6 An example of coding by punched holes (called *kimbals*), formerly used in M & S stores.

All price tickets are coded in chain stores by means of punched holes (see Fig. 4.6) a number code or a bar code. Where stores have a modern computer system the sales assistant will enter the number code in the till, or pass a light pen over the bar code: the till automatically shows the correct price, itemises the receipt and alters the stock records. If the store does not have this system the price tickets are collected up and sent to the computer centre to be "read". This imformation tells the company about branch sales performance and stock levels and helps to decide when certain lines of stock need to be reordered.

Department stores

Department stores are usually found in town and city centres. They sell a wide range of goods: clothing, food, toys, cards and stationery, furniture, electrical goods, cosmetics, etc. Credit facilities are available. Restaurants, coffee shops and cloakrooms help attract customers who stay to browse and buy.

A department store is really a collection of shops under one roof. In fact, in the case of Debenhams, shop space is rented to other firms, which do business independently of each other. But in other stores, each department is under the control of a buyer or manager, who in turn is responsible to the general manager.

During recent years there have been several mergers of department stores. For example, both House of Fraser and Debenhams are the owners of a number of stores, and this enables them to form large multiple chains which makes the bulk buying of goods more profitable. Customers benefit from lower prices.

Co-operatives

The history of the Co-operative Movement is described in Unit 7, section 7.3. Co-ops span all forms and sizes of retail outlet. At one end there are the unit shops, such as butchers; at the other, large city-centre outlets that are department stores. Somewhere in-between are the milk roundsmen carrying dairy produce (who are really itinerant traders), the wedding and funeral services, the Co-operative Bank and the Co-operative Insurance Service. In total the range of services provided by the Co-operative Movement makes it one of the largest distributive organisations in Britain.

● SOURCES OF INFORMATION

1. Marks & Spencer Financial Services Ltd, North-West House, City Road, Chester CH1 3AN
2. House of Fraser (Stores) Ltd, 69 Buchanan Street, Glasgow G1 3LE
3. Harrods Ltd, Brompton Road, London SW1X 7XL
4. Selfridges Ltd, 400 Oxford Street, London W1A 1AB
5. Debenhams Ltd, 334 Oxford Street, London W1A 1EF
6. Yellow Pages and the telephone directory

● QUESTIONS

1. From your area, write down the names of: (a) as many chain stores as you can and detail the range of products available; (b) as many variety chain stores as you can; again detail the range of products available; (c) department stores: detail the range of separate departments.
2. Trading stamps are now being offered at certain retail outlets. When you are buying goods, which do you prefer: (a) lower-priced goods, or (b) usual-priced goods plus trading stamps? Give reasons for your choice and describe any advantages of trading stamps: (i) to the buying public, (ii) to a retailer, and (iii) to the trading stamp firm.

● THINGS TO DO

1. Next time you buy an item from a chain store, look at the sales tag (Fig. 4.6). Note all the details and punched holes that are used to record details of stock and sales. Notice what the assistant does with the tag. Ask him or her politely to explain what happens to the tags after he or she has collected them.
2. Assume you are over 18 years of age. Copy out and then complete the credit application form shown in Fig. 4.5. Give reasons why the company requires the information requested in boxes 2, 3, 5, 6, 7 and 8.
3. Conduct a survey of shoe sizes of 100 people in your school (either all female, all male, or 50 female and 50 male) and draw a graph showing the range of sizes. How would this information influence your stock levels if you were managing a shoe shop?
4. British Home Stores, Mothercare and Habitat all belong to the same retail combine. Do you feel that these retail outlets have anything in common, and what advantage is to be gained from such combinations?

UNIT 4.4
Supermarkets, Hypermarkets and Discount Selling

Supermarkets

A supermarket is a large self-service shop selling food and household goods. The stock sold is bought in bulk, and a quick turnover is expected. All perishable produce must be fresh when it reaches the shop, otherwise customers will be dissatisfied and sales will decline.

'Sell by' dates on produce must be carefully checked, and quality control must be observed. Shelf stacking is practiced in a 'menu plan' to attract customers. Sweets, chocolates and seasonal goods, e.g. Easter eggs, are usually placed near the check-out to encourage *impulse buying*. Some people are employed solely as shelf stackers; this work is often done when the shop is closed.

Supermarkets are virtually fully self-service, except in some cases for sales of fish, meat and *delicatessen*. Most supermarkets offer late shopping every day of the week.

Branches of supermarket companies like Tesco, Sainsbury and Fine Fare are locally managed. But stock levels, presentation and pricing are the result of group decisions taken centrally at the company's head office. Head office also controls a bulk buying-in policy for all branches. Delivery is by an own-transport fleet from warehouses maintained by the group.

Hypermarkets

Hypermarkets (sometimes called *superstores*) can cover an area as large as a football stadium and carry a wide range of goods. Hypermarkets are usually situated just outside a town, providing plenty of space for car-parking; they often have car-park attendants. Shopping trolleys are placed outside the store, and in some places a deposit has to be paid before a trolley can be used. The deposit is refunded when the shopping trolley is returned, reducing the likelihood of shoppers leaving trolleys in random places. Hypermarkets have restaurants and coffee shops, and remain open for late shopping every day except Sunday.

Electronic tills are increasingly used at hypermarket check-outs. This system is called *electronic point of sale*. The bar code on the produce is passed through a beam at the check-out, which is read by a computer; the sales, stock and customer flow are recorded, providing a check on stock levels and the need to reorder (Fig. 4.7). Often, items are not individually priced, but the price is shown on the display shelf. However, the name of the product in addition to the price is recorded on the receipt slip from the electronic till.

In both hypermarkets and supermarkets, 'food tasting' is sometimes offered by a representative of a company wishing to launch a new product. A variety of methods are used to attract new customers and to encourage existing customers to make regular visits, e.g. free draw tickets are delivered to each household in the area of the store.

Closed-circuit television is used in hypermarkets, as in most large shops, in an attempt to prevent *pilfering* (people stealing small items).

Fig. 4.7 A bar code

Discount stores

Comet, MFI, Magnet Southerns, Queensway and Argos are some of the well-known discount stores which buy a range of household goods in large quantities from the manufacturer and sell direct to the consumer. This direct buying enables them to sell at discount prices, cheaper than the manufacturers' recommended prices. Products sold in discount stores include furniture, 'white goods' such as washing machines, TV sets, lighting and soft furnishings. Some stores now offer credit facilities and a delivery service. If a delivery service is not available, self-drive van hire can be obtained for the customer to transport bulky purchases. Discount stores advertise their goods in local and national newspapers, as well as on television.

This form of shopping has both advantages and disadvantages for the customer. Besides the discount price, customers benefit from large stocks and ranges of goods to choose from, together with the convenience of weekend and late-night opening hours. Disadvantages include a lack of advice and personal attention from sales staff if the store is very busy and the possibility that some of the lines of goods on offer may be out of stock.

●QUESTIONS

1. What are the advantages and disadvantages to the customer of supermarket selling? What improvements would you suggest in a supermarket well known to you?
2. Give reasons for the recent development of hypermarkets. Why do they not appear in city centres?
3. Why are discount stores so popular with the public? What do such stores offer which is missing from, say, department stores?

VIRGINIA. A soft acrylic velvet fabric with twin tiered back for extra comfort. This traditional suite has a delicate piping, edged along the top of the deep valance. In a choice of 3 colours. Suite consists of 3 seater settee and 2 armchairs. Available as individual items including 2 seater settee.

ONLY £699.99

FOR YOUR GREATER SAFETY

No wonder we call it The Premier Collection! For nowhere else will you find a range that so excitingly combines style, comfort, value and, above all, safety, with every suite upholstered with Combustion Modified High Resilient Foam. This foam complies with all current and proposed government legislation.

MONTROSE. With cushions that virtually wrap themselves around you. One of the most luxurious designs with gleaming 'Show-wood' trim. Upholstered in attractive diagonal stripes in 3 dominant shades. Suite consists of 3 seater settee and 2 armchairs. Available as individual items including 2 seater settee.

Normal Price	Save
£674.99	£75.00

NOW ONLY £599.99

FOR YOUR GREATER SAFETY

We offer a beautiful choice of fabrics too. Just choose the style and pattern you like and, in no time at all, your purchase will be delivered direct-from-manufacturer **FREE!** (to mainland addresses only).

TAKE A LOOK AT US NOW!

SHOPPING HOURS

Mon	10-8	Thurs	10-8
Tues	10-6	Fri	10-8
Wed	10-6	Sat	9-6

Scottish stores open Sun 10-5
N. Ireland exceptions Mon 10-6, Wed, Thurs, Fri 10-9

* Ring 01 200-0200 for the location of your nearest MFI Upholstery store.
* Access, Visa, Connect, American Express and Diners Cards accepted.

* Up to £2000 Instant Credit is available with the MFI Credit Card, subject to status. APR 32.9% variable (with Bankers Order). Written Quotations from any branch upon request. MFI are licensed Credit Brokers.

MFI

Prices do not include ornaments, accessories etc. Delivery service is to Mainland addresses only. Normal price is the price charged in all MFI stores not necessarily for 28 consecutive days in the past 6 months.

Fig. 4.8 MFI advertisements include details of their own credit card facilities

●THINGS TO DO

1 Go into a supermarket or hypermarket and make a diagram of the layout in the food department. Give reasons for the 'menu plan'. Compare the layout with that of another store, and account for the differences, if any.

2 Fig. 3.1 (in Unit 3, section 3.1) shows the story of how a lettuce arrives at the supermarket in a fresh condition ready for purchase. Illustrate the journey to the shops of fresh produce, such as bread or milk.

3 Look at Fig. 4.7 and find out how many items in your food cupboard have a bar code on the label. When you next shop at a store which uses an electronic till, watch the operation at a check-out and suggest how the bar code assists accuracy. Describe the advantages to both the retailer and the consumer.

4 Discuss the methods of security operated in large stores. Write down all the aspects of security you have noticed. How effective are they?

5 Fig. 4.8 advertises the MFI credit card. Write a polite letter to your nearest MFI store, asking for details of the MFI credit card. How does this sort of card compare with Access or Visa?

6 Write down the price of six good-quality items in a discount store and compare the price charged in a department store or specialist outlet. Make a case for buying from: (a) a discount store, and (b) a department store. Discuss any advantages of paying a higher price in a department store.

●SOURCES OF INFORMATION

1 Yellow Pages and the local telephone directory
2 Article Number Association (UK) Ltd, 6 Catherine Street, London WC2B 5JL. This organisation allocates the bar codes for the whole of Britain.

UNIT 4.5
Location of the Retail Trade

Corner shops
In many parts of Britain, small unit shops are situated at street corners in residential areas. They are 'open all hours' and serve a local need; they are used mainly by regular customers, most of whom are known to the owner.

Markets
Not all towns have market days, but those that do erect temporary stalls in a central square on perhaps two or three days each week. Market trade does not usually clash with the established shops in the area, but attracts customers who may not otherwise visit the town centre. Market traders travel the country, selling in different towns during the week.

Stall holders enjoy more freedom than shopkeepers; for example, small farmers can sell their own produce by having a part-time market stall. For the customer, markets offer variety, a day out and the chance of finding bargains.

Shopping centres
A shopping centre is where a number of shops are grouped together, often near housing estates, in shopping arcades or shopping parades, and they provide for people's everyday needs, i.e. grocers, chemists, greengrocers, bakers, butchers, hairdressing, clothes and shoe shops.

Shopping precincts
Precincts are found in the centre of a town. They are free from traffic, which makes it easy to browse as you walk from shop to shop. Car parks are sited within a short walk of the precinct. There is a wide range of shops – chain and department stores as well as small shops.

Shopping malls
A shopping mall is a collection of shops under one roof. The car park is usually conveniently situated. Outlets range from small individual shops to chain stores, department stores, banks and building societies.

Two well-known shopping malls are Brent Cross in London and the Bull Ring in Birmingham; others include the Arndale Centre at Eastbourne, the Plaza at East Kilbride and the Stoneborough Centre at Maidstone. Shopping malls attract a large number of customers, and many people spend a whole day in the centre, perhaps enjoying a meal in one of several eating places.

Regular excursions are available to shopping malls, and they are especially popular during Christmas and the holiday season.

The main advantage of shopping malls is that they provide a wide range of town-centre type shops in a pleasant, clean environment out of wind or rain.

Out-of-town centres and one-trip shopping The American system of out-of-town shopping malls is catching on fast in Britain where we are becoming used to the concept of superstores (like MFI, Halfords, Toys R Us, Texas, Carrefour and Wickes) all of which display goods in a warehouse type store with check-out counters and large car parks for the use of customers. Indeed the motor car is essential to the development of out-of-town shopping and specialist superstores.

The next step is for the grouping of superstores on sites well away from the traditional town centre, possibly on the edge of a town on what used to be farmland. An example of this is the Metro Centre at Gateshead (2000 parking places) which is the largest covered shopping area in Europe offering hypermarkets, superstores, Fantasy Land, Space City, restaurants, children's play areas, banks, hairdressing, shoe repairs, etc. A similar development, the Merry Hill Centre is now open at Wednesbury in the West Midlands.

Such centres are large, convenient, offering one-stop, pleasant, relaxed shopping. They are so popular with motorists that they threaten the future of traditional high-street trading upon which much commercial activity (banks, solicitors, building societies, insurance companies) depends. Cars are now motorised shopping trolleys and a trip to the Metro Centre provides a day out for all the family.

Out-of-town malls have destroyed city-centre shopping in the United States. Metro Centres may well have the same effect on shopping patterns in Britain.

Town and city centres
All large towns have shopping centres. London is the prime example, with Regent Street, Oxford Street, Bond Street and Knightsbridge, with nationally known shops attracting customers from an extremely wide area. You may wish to consider your own town to determine the advantages offered by city-centre shopping.

Changing patterns
The retail trade is changing. Many of the old corner shops have gone, although there are still plenty of 'open-all-hours' mini-market grocery stores. More and more large-scale schemes – hypermarkets, discount stores, shopping precincts and malls – are being built. At the same time, town- and city-centre shops are becoming more stylish and streamlined, using *atmosphere* (e.g. music and special lighting) to help sell their goods. As a result consumer choice is wider than ever before.

●QUESTIONS

1. Why might you decide to shop at your local shops rather than make a journey to the city centre eight miles away?
2. Why do you think special excursions to markets on market days are so popular?
3. Write down a list of shops you would expect to find in a shopping mall. Justify your choice.
4. When a new shopping precinct is established, why might existing retailers outside the precinct lose trade even though their products are competitively priced?

●THINGS TO DO

1. Draw up a questionnaire to discuss the shopping patterns of consumers near your school. Include questions such as: 'How often do you visit (a) your local shops; (b) the precinct/mall in town; (c) the shopping centre out of town?' And: 'Do you travel by car or by public transport? From the information you obtain, choose a suitable method of showing the shopping pattern, e.g. graphs and charts.
2. Where would you expect to find each of the retail outlets shown in Fig. 4.9? What circumstances influence that location? What particular service does each provide in order to attract custom? Do they compete by price or non-price methods?
3. In small groups, draw up a plan for a new shopping centre, precinct or mall in your area (it can be large or small). Choose a place where there are not enough shops and where the local community will benefit. On a large sheet of paper, design the layout of your shopping area; decide which will be the most useful shops to include, and give each one a suitable position. Will new buildings be needed, or can you adapt existing (perhaps empty) buildings? Will new roads or bus routes be required? How can the new shopping scheme be made as pleasant for people as possible? Compare your scheme with those of others in the class.

●SOURCES OF INFORMATION

1. Yellow Pages and the telephone directory
2. Local area guide and map
3. Your town hall and Chamber of Commerce

Fig. 4.9

5 COMMERCIAL DOCUMENTS

UNIT 5.1
Paper Transactions

When we shop we usually pay for the goods there and then and we are given a till receipt as proof that we have paid. The shopkeeper keeps a copy to record each sale. In the business world, payment is often not made until *after* goods have gone from seller to buyer. This practice is called *credit*, meaning 'have now, pay later'. Commercial transactions between business people where credit terms are allowed are also recorded by the issue of documents, and copies are kept for book-keeping purposes. This section explains these credit documents and provides examples in common use.

Letter of enquiry
Someone wishing to open a credit account will write to a number of suppliers asking for details about the products, delivery time, prices and special discounts.

Quotation
The seller will reply with a quotation, detailing a range of standard products, delivery arrangements, prices, special discounts and minimum orders.

Opening an account
Credit facilities will be given by a supplier (seller) to a new business customer only after satisfactory references from a bank or previous supplier have been obtained. Once an account has been approved the buyer will be able to order goods but not have to pay for them for a month or so.

The order
If the buyer finds the quotation satisfactory then an official order will be sent to the seller (Fig. 5.1). The order will state exactly the goods which are required, the price, the quantity required and where the goods are to be delivered.

Order forms are usually pre-printed and numbered in sequence. Some companies will accept orders over the telephone but the buyer will still send a written order confirming the telephone call.

Acknowledging the order
Most sellers will acknowledge an order. This may be a letter or a pre-printed form. The acknowledgement repeats the information from the order and the buyer should check that all the details are correct.

Advice note
This is sent by the seller to the buyer saying that the goods are on the way. If the goods do not arrive within a reasonable time then the buyer can contact the seller who will find out what has gone wrong.

Delivery note
This is usually packed with the goods and the buyer should check that (a) the delivery note is the same as the order and (b) that all the items on the note have been delivered.

ORDER FORM — O/N 123

To Thompson's Ltd.
London Road,
Chelmsford.

Date 3rd. December, 1990

Please supply DOMESTIC SUPPLIES LTD.,
HIGH STREET,
CAXTON,
ESSEX

with the following goods: Ref: EDA/AM

Quantity	Description of Goods	Price £	Value £
5	Cocktail cabinets	160	800
6	Fireside chairs	100	600
10	Coffee tables	80	800
10	Dining chairs	40	400
		Total £	2600

Fig. 5.1 An order form

V.A.T. Reg. No. 12/960   **INVOICE**   Invoice No. 1423
THOMPSON'S LTD.
LONDON ROAD
CHELMSFORD

To Domestic Supplies Ltd.,
High Street,
Caxton,
Essex.

Date 6th December, 1990

Our Ref. AM/5   Your Ref. EDA/AM

Quantity	Description	Recommended Retail Price £	Amount £
5	Cocktail cabinets	160	800.00
6	Fireside chairs	100	600.00
10	Coffee tables	80	800.00
10	Dining chairs	40	400.00
		£	2600.00
	Less: 20% Trade Discount		520.00
		£	2080.00
	Add: 10% V.A.T.		208.00
	Total	£	2288.00

Terms: $2\frac{1}{2}$% Discount 7 Days
E. & O.E

Fig. 5.2 An invoice

The buyer will be asked to sign a carbon copy of the delivery note as proof of receipt.

The invoice

This is sent from the seller to the buyer stating how much is owed for a particular order (Fig. 5.2). It will state the buyer's order number, detail all the goods sent and their price. Each invoice has its own number.

An invoice is not necessarily a request for payment – the buyer may wait until the end of the month and make several payments together.

The acknowledgement, advice note, delivery note and invoice can be bought as either a pack interleaved with carbons or NCR (no carbon required). The *multicopy method* as this system is called, ensures that the correct information is on each document and the transaction only needs to be recorded once.

The credit note

Despite every precaution, mistakes are sometimes made in dispatch and goods do have to be returned. Returned goods are often accompanied by an advice note (see above), but the original supplier will issue a *credit note* (Fig. 5.3) to acknowledge the return. Credit notes are printed in red; the value shown cancels the relevant part, or all, of a previous invoice.

The statement of account

At the end of the month, suppliers send a *statement of account* (Fig. 5.4) to each customer. As well as any unpaid balance from a previous month, the statement gives details of all transactions during the month, showing balance due and often offering a cash discount for prompt payment. It also shows any credits given and any payments made with discounts taken.

Fig. 5.3 A credit note

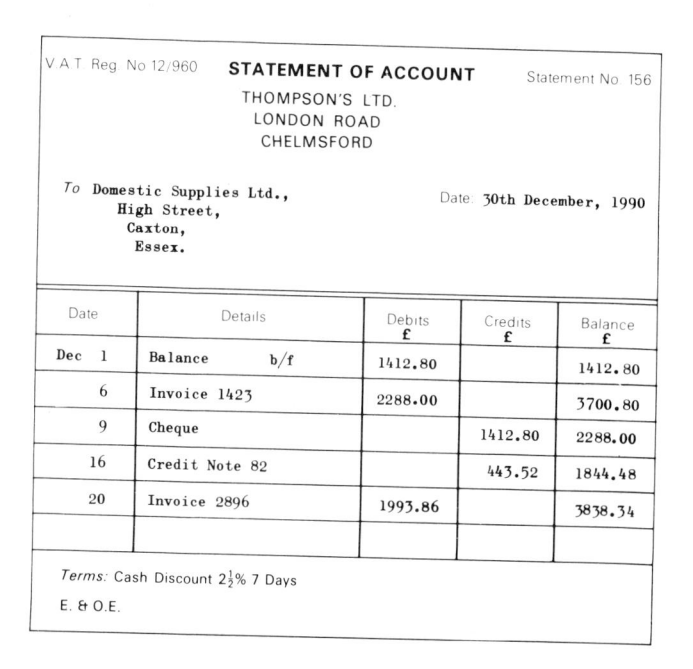

Fig. 5.4 A statement of account

The cheque

All customers are expected to settle their accounts promptly, usually by the issue of a *cheque* (Fig. 5.5) sent off to the supplier with the statement. However, payment can also be made by credit transfer or direct debit (see Unit 9, section 9.3).

Fig. 5.5 A cheque

Commercial terms

VAT (value added tax), currently 15 per cent, is added to almost all goods and services at the point of sale (in the case of goods) or on completion (in the case of services). For simplicity a VAT rate of 10% is used in this example.

E&OE (errors and omissions excepted) is a term used to denote that any mistakes made in the document will be rectified.

Estimates or *tenders* are often required when several firms are competing for an order. The estimate or tender that the customer accepts will be the one that offers the best combination of low price, early delivery and reliable service.

●SOURCES OF INFORMATION

1. As a group, your class should collect *all* types of commercial documents available. If any parents work in commercial business, ask them for sets; mark such documents 'specimen'. When your collection is complete, make a wall chart.
2. Banks provide booklets containing specimens of commercial documents. Ask around and collect as many examples as you can.
3. When you go on a visit, expecially to a business efficiency exhibition, collect any examples of commercial documents, particularly those associated with micro-computing.
4. Write politely to the local Customs and Excise offices (see your telephone directory) and ask for a brochure on VAT.

●THINGS TO DO

1. Write to an imaginary supplier, introducing yourself as a new business man or woman in the area. Describe your business and the kind of goods and credit facilities you will need; suggest people to whom reference may be made. Compare the letters written by members of your group to find good and bad points.
2. Write a letter from your bank manager to the imaginary supplier suggesting that you are a person to whom credit terms can safely be offered.
3. Draft a letter from the supplier to yourself, agreeing to credit facilities; include details about supply terms and payment.

Answer the following questions using Figs. 5.1 to 5.5:

●QUESTIONS

1. Who are the two firms involved in this model transaction?
2. Which is the customer and which is the supplier?
3. What trade do you think they are both involved in?
4. What do you understand by *trade discount* and what does it represent?
5. What effect does Credit Note No. 82 have on the balance shown on Statement No. 156?
6. Who owes who £3838.34 on 30 December?
7. If Domestic Supplies Ltd had been able to settle their account earlier, how much could they have deducted for prompt payment?
8. What will Thompson's Ltd do with the cheque shown when it is received?
9. What balance carried forward will Thompson's Ltd show on the statement issued to Domestic Supplies Ltd at the end of January?

UNIT 5.2
Settling Debts

In every commercial transaction there comes the time when payment is expected. These payments are not necessarily expressed in cash terms.

Barter

All cultures use, or have used, a system of *barter*, exchanging goods for other goods or one form of service for another (Fig. 5.6). Barter is mainly confined to underdeveloped societies, many of which don't have money. But even in Britain, simple forms of barter still persist. Groups of families organise a mutual baby-sitting service based on tokens. Neighbours look after your house when you are on holiday, for similar services when they are away. Even countries may barter: Saudi Arabia might swop oil for American wheat.

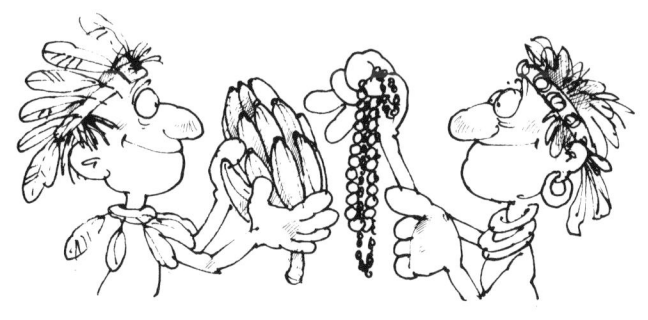

Fig. 5.6

Cash

Most of us offer money – notes and coin (Fig. 5.7) – to settle our bills, either for goods such as petrol, groceries and newspapers, or for services like railway fares, hairdressing or dry cleaning. Business people also use cash (e.g. when giving change to retail customers), but on far fewer occasions between themselves. In the commercial world, payment is often required in thousands of pounds, or the amount involved may be due to a supplier hundreds of miles away. For large amounts or over long distances, payment in cash is inconvenient and time-consuming. However, 'cash on the nail' (immediately) was once expected in most transactions. Fig. 5.8 shows a 'nail' (it was in fact a flat-topped stand, shaped like a nail) outside the Bristol Corn Exchange which was used to count out the money due on completion of a deal.

Fig. 5.7

Fig. 5.8 The 'Nail' at Bristol Corn Exchange

Today cash tends to be used for small amounts and on those occasions you meet your creditor (the person you owe money) face-to-face. There are, however, methods of cash payment (described below) which require the services of a bank or the Post Office. Cash has one major advantage: it is accepted without hesitation by both the general public and all trading concerns.

Legal tender

No one has to accept anything you may offer in settlement of a debt. If you offer a pig in payment, your creditor can accept this but is not legally required to do so, even if what you offer has a value beyond the amount you owe.

A trader is not obliged to accept a cheque or a credit card. He or she can insist on notes and coin, which are *legal tender* in any situation. All notes (£5 and above) together with £1 coins are legal tender up to any amount; bronze and cupro-nickel (silver) coins can be offered, but only in limited quantities. For example, a bus driver would be legally entitled to refuse 100 individual pennies in payment for a £1 fare.

Cheques

Books of cheques are issued to current account customers by banks and building societies. Each cheque (see Fig. 5.9) is an instruction to your bank to transfer a stated amount of money from the balance of your account to the account of the person or firm named on your cheque.

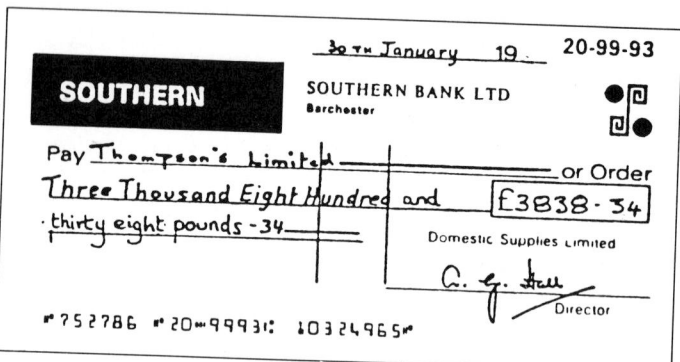

Fig. 5.9

In Fig. 5.9 the writer of the cheque has instructed his bank in Barchester to pay Thompson's Ltd (who are in Chelmsford) the sum of £3838.34, adding his signature which can be checked by reference to a specimen held on the bank's file. Thompson's Ltd will then pay the cheque into the National Westminster Bank in Chelmsford, and the money transfer is completed through the *Bankers' Clearing House* (Unit 9, section 9.4). The payer's current account is reduced, and that of Thompson's Ltd is increased, by the amount in question.

In the same way, the payer's customers will send *him* cheques in settlement of an invoice or statement, and these cheques are paid into his account for collection.

Bank credits, Giro transfers, Transcash

Cash values can be moved form one part of the country to another (or abroad) using the facilities of a bank or Post Office. It is not necessary to have a bank or Giro account yourself, but the Post Office may charge a small fee for its services.

Large companies and organisations who regularly issue bills (e.g. Access, Visa, British Telecom, hire purchase companies, the electricity boards and local authorities) use a form of bank transfer. They attach a paying-in slip to individual bills or provide a book of printed vouchers corresponding to the number of payments required for any transaction. Each Giro in-payment is scheduled for a named payee with a stated account number (see Fig 5.10) at a particular bank and branch.

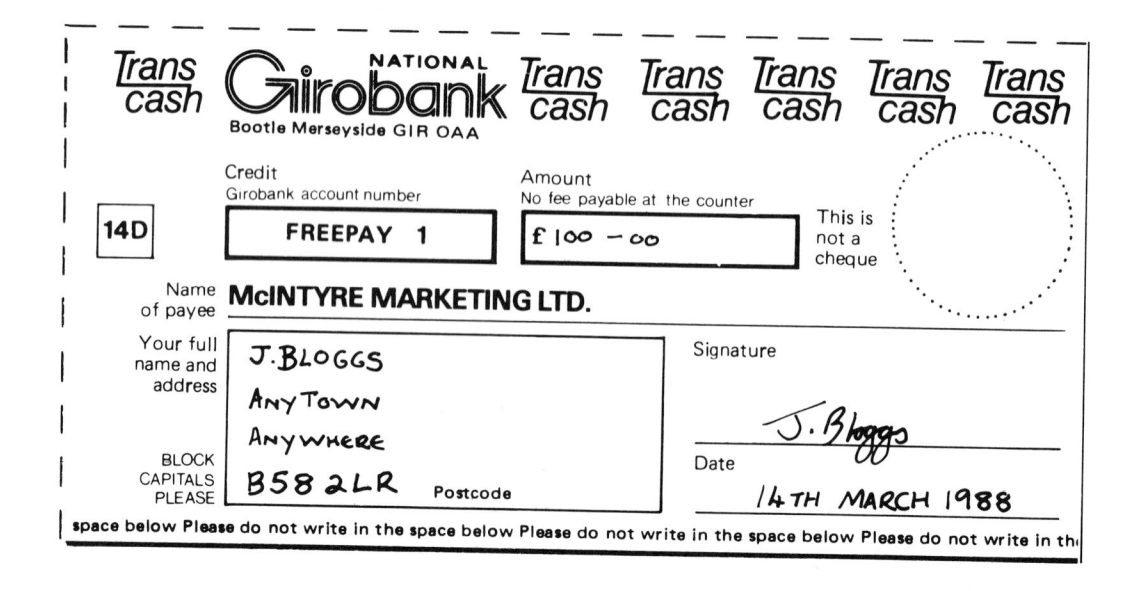

Plastic money

The best-known credit cards are Access and Visa, which provide credit facilities for goods and services. There are now also many 'in-house' schemes (Fig. 5.11) whose credit cards can be used only at specific stores (e.g. you can use an M&S card only at an M&S store). Customers pay for their goods by presenting their card at the check-out counter. The sale is recorded by the issue of a voucher carrying the name and account number, which the customer is required to sign. At the end of each month an account is sent to the customer showing the total due for the month and any arrears. Customers may pay in full or pay part of the total due. Any outstanding balance (money left owing) attracts interest at a rate well above 20 per cent (See Unit 10, section 10.2 on APR).

Charge cards such as American Express and Diners, operate in a similar way, but are not accepted at all retail outlets.

Connect cards, issued by Barclays Bank as well as their Visa cards, act like a 'plastic cheque'. The transfer of funds is made automatically by computer from the account of the buyer to the account of the seller– just as if a cheque had changed hands.

Standing orders and direct debit

A current account holder may issue instructions to his or her bank: (1) to pay a given sum at agreed intervals (annually, quarterly or monthly), which is a *standing order*, or (2) to meet a request for either a stated or an unspecified sum from a named organisation (again annually, quarterly or monthly), which is a *direct debit*. The instruction, once issued, will be followed by the bank until an instruction to stop is given.

Fig. 5.10

Fig. 5.11 'Plastic money'

For example a *standing order* might be used to pay a given sum monthly for a year to Wessex Water Board for water and sewerage charges. A *direct debit* could be used to pay a quarterly charge for electricity, where the amount *varies* each quarter. The electricity board, having drawn its money from the customer's bank account, will issue the usual bill marked as paid.

Standing orders and direct debits are used both by individuals and by companies to ease the problems of regular payments. Once the instruction is issued, an individual can forget the transaction and let the bank do the worrying. The person owed the money can rest assured that payments will be made regularly and on time. Some companies even offer a small discount for any customer willing to use either of these schemes.

Computerised records

At any one time, there is so much money in transit that the financial records are maintained by computer. Without computerised records, our systems for settling debts would collapse in chaos.

EFTPOS (short for Electronic Funds Transfer at Point of Sale), is a new system still at the trials stage. Eventually most cash tills, especially in supermarkets, will be able to transfer funds electronically from one bank account to another, no cash being involved. Your account will be reduced by the value of the goods purchased, and the trader's account will be increased by the same amount. No cash will be necessary, and the machine will signal that the transfer is complete. A credit card can also be used to charge the amount involved to your Access or Visa account.

● QUESTIONS

1. What forms of barter are you familiar with in your own experience? How do you decide when a satisfactory deal has been arrived at?
2. List ten situations where you would use cash in payment.
3. For what would the Bristol merchants be paying 'cash on the nail'?
4. What is contained on the reverse of an Access or Visa card? Why is this important? What is the brown strip used for?
5. In Fig. 5.10, to whom would the amount due be paid? What is the little circle on the right used for?

● THINGS TO DO

1. Working in groups, obtain as much information as you can about the credit cards mentioned in this section. Compare the services they offer. Who is entitled to a card? What are the credit limits? What percentage rate is charged on outstanding balances?
2. Look at an Access or Visa statement. Compare the paying-in section with the Giro transfer. Compare the information contained in each, and suggest reasons for any difference.
3. Find out what people are recommended to do after losing a credit card. Why is speedy notification essential?
4. Imagine you are in business selling records, cassettes and videos. Consider the methods of payment you would accept from your customers. Discuss the methods you would consider when settling invoices from your suppliers. What methods of payment are available for: (a) telephone/gas/electricity; (b) rent and rates; (c) advertising; (d) insurance; (e) assistants' wages?

● SOURCES OF INFORMATION

1. Any post office, for details of Transcash
2. National Westminster Bank plc, Access House, Southend-on-Sea, Essex SS99 9BB
3. Any bank, for student packs on current accounts, cheques, service cards, etc.
4. Marks & Spencer Financial Services Ltd, North-West House, City Road, Chester CH1 3AN
5. Royal Mint, Llantrissant, Wales
6. National Girobank, 10 Milk Street, London EC2V 8AN

6 ADVERTISING

UNIT 6.1
How Consumer Advertising Works

Advertising means using channels of information such as newspapers, TV and radio and outdoor posters to tell the public about the benefits (or dangers) of something. This does not have to be commercial. For example, the government uses advertising to warn about the dangers of drinking and driving, or of AIDS. Adult education classes use advertising to attract students.

However, as far as the subject of commerce and business is concerned, advertising means publicising the good qualities of the commercial product or service. This may be in the form of *trade* advertising, directed not at the general public but at one group of people, e.g. drug manufacturers advertising their medicines in doctors' journals; or it may be *consumer* advertising, aimed at the buying public in general. Here we look at consumer advertising in detail.

The Kellogg approach

There can be few countries where the name of Kellogg's is not synonymous with breakfast cereals. For many years this company has run such a persuasive advertising campaign that its products are immediately identified with the brand name and the company involved. Consider the following points:

Branding The packaging is easily recognisable, as is its *logo* (the design used for the company or brand name). Its shape and design rarely change and the name Kellogg's is a universal household word. It is a *brand leader*.

Image 'Pour out the sunshine' is a Kellogg's catch-phrase. Stored-up 'sunshine' in the wheat, together with milk and sugar, provides a wholesome image of goodness.

Association Kellogg's suggest an association with happy morning breakfasts, family togetherness, friendship, golden days of continuous sunshine, belonging to a world-wide club of cornflakes eaters.

Convenience What could be easier on a busy morning? Packet from the larder, milk from the fridge, add sugar, that's it! No mess or cooking, and you have a contented and smiling family, ready to face the day.

Economy The packet is large, reasonably cheap, easily obtainable, constantly available. By comparison, bacon and eggs are expensive, messy and time-consuming.

Medium The use of TV and cinema advertising makes contact with consumers at a time when they are relaxed and enjoying themselves, and (important point) when the next meal is supper or breakfast.

Brand loyalty Kellogg's sales of breakfast cereals exceed those of any other competitor. Buyers are convinced of their superior qualities.

The Kellogg's advertising campaign is successful because it projects a brand image of convenience, economy and happy, healthy people.

The media

Advertising is big business, and advertising agencies (see below) can earn huge sums of money planning and designing campaigns for their clients. The advertising *media* (information channels) at their disposal – as long as they can pay for them! – include the following:

1. TV and cinema commercials.
2. Commercial radio.
3. Newspapers and magazines.
4. Outdoor posters in the street, on buses and tube trains.
5. Railway and bus stations, airports, docks and garages.
6. Sponsorship deals with, for example, football teams.
7. Shop windows and retail displays inside shops.
8. Free promotional gifts, such as calendars, diaries and carrier bags.
9. Pamphlets and brochures.
10. Letterheadings, special postal franking, names on cars, vans and lorries.

Using these media, consumer advertising aims to obtain and maintain a share of the market, to increase sales and to promote desires we never knew we had! It is designed to *create a market* for goods or services and, once obtained, hold consumers for a lifetime.

Codes of practice and consumer protection

Buying from a catalogue or from an advertisment involves an element of trust that someone, somewhere is looking after your interests, i.e. that you are not being tricked or cheated. The Association of Mail Order Publishers, the Mail Order Traders' Association and the Mail Order Publishers' Authority all publish *codes of practice* which their members must follow.

Even so, dishonest advertisements do sometimes appear. The Advertising Standards Authority (a government agency) represents and protects the public against unfair trading through advertising (Fig. 6.1). The Authority receives and investigates complaints, reporting dishonest advertising to the Director-General of Fair Trading.

Consumer protection is dealt with in Unit 15, and the remedies described there cover the goods purchased by mail order and any misrepresentation (dishonest description) of goods and services generally.

Advertising agencies

Manufacturers and suppliers rarely organise their own advertising campaigns. Instead they rely upon agencies who specialise in image-making and employ staff who understand how to sell a product. These staff include *copywriters*, who write the words printed or spoken in advertisements, *designers* and *photographers* who decide

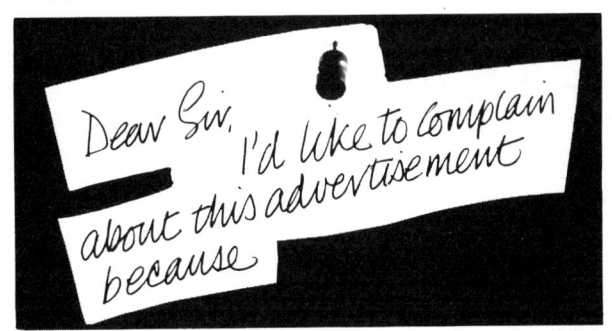

Fig. 6.1 The Advertising Standards Authority protects the public against dishonest advertising

how it will look, and *media buyers*, who decide when and where to advertise.

'Soft sells' amuse, interest or relax the public (e.g. Fig. 6.2). 'Hard sells' create anxieties (like the need for insurance, or 'Mothers who care use Persil') or they make people feel they have to rush out to buy something at once (e.g. Fig. 6.3). See if you can recognise each style in current advertisements.

Fig. 6.2 'Soft' sell

●SOURCES OF INFORMATION

1. Advertising Standards Authority, 2–16 Torrington Place, London WC1E 7HN
2. London Weekend Television Ltd, Kent House, South Bank, Upper Ground, London SE1 9LT
3. Pearl & Dean Ltd, Summit House, 27 Sale Place, London W2 1PP
4. Saatchi & Saatchi Advertising Ltd, 80 Charlotte Street, London W1P 1LR
5. Yellow Pages – advertising agencies; marketing and publicity consultants.

Fig. 6.3 'Hard' sell

●THINGS TO DO

1. Collect some Saturday and Sunday newspaper colour supplements. Do similar advertisements appear in each? Who are most of them aimed at? Compare this advertising with that contained in women's magazines and explain any differences you find.
2. Video-record all the adverts on TV over a 60 minute period, perhaps 7.30 – 8.30 pm (about 20 minutes in all). Play them back in class. How many times is an advert repeated? Do the adverts on TV differ from those in colour supplements? Explain any differences.
3. Conduct a survey of all advertising media (TV and radio, cinemas, newspapers, hoardings and so on). In your view, which of the following is the highest-spending industry: (a) food and drink; (b) motor cars; (c) soap and detergent; (d) travel and leisure; (e) other? Can you explain why?

UNIT 6.2
Brand Names and Image-Building

Consumer advertising is part of the competition between *branded* goods. Branded products are specially wrapped and labelled or marked with the maker's name and a distinctive form of packaging. The manufacturers use advertising to inform and persuade consumers that their brand of a product is better value or superior to another brand. They try to build up an *image* in people's minds that their product is better than the competition.

Brand image

'Beanz meanz Heinz!' 'Lassie promotes strong bones and healthy teeth!' 'Mash means Smash!' and so on. Advertisers try to differentiate their product, give it a name and a 'personality' of its own, surround it with thoughts of health, happiness and well-being. That is the secret of brand image. Slogans like these are repeated, often to music, over and over again; the constant repetition of a phrase or a brand name helps to persuade people to buy and keep on buying.

Many of our personal choices are influenced by the images created by advertising, although we may not be aware of it. Advertising consultants design their campaigns to exploit the way we like to think of ourselves. For example, men usually want their choice of beer to stress their 'manly' qualities or their choice of car to indicate success; women usually want their choice of perfume or stockings to stress their 'feminine' qualities, or their choice of food to show they are a 'good' wife or mother.

Product identification

To shape people's preferences, it is important that a product is easy to spot, packed in a popular, easily recognisable container (remember Kellogg's cornflakes), given a catchy name (e.g. Coca-Cola or Coke) and promoted as a brand leader (e.g. Nescafé).

Then the product must be given an image, i.e. a personality. Think of the advertising used for Heineken, Daz, Pedigree Chum and Shell, each of which is said to offer much more than the rival product. Also, customers must be convinced that no other product gives quite the same value or satisfaction in use.

Once you have done all this, you have created a strong market for your product, with loyal customers who will not want to desert you. This process is called *product identification* or *brand awareness*.

Market research

Advertising is expensive and needs therefore to be aimed at the consumer most likely to be influenced by the campaign. To test the market, companies employ *market researchers*, whom you may have seen in the high street. Some market research is conducted by telephone or door to door. All such research helps advertisers find out what people think about their products.

Questionnaires are designed to obtain information on the popularity of one or more products and who uses them most, e.g. men or women, which age groups, the jobs they do, whether they are married or single, etc. All the

Fig. 6.4

answers received are then fed into a computer, which analyses consumer preferences and market trends.

Sampling To obtain a fully accurate response, market researchers would have to ask the same questions of each and every person in the country, which would be a long and expensive task. Instead they choose a representative sample (say, 2000 people) to include both sexes, all age groups, rich and poor and people from every part of the country. From this very small sample, statisticians can predict the response over the country as a whole or even produce answers about area preferences, as the popularity of products varies from one area to another.

Sales Promotion

Some companies give away samples of their goods (e.g. a packet of detergent in a new washing-machine). Others offer prizes if householders will buy, for example, books described in a brochure sent through the post. 'Two for the price of one'; '10p off your next purchase'; collecting tokens for a reduction on goods or services – all these are forms of sales promotion, where free gifts or tempting offers are part of the 'subtle sell'.

●SOURCES OF INFORMATION

1 Yellow Pages – look up 'market research and analysis' and 'marketing consultants'.
2 Mass Observation (UK) Ltd, Alexandra House, Church Road, London W3
3 MORI, 32 Old Queen Street, London SW1H 9HP
4 Write to the marketing boards (e.g. Milk Marketing Board) for brochures and leaflets etc.

●QUESTIONS

1 What is an *own brand* label? What is a *brand leader*? Why do you suppose that supermarkets stock brand leaders and own brands side by side on the shelves?
2 What is contained in the consumer magazine *Which?* (available by annual subscription and in some public libraries). To what extent does this magazine publish market research? Who receives copies of *Which?*?
3 Who is most likely to promote a large advertising campaign: (a) a shopkeeper; (b) a wholesaler; (c) a manufacturer? Give reasons for your answer.
4 How are eggs advertised? Who promotes the sale of eggs? How is it done? Who provides the money?
5 What is the function of a *marketing board*? How does it assist: (a) the producer and (b) the public? How is it financed? Research the names of as many as possible and write down what their special areas are.
6 What 'image' do you think that the advertisers in Figs. 6.4 and 6.5 are trying to promote? What does each include in its effort/attempt to influence the buying public? Are they 'hard' or 'soft' sells?
7 Who pays for free newspapers issued in your area? Is anything really free?

●THINGS TO DO

1 Split into four groups. Each team should make up a (coloured) wall chart to include adverts showing famous brand names. Remember Ford motor cars and Shell petrol are branded goods, even though they are not small packaged items like instant coffee. Try to agree a different theme for each group, e.g. food, transport, banking, insurance, government services, drinks, clothes. Do you notice a similarity in style and presentation? Which is a 'hard' and which is a 'soft' sell? Elect a spokesperson from each group to talk to the class about the group's findings.
2 See the market research assignment in Unit 18.

Float into retirement with a pension from Legal & General.

Legal & General

Fig. 6.5

7 BUSINESS ORGANISATIONS

UNIT 7.1
The Private Sector

The private sector contains those firms and companies which are *not* owned and run by the government. These business firms can be classified according to ownership. A *sole proprietor* (a person in business on his or her own) or a *partnership* (two or more people running a business together) are usually small-scale firms; they have to rely on their own funds and bank credit if they want to expand. *Limited companies* are larger organisations owned by shareholders and managed by a board of directors.

Sole proprietors

Sole proprietors (sometimes called sole traders) control small businesses like a shop, a garage or a nursery, or provide a service such as printing, window-cleaning or television repairs. Individual proprietors, responsible to no one but themselves, are often helped by members of their family. The size of the unit is restricted by the amount of personal capital (investment funds) available and the credit facilities provided by the bank. Sole proprietors mostly offer local services, which are easily controlled. Once all expenses are met, any profit belongs to the proprietor.

Many sole proprietors are very efficient at keeping their costs down and providing a personal service; so they are very successful. New business start-ups are offered government help. Some of these firms become quite large, but are still owned by only one person. However, a sole proprietor has *unlimited liability*. This means that if the firm gets into difficulties and owes large sums of money, the proprietor has to pay all these debts out of his or her own pocket – even if this means selling house, car and every personal possession.

Partnerships

Two or more people in business together with a view to making a profit are called a partnership. The number of partners trading is limited to twenty by the Partnership Act 1890. (However, professional firms, such as accountants and solicitors, may have more than twenty partners.) Two or more people can provide more capital than a sole trader, and each individual contributes additional skills. So a partnership is likely to be larger than a business conducted by a sole proprietor; it will also often be more efficiently run and show a greater return of profit for each pound of capital invested.

Partners agree (usually in writing) on how the business shall be run, how the profits shall be shared and who is responsible for what. The Partnership Act 1890 provides a guide. As with a business conducted by a sole proprietor, at least one of the partners must accept *unlimited liability*. If the business fails, leaving large debts, not only will business assets be sold to satisfy creditors, but the personal possessions of the proprietor(s) concerned may also be sold to pay the debts.

Limited liability

Limited liability means that people can invest in a company without the risk of losing all their personal possessions if something goes wrong. If a company has debts or goes bankrupt the only money an investor (owner) will lose is the money that he or she agreed to pay for shares in the first place.

Private limited companies

A private limited company can be owned by any number of individuals. The capital of the company is divided into 'shares' which are bought by investors. The shares cannot be bought on the Stock Exchange (see Unit 11) and they cannot be advertised; they can only be bought privately – and so the name *private limited company*. This type of organisation is still popular as a family business because ownership can be kept to a chosen group of people. Some quite well-known companies are privately owned – SavaCentre Ltd for example, which is owned partly by Sainsbury plc and partly by BHS.

Public limited companies

Most companies which are household names are public limited companies: Marks & Spencer plc, Barclays Bank plc, British Telecom plc. There are more than 5000 PLCs in the United Kingdom. To be a PLC a company must have at least 2 shareholders, £50 000 of share capital and be registered with the Registrar of Joint Stock Companies. Shares of public limited companies may be bought and sold on the Stock Exchange.

Being a shareholder of a public limited company does not entitle you to run the business but you may attend the Annual General Meeting (AGM) where you can elect directors to run the company for you. You may also question the directors about what they have done and how they intend to manage the company in the future.

Company law

Company law is contained within various Companies Acts from 1948 to 1986. There are two types of company, the *private company* and the *public limited company* (*PLC*). The *board of directors* maintains day-to-day control of a PLC. It must issue an annual report and accounts to every shareholder, sending a copy to the Registrar of Joint Stock Companies, who also holds the original description of the company called the *Memorandum and Articles of Association* issued when the company was first formed (or *incorporated*, as the process of setting up a company is known). All the documents connected with a PLC may be inspected by the general public. Private companies still have to register documents and to issue annual reports and accounts, but these are not necessarily available for public inspection.

Fig. 7.1 From sole proprietor to public limited company

Holding companies

The very largest PLCs own all or a large part of the share capital in other companies. They are then called *holding* (or *parent*) companies. Such companies often do not trade themselves, but organise the activities of several subsidiary companies that do. One of Britain's largest holding companies (the American word is *conglomerate*) has interests in property, hotels, shipping, food processing and the manufacture of drugs and cosmetics.

Multinational corporations

Multinationals (sometimes called *transnationals*) are companies of huge size and influence which trade worldwide, dominating international markets in their field. Examples are the Ford Motor Company (USA), Roche (drugs and medicines – Switzerland), Barclays International (commercial and industrial bankers – Britain), the Coca-Cola Corporation (soft drink manufacture – USA) and Bosch (electronic equipment – West Germany). Multinationals have their headquarters in a particular country but maintain offices and factories all over the world. These corporations employ many hundreds of thousands of workers of all nationalities and they deal in billions in every major currency. They are very powerful, and one multinational company can easily dominate the economy of a small country.

●SOURCES OF INFORMATION

1. Granada PLC, 34–6 Golden Square, London W1R 4AH
2. Courtaulds PLC, 18 Hanover Square, London W1A 2BB
3. Cadbury Schweppes PLC, 1–10 Connaught Place, London W2 2EX
4. Commercial Union Assurance Group PLC, 1 Undershaft, London EC3P 3DQ
5. Rank Organisation PLC, 6 Connaught Place, London W2 2ES
6. Unilever PLC, Unilever House, Victoria Embankment, London EC4P 4BQ
7. ICI PLC, ICI House, Millbank, London SW1P 3JF
8. Trust House Forte PLC, 166 High Holborn, London WC11V 6PA
9. Allied Lyons PLC, Allied House, St John Street, London EC1V 4QJ
10. BAT Industries PLC, 50 Victoria Street, London SW1H 0NL

●THINGS TO DO

1. Working in pairs, write politely to the companies listed above for brochures and information about themselves.
2. Construct a wall chart illustrating the industries in which each PLC is involved. Compare the products or services offered by each. Say why, in your view, each is a PLC rather than a private limited company.
3. Find out about one or two really large *private* companies. What products or services do they offer? Why have they stayed private?
4. What do you understand by the term *logo*? (A dictionary may help.) Start a collection of logos to include every size of company. Why, in your view, do firms adopt a logo?

UNIT 7·2
The Public Sector

The public sector contains those business organisations which are owned by the state. In every developed country some part of the economic system is owned by the state. Contrail and Amtrack are government-owned railroads in the USA. Elf is the French state oil company. The West German government owns 40 per cent of Volkswagen. Renault is completely owned by the French government.

In Britain, British Coal, British Rail and the Post Office are all examples of state-owned corporations (often called *nationalised industries* or *public corporations*). Each of them plays an important role in the extractive, manufacturing or tertiary sectors of the economy. Government agencies are also active within the private sector. The Central Electricity Generating Board places many orders for plant and equipment with private companies. G.E.C. and Marconi, two private-sector technological giants, are involved in government-funded research and development for the armed forces. Motorways, a government responsibility, are levelled, surfaced and maintained by private contractors. Schools and hospitals, which are run as part of the non-business public sector, are built and supplied by firms operating in the private sector.

Public ownership began in Britain early in the twentieth century. The Metropolitan Water Board (1902), the Port of London Authority (1908), the British Broadcasting Corporation (1927) and the London Passenger Transport Board (1933) were all early examples of state ownership.

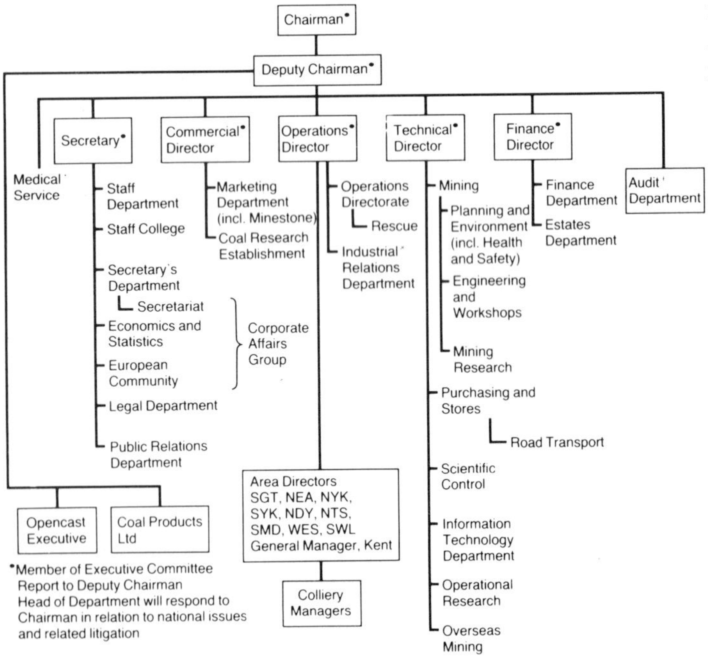

Following 1945, many more industries and organisations were *nationalised* (taken into public ownership), e.g. the coal and steel industries, shipbuilding, the railways, road transport, gas and electricity.

Nationalisation and privatisation

Many of these public-sector industries and organisations have been *privatised* (sold back into private ownership) since 1979. British Telecom, British Steel, British Gas, British Airways, British Aerospace, Britoil, the National Freight Corporation, Sealink/Seaspeed and the British Airports Authority have all been sold back to shareholders. The various electricity boards and water boards are also in line for privatisation. However, with coal, the Post Office and the railways still in public hands, the state continues to control a large slice of the economy. British Coal will serve as a model for the rest.

British coal: a nationalised industry

The coal industry was first nationalised in 1947. Before then, it was made up of a number of private firms mining coal in a particular coalfield and selling their products wherever there was a market. After 1947 the Coal Board, under a chairman, became responsible for the whole of the industry, involving both deep-mined and open-cast sites. Despite gas and oil developments in the North Sea, and decisions to extend the role of nuclear power stations, coal still meets around 36 per cent of the nation's total energy needs; and it generates up to 75 per cent of our electricity. At present rates of production, Britain has enough coal reserves to last 300 years.

Ownership and control

There are no individual owners of a nationalised industry in the same sense as a public limited company is owned by its shareholders. All public corporations are owned by the state on behalf of the general public, who jointly own land, buildings, plant, equipment, pipelines, rails, transport, furniture and mineral rights worth many millions of pounds. All these assets are held in trust by the government of the day.

The day-to-day activities of public corporations are controlled by a *board* or *commission* under a *chairman* (Fig. 7.2). The chairman and members of the board are appointed by a government minister, usually the *Secretary of State for Trade and Industry*. Our example industry, British Coal, employs many thousands in its workforce within the collieries themselves and at regional and national headquarters. The industry is divided into areas, each of which has responsibility for mines in its region, for productivity and for profitability.

Fig. 7.2 British Coal management organisation

Responsibility for profit and loss

It was never intended that the nationalised industries should make huge profits. But they were expected to *break even*, taking one year with another (i.e. a loss in one year should be offset by a profit in the next year). Unfortunately, the task of redevelopment proved difficult, and foreign competition has been fierce, so large losses have been made in some cases. State *subsidies* (i.e. extra funding) for development and research were often necessary for survival.

Most governments would be happy to leave the boards of public corporations to conduct their own affairs. However, because many of these industries have made large losses, successive governments have become involved in an attempt to solve the problem. MPs in Parliament see the accounts and can question the minister responsible for overall control of the public corporations.

Many drastic cuts have been made. In the case of British Coal, recent reorganisation has included the closure of 'uneconomic' (loss-making) pits, a slimming down of the workforce and the application of productivity targets. Currently, British Coal is in sight of profitability, at which point state subsidies will stop.

Nationalisation and privatisation are political 'footballs'; whatever one government does, the opposition tends to criticise. There is perhaps no 'right' answer, only political opinion.

Product range

It would be easy to suppose that the coal industry produces only coal which is burned to provide heat or energy (Fig. 7.3). But in fact the industry manufactures a range of products including petrol and jet fuels, plastics, disinfectants, medicines, road-surfacing materials, paints, fertilisers and animal feed. People in the industry suggest that coal is really far too valuable to burn.

●SOURCES OF INFORMATION

1. British Coal, Public Relations, Hobart House, Grosvenor Place, London SW1X 7AE
2. Mining Museum, Blaenavon, South Wales.
3. Chatterley Winfield Mining Museum, Tonstall, Stoke, Staffordshire.
4. National Mining Museum, Lound Hall, Retford, Nottinghamshire.
5. British Railways Board, 222 Marylebone Road, London NW1 6JJ (or Yellow Pages for regions)
6. British Waterways Board, Melbury House, Melbury Terrace, London NW1 6JX
7. British Airports Authority, Gatwick Airport, Gatwick, West Sussex

●THINGS TO DO

1. Write politely to all the nationalised or former nationalised industries requesting brochures and information. Split into four groups to produce wall charts on the history, growth, products, finance, structure, etc. of four separate industries which are, or have been, public corporations. Try to obtain some material to illustrate the pre-nationalisation period and the history of each.
2. Using your reference library, trace the origins of coal. Why is it found only in certain districts?
3. Construct a management organisation chart like the one shown in Fig. 7.2 for your own school or college. To whom is the headteacher or principal responsible?

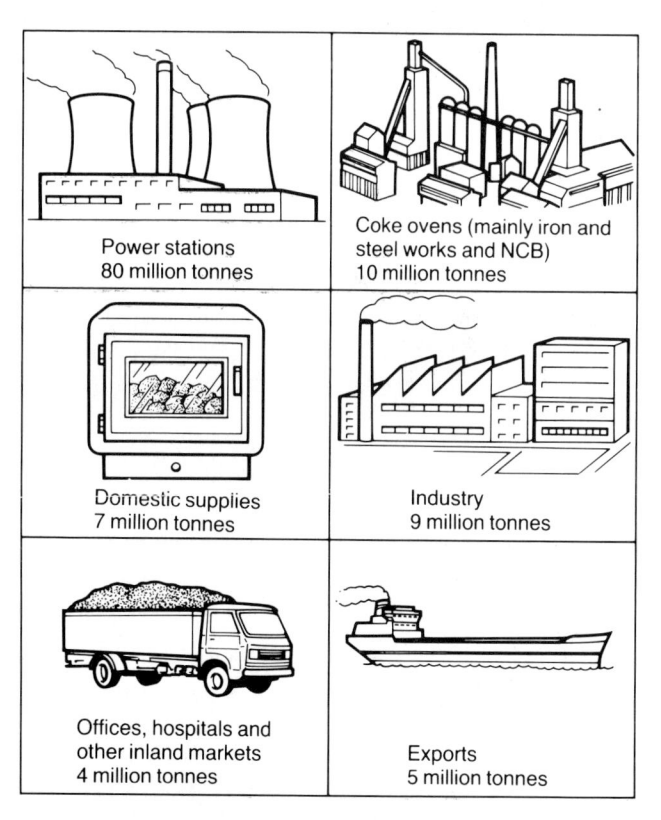

Power stations 80 million tonnes	Coke ovens (mainly iron and steel works and NCB) 10 million tonnes
Domestic supplies 7 million tonnes	Industry 9 million tonnes
Offices, hospitals and other inland markets 4 million tonnes	Exports 5 million tonnes

Fig. 7.3 Where the coal goes in a year

UNIT 7.3
Co-operation and Co-ownership

The Co-operative Movement began in Lancashire in 1844. A group calling themselves the Rochdale Pioneers each contributed £1 to set up a small grocery warehouse buying basic commodities in bulk, and selling cheaply to members in small, family-sized quantities.

Samuel Smiles (1812–1904) and 'Self-help'

The term 'self-help' was made popular by Samuel Smiles, a writer who, in about 1859, argued in favour of self-reliance and independent enterprise. Smiles suggested that working people could help themselves by forming associations through which people's thrift (carefulness with money) could be used to the benefit of the group. This approach led to the spread of the co-operative movement and the development of Friendly Societies.

Friendly Societies were formed by neighbours, and members paid in a few coppers each week. When a member died the collected funds were used to pay for a funeral. (Life assurance has developed from this). A few of the old Friendly Societies still remain, with grand titles indicating their origins: the Independent Order of Foresters Fraternal Benefit Society, the Manchester Unity of Oddfellows, and the Ancient Order of Druids United Family Society.

The *Trustee Savings Bank* (privatised in the mid-1980s) also grew out of working-class thrift, as a bank where people could deposit their small savings. *Building Societies* began as small self-help groups, enabling members to build their own homes. Many of the *trade unions*, which also have their origins in the Industrial Revolution, provide commercial benefits for members in terms of insurance or mortgage schemes; the Teachers' Provident Society is a good example.

The co-operative movement

The co-operative movement, spread throughout the country, will serve as a model for a study of co-ownership.

Each co-operative society belonging to the movement is an independent organisation, often covering a wide area (e.g. Greater Nottingham Co-operative Society) and affiliated to the Co-operative Wholesale Society. In recent years the retail societies which run shops and supermarkets have come under heavy pressure of competition from retail chains such as Tesco and Fine Fare, which have captured a large share of the market. Much thought has had to be given to more modern methods of selling, resulting in a reduction in the number of Co-operative Societies to enable them to compete more

Fig. 7.4 Early co-operative society

effectively. The top 22 societies now account for over 75 per cent of all retail trade by the Consumer Co-operative Movement in the UK.

Co-operative ownership Anyone can become a member of a retail society by depositing just £1 in a share account, to which he or she can add other deposits large or small, just as in a bank. In this way a member may build up a savings account with the society and draw on that balance when necessary. When the time comes to elect the management committee which runs each society members have only one vote each (no matter how many shares they own), so that no one member or group of members can control the society. Retail societies are registered under the Industrial and Provident Societies Acts and not under the Companies Act as in the case of a limited company.

The Co-operative Wholesale Society Retail societies are free to obtain their stock from whatever source may be available. However, each society is a member of the Co-operative Wholesale Society which imports from abroad, manufactures its own goods under its own brand names and is able to obtain the advantages of bulk buying; so in fact many societies rely upon the CWS for most of their stock. The CWS is itself owned by the Retail Societies who elect a Board of Directors to run it.

Other Co-operative interests The Co-operative Bank, the Nationwide Building Society and the Co-operative Insurance Society are themselves very large concerns. Each has assets of many millions of pounds and is conducted in competition with other organisations in the same line of business.

Modern *housing associations* are reviving the original idea of the building societies. Groups of people are once again forming 'societies' to acquire land upon which to build houses for their members. When the scheme is completed and everyone is housed, the association is wound up.

Producers', workers' and retailers' co-operatives

The earliest attempt at co-operative production was organised by *Robert Owen* (1771–1858), who formed producers' co-operatives in Scotland. The more successful co-operative societies have already been discussed. Producers' co-operatives are well organised on the continent of Europe, especially in Belgium (farming co-operatives) and in France (wine co-operatives) (Fig. 7.5). In the United States there are also farm co-operatives supervising the sale of products from a number of associated small producers. Workers' co-operatives are well-established methods of production in many countries. In Britain the Worker Co-operative Sector has expanded rapidly in the last decade, with a growing network of support organisations such as the government funded Co-operative Development Agency, local authority supported Co-operative Development Agencies, and the Industrial Common Ownership Movement (ICOM). In 1988 there were over 1800 worker co-ops in the UK.

Co-operatives have a number of advantages. Many French villages in the wine-growing areas are organised as co-operatives to market their produce, often world-wide.

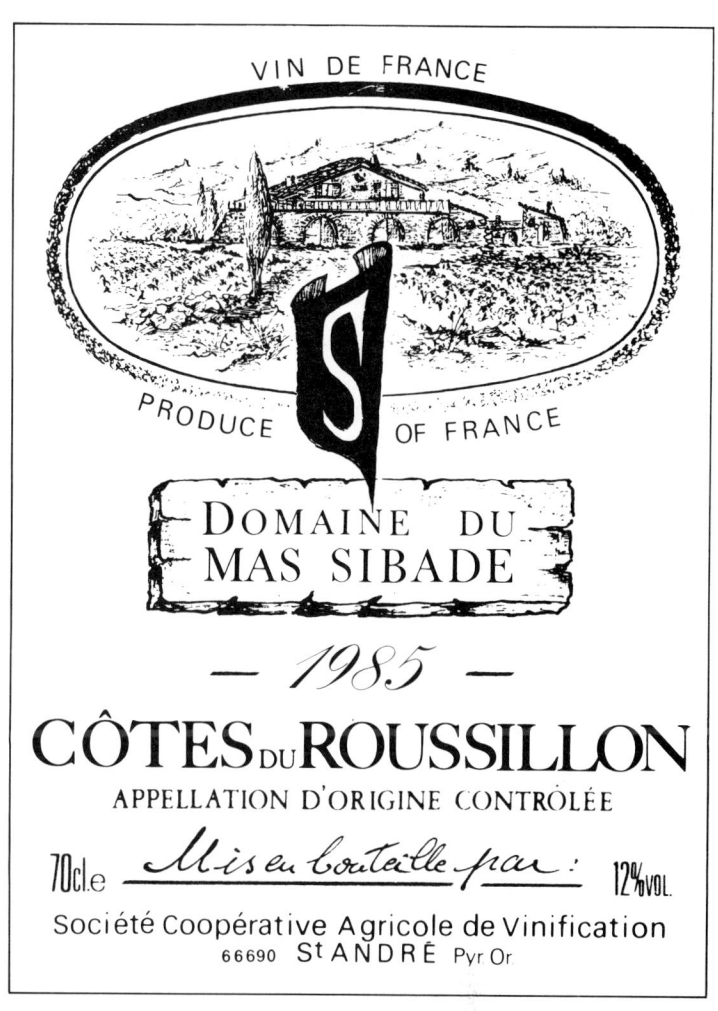

Fig. 7.5 Label from a French wine co-operative

There are no bosses as such, but managers, elected by the members, organise the collective (which owns the land and the necessary machinery) to achieve efficient methods of production and to maximise the crop. Left to themselves, individual smallholders would be inefficient and (relatively) unproductive.

In Britain small grocery chains like Spar, Mace and Wavy Line are organisations of independent retailers co-operating to achieve the economics of bulk buying to combat competition from giants like Asda and Sainsbury. Such co-operatives are formed and maintained for much the same reason as the French collectives.

●THINGS TO DO

1 Assess your local Co-operative Society organisation. How many stores or shops are there? Ask about membership.
2 Organise a workers' co-operative in your school. What is your product? How will you market it?
3 Go to the library and read up on Samuel Smiles and Robert Owen. What were their aims?

UNIT 7.4
Planned Economies and Market Economies

A contrast of style

The business organisation of the two superpowers, the Soviet Union and the United States, provide an interesting contrast.

The USSR has a *planned* economy. The government sets plans and targets for industrial production and business. All major enterprises are state owned (a bit like our public corporations), and the state provides free services like health and education. Nearly every worker, therefore, is employed and paid by the state. However, in the USSR and most communist countries private enterprise markets in some goods, particularly in farm produce, are now encouraged; productivity has increased as a result. China, the other communist giant with a planned economy, has agreed to allow Hong Kong to continue its present (Western-style) economy when that colony reverts to China in 1997. There are real signs of changing attitudes in both the East and West. Consequently, trade between the communist countries and the West is increasing, which benefits both sides.

The USA, on the other hand, is a *market* economy. Free choice by consumers in the market-place is considered all-important. Major US industries and commercial institutions are owned by private companies which are responsible to shareholders. The government regulates economic activity to some extent but doesn't interfere with or influence business decisions. There are public corporations (like the US state-owned railways) and there are some free services, like education and welfare benefits. But the vast majority of manufacturing and service corporations – large and small – are run for private profit.

There are faults in both systems, each of which represents one extreme of economic organisation. However, though the majority of citizens in each country seem to prefer the style of government they are used to, business attitudes are demanding major concessions to change and prosperity.

A mixed economy

Britain, like most West European countries, has aspects of both the planned and the market economy. This combination of the two is known as the *mixed economy*. The British mixed economy is made up of the following parts:
1 *Private firms* in private hands, ranging from the sole trader, through partnerships, limited companies and public limited companies, conducting every kind of business, with profits going to proprietors and shareholders.
2 *Public corporations* offering goods and services in such areas as communications, coal and transport. All of these are owned by the state, responsible through appointed boards to Parliament. Profits go to the state; losses are met out of taxation.
3 *Co-operatives and co-operative ventures*, like building societies, (at the time of writing), the Co-operative Movement (distributive, insurance and banking), workers' collectives and Friendly Societies. None of these exists primarily to make a profit; none has owners, proprietors or shareholders (in the accepted sense of those words).
4 *Government and local government services*, like the social services, police, health, education, roads, parks and gardens, libraries, swimming pools and other leisure outlets. Some of these services are free; in other cases a charge is made. Paid for out of income tax and rates, which will shortly become poll taxes, as in Scotland. (You may be more familiar with, the term 'community charge'.)
5 *The voluntary sector*, mostly charities like Barnardo's, Help the Aged and Oxfam. Large organisations with a paid workforce, distributing welfare services to the needy provided by donations from the general public and income from investments and shops.

This is a *mixed* economy because Britain does not rely entirely on any one sector to provide all the goods and services needed by the public. Many suppliers of goods and services are in competition. The railways compete with private airlines and road transport; British Coal competes with private suppliers abroad; the Post Office competes with private carriers.

Supply and demand

A communist planned economy, which controls all *factors of production* (land, labour and capital), must also become its own risk-taker, regulating output by the application of plans, quotas and targets. Wages are determined by the state, and there are none of the extremes of income which exist in a capitalist economy. Any committee decision will go wrong from time to time, and despite rolling acres of farmland the USSR needs to buy vast quantities of cereals each year, mainly from the USA.

A capitalist economy is a free-for-all. Produce as much as you wish, sell it where you can; if you can't, you go out of business. Prices (fixed by the state in a communist society), are determined mostly by *supply and demand* (see Figs. 7.6, 7.7 and 7.8). If the supply is too great, then the price must fall to tempt people to buy more. If demand increases above supply, then prices are likely to increase rapidly out of control. Despite the efforts of trade unions in a Western economy, wages also depend on supply and demand. The supply of unskilled workers is huge, demand is poor, and so wages are low. Again, there are mistakes and miscalculations, some of which, like the overproduction of butter in the European Community, leads to the produce being sold very cheaply to other countries or to the destruction of the produce.

In Britain we tend towards a supply-and-demand economy. We do not generally fix prices (but see below) and instead rely on competition to regulate prices and standards.

The EC and the CAP

We have one example of state-style price-fixing, however, which is associated with our membership of the European Community. The EC has a *Common Agricultural Policy* (*CAP*) which fixes prices for dairy and farm produce. This system has led to overproduction of butter (the 'butter mountain'), wine (the 'wine lake') and tonne upon tonne of meat in constant cold storage. At the prices offered to farmers for their produce, they oversupply. At the price charged for farm produce in shops, the public have declined to buy. Hence the mountain of produce in cold store. The outcome is that the surpluses are often sold to the USSR at less than cost price. Produce is also given away to the old and needy; some is destroyed.

●THINGS TO DO

Read through this exercise together with your teacher. Then discuss the questions on oversupply, surplus produce and shortages.

Figs. 7.6, 7.7 and 7.8 show three graphs: of demand; of supply, and of supply and demand in balance. The demand graph shows that: (a) at a price of 6000, 15 000 tonnes of produce will be bought, and (b) at a price of 1000, 92 000 tonnes will be bought.

The supply graph suggests that, at a price of 5000, 103 000 tonnes of produce will be offered for sale. However, at a price of 1000, no supplier is prepared to sell at all.

The supply–demand graph shows the price at which the amount offered for sale just equals the price which the purchaser is prepared to pay, assuming the same quantity for sale. At 3000 the amount demanded and the amount supplied just agree at 52 000 tonnes, and that (in a free market) would be *equilibrium*.

1 What would happen to demand if the EC fixed the sale price at 4000?
2 What would be the amount offered for sale at 4000?
3 If this commodity was apples, how would you deal with the problems arising from price fixing?

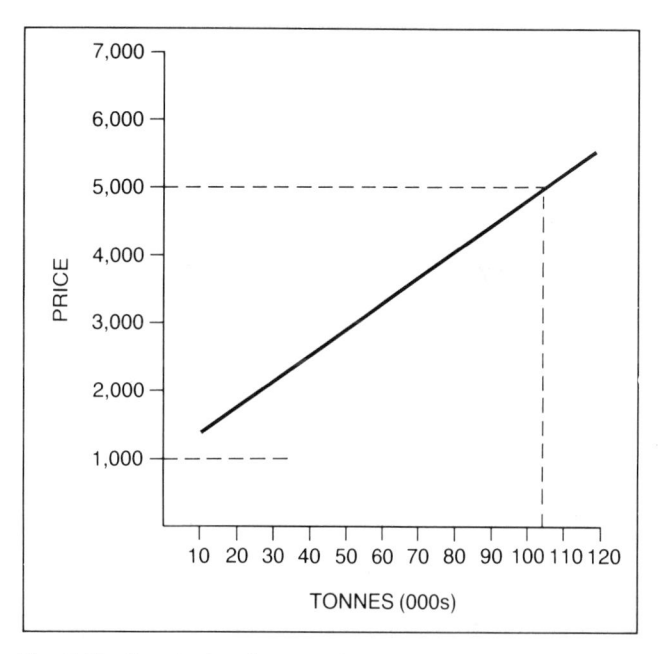

Fig. 7.7 Graph showing supply

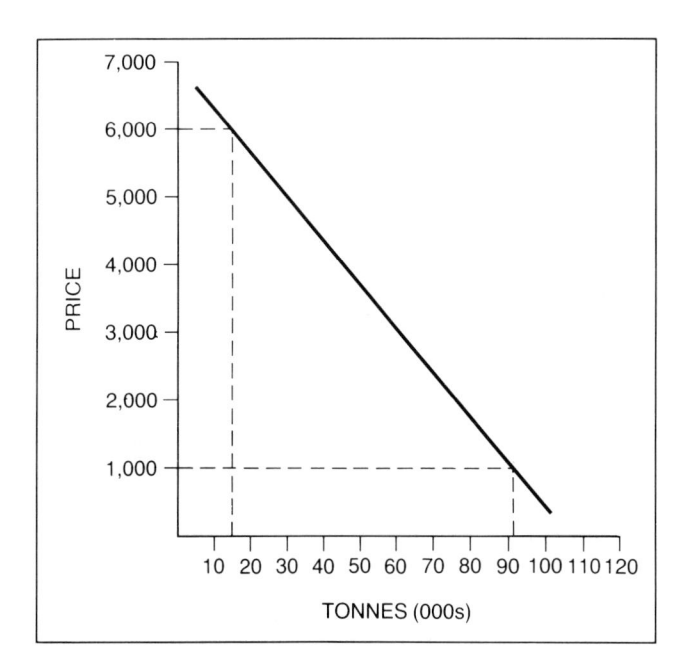

Fig. 7.6 Graph showing demand

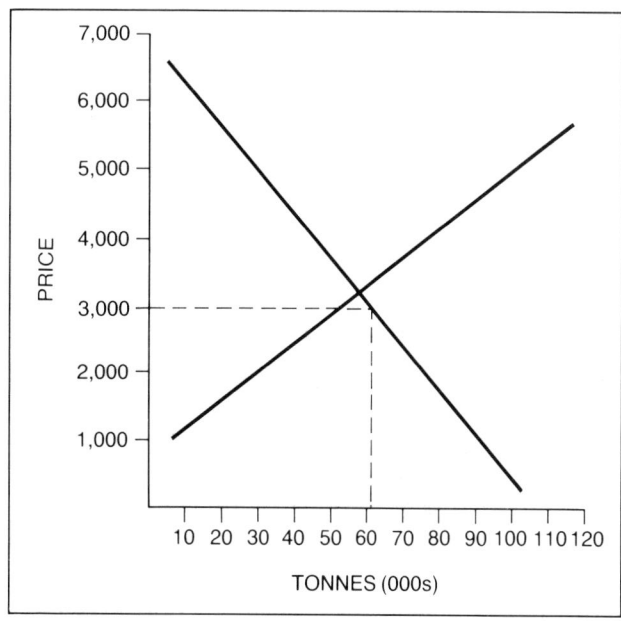

Fig. 7.8 Supply and demand in balance

8 BUSINESS FINANCE

UNIT 8.1
Formation and Investment

Start-up capital

Whoever owns a business and whatever the size of that business, someone invests a sum of money to get the business going; this first investment is known as *start-up capital*. A market trader needs only enough capital to cover the cost of stock and other expenses like petrol for the van and the hire of the stall. A shopkeeper holding considerable stock will have to invest money for shop fittings and may own the premises. Multiple shops (like Marks & Spencer) or department stores (like Harrods) carry enormous stocks, have expensive fittings, own their own premises and maintain fleets of motor vehicles. Anyone can start a business, but the level of capital investment needed will depend upon the size, stock levels, fixtures and premises.

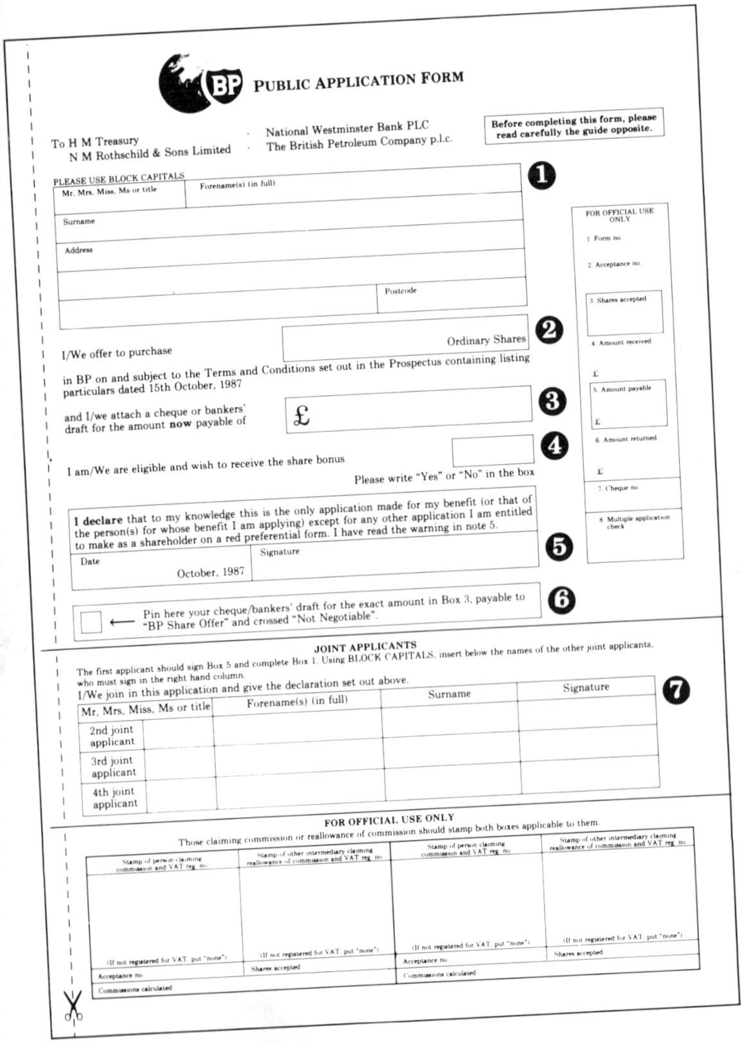

Loans and overdrafts

Banks (and other institutions) offer loan facilities to customers. A *loan* is usually sought for a capital purchase such as machinery, where the total amount agreed is advanced in one lump sum and repayments are made in equal instalments, with interest, over (say) two or three years. A loan, then, is an agreed sum borrowed for a particular purchase.

On the other hand, where a business is temporarily short of ready cash, or where its income is not received regularly at the end of each month, the bank may approve *overdraft* facilities on a current account up to an agreed maximum. With an overdraft, unlike a loan, the customer may at different times have either a credit balance on his or her current account (which means money at the bank) or a debit balance (which means he or she is overdrawn and owes money to the bank).

For both a loan and overdraft facililties the bank will charge interest. The bank will require some form of security, such as a second mortgage on your house, which can be sold if you default.

Public limited company (PLC) share issues

Our very largest companies (Plessey, Ford, Tesco, etc.) need so much capital that they issue shares to the general public in an *offer for sale* (the *prospectus*) which appears in the national newspapers. If the amount of share capital already agreed (*authorised capital*) is to be increased, then the Registrar of Companies must be informed, and any additional documents (like the prospectus) must be deposited with the Registrar. Finally, the directors must seek Stock Exchange approval if the new shares, when issued, are to be bought and sold on the market. (For the buying and selling of stocks and shares, see Unit 11.)

Issue price Once the *face value* of the shares has been agreed, the directors must decide the actual selling price. The BP shares (see Fig. 8.1) have a face value of 25p, but were sold at £3.30, payable in three instalments of £1.20, £1.05 and £1.05. Any shares issued (sold) at face value are said to be issued *at par*. Any sold at more than face value are issued *at a premium*. Any securities sold at less than face value (usually only debentures – see below) are issued *at a discount*. Once issued, the value of stocks and shares goes up and down according to supply and demand.

Preference and ordinary shares

All shares carry a *dividend*. *Preference* shareholders receive the amount of dividend stated at issue; (for example, 6 per cent on a £1 share would yield 6p per annum on each share). Once the preference shareholders have been paid, all the remaining profit belongs to the *ordinary* shareholders, whose dividends are declared by the directors and agreed at an annual meeting of

Fig. 8.1 BP share application form

shareholders; for example, 15p on every £1 share held at the time the dividend is declared would equal an ordinary dividend of 15 per cent.

Debentures

Debentures are a special method of borrowing money, available only to limited companies. Debenture holders are not shareholders and do not participate in profits. They are issued with a bond (which looks very like a share certificate) and receive fixed interest on their loan. Debentures are issued like shares, the interest being (say) 8 per cent, which will amount to £8 for every £100 debenture held. Once issued, debentures can be bought and sold just like shares.

Yield

Dividends and debenture interest are calculated on the face value of the security, which may be quite different from the price you actually paid. For example, a share with a face value of £1 may well cost £3.50 to purchase (i.e. at a premium of £2.50 per share). The company declares a *dividend* on the face value, while *yield* is calculated on the price you actually paid.

Difference between dividend and yield Let us suppose that you buy £100 (face value) of debenture stock for £85 and the stock carries a fixed rate of interest of 8½ per cent. You will receive £8.50 annually, but the rate per cent on the money paid (£85) = 8½ × (100 ÷ 85) = 10%. Therefore your *actual* yield is 10 per cent.

Similarly, you buy shares with a face value of £1, paying £1.50 for each share. A dividend of 21p per share is declared, which is 21 per cent on the face value, but you paid £1.50. Therefore your yield is (100 ÷ 150) × 21 = 14% expressed as a percentage of the price you paid.

Yield will greatly influence the market value of a share, as a higher-than-average yield is attractive to investors.

●SOURCES OF INFORMATION

1. National Westminster Bank PLC, New Issues Department, 2 Princess Street, London EC2P 2BD
2. *In Business Now*, Freepost, London SW1P 4BR
3. Confederation of British Industry, Centre Point, 103 New Oxford Street, London SW1P 4BR
4. Small Firms Centre, 2–18 Ebury Bridge Road, London SW1W 8QD
5. Companies Registration Office, Companies House, Crown Way, Maindy, Cardiff CF4 3UZ

●THINGS TO DO

1. Make a copy of Fig. 8.1. Work in pairs and apply for 1000 ordinary shares. Use Fig. 8.2 to calculate payment. Fill in the application form you have copied in the names of the joint holders. Copy and complete the cheque in payment (Fig. 8.3).
2. How much will the second and third instalments be on your 1000 shares? Have the shares been issued at par, at a premium or at a discount?
3. If your first dividend is 20p per share, what is the yield per cent on the price you actually paid?

Number of shares you are applying for	Amount you pay now (120p per share)	Your total investment (330p per share)
80	£96	£264
100	£120	£330
200	£240	£660
300	£360	£990
400	£480	£1,320
500	£600	£1,650
600	£720	£1,980
700	£840	£2,310
800	£960	£2,640
900	£1,080	£2,970
1,000	£1,200	£3,300
1,500	£1,800	£4,950
2,000	£2,400	£6,600
2,500	£3,000	£8,250
3,000	£3,600	£9,900
3,500	£4,200	£11,550
4,000	£4,800	£13,200
4,500	£5,400	£14,850
5,000	£6,000	£16,500

Above 5,000 shares, applications must be in the following denominations:

Applications	Multiples of
5,000 to 10,000 shares	1,000 shares
10,000 to 50,000 shares	5,000 shares
50,000 to 100,000 shares	10,000 shares
over 100,000 shares	50,000 shares

Fig. 8.2 How much your shares will cost

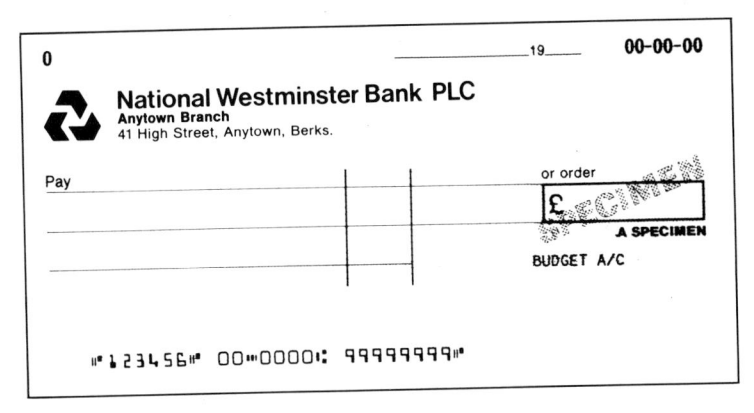

Fig. 8.3 Your cheque

UNIT 8.2
Capital, Assets and Liabilities

Authorised and issued capital

Capital to start a business is provided by the owner(s). Extra capital can be obtained by borrowing, by issuing more shares or by retaining (rather than distributing) profits.

Authorised (sometimes called *registered*) *capital* is that capital (divided into preference and ordinary shares) authorised by the Registrar of Joint Stock Companies when the company was formed. The number of shares involved cannot be exceeded, but a company is not obliged to *issue* (sell) all the shares with which it was registered. Some may be retained for issue at a later date. In the example in Fig. 8.4, *all* the preference shares and *half* the ordinary shares have been issued. The remaining (100 000) ordinary shares are available for issue when more capital is required for expansion.

The balance sheet

The *balance sheet* is a formal written statement of a company's *assets* (what it owns) and *liabilities* (what it owes). Most balance sheets look very similar but those of a limited company must be presented in a legally acceptable form.

Balance sheet liabilities   Anything that a business owes is called a *liability* and is shown on the liabilities side of the balance sheet. Liabilities include:

1 *Issued capital* – the amount due to the shareholders.
2 *Reserves* – usually undistributed profits which are the property of the ordinary shareholders.
3 *Debentures* – borrowed capital, showing the amount due to debenture holders.
4 *Creditors* – people to whom the business owes money, usually for goods and services. These are called *current liabilities*, due for repayment within the financial year.

Balance sheet assets   What the business owns is divided into *fixed* and *current* assets. The fixed assets include:

1 Land and buildings (freehold or leasehold).
2 Plant and machinery.
3 Motor vehicles.
4 Fixtures and fittings.

The current assets include:

1 Stock in trade.
2 Sundry debtors (what people owe to the business).
3 Cash at bank.
4 Cash in hand.

The balance sheet shown in Fig. 8.4 is a simplified version of that suitable for a limited company. Note that the total value of the assets equals the total value of the liabilities. In other words, what the business *owns* is equal

Modern Fashions Ltd.
Balance Sheet as at 31 December, 1989

Liabilities	£	Assets	£
Authorised Capital		*Fixed Assets*	
100,000 6 per cent Preference Shares of £1 each	100,000	Land and buildings	160,000
200,000 Ordinary Shares of £1 each	200,000	Plant and machinery	40,000
	£300,000	Motor vehicles	20,000
		Fixtures and fittings	15,000
Issued Capital		*Current Assets*	
100,000 6 per cent Preference Shares of £1 cash	100,000	Stock in trade	15,000
100,000 Ordinary Shares of £1 each	100,000	Sundry debtors	40,000
		Cash in bank	12,000
Reserves		Cash in hand	3,000
General Reserve and undistributed profit	25,000		
Loan capital			
500 Debentures of £100 each	50,000		
Current Liabilities			
Sundry creditors	30,000		
	£305,000		£305,000

Fig. 8.4 A company balance sheet

to what the business *owes*; assets and liabilities are in balance, hence the term *balance sheet*.

Calculation of a dividend

The way profits are shared out is a matter for the directors, who decide and declare the annual dividends. If a shareholder is not satisfied, he or she can sell his or her shares in order to make a more rewarding investment offering a higher yield.

The amount of preference dividend is determined by the rate per cent at which the shares were issued so, for example, 6 per cent preference shares require that the shareholders shall be paid 6p for every £1 share they hold. The total preference dividend will be determined by the total amount of preference capital issued to the general public. Assuming a total preference capital issued of £100 000, then the preference dividend will be:

$$£100\,000 \times \frac{6}{100} = £6000 \text{ in any one year}$$

Also assuming a total issued ordinary capital of £100 000, the directors will now declare a dividend on the ordinary shares, expressed as a rate per cent. Suppose they declare an ordinary dividend of 10 per cent, then the total ordinary dividend would be:

$$£100\,000 \times \frac{10}{100} = £10\,000 \text{ for that financial year}$$

The amount of dividend to be distributed to the shareholders is now £16 000 out of a total profit available of £25 000. It is sensible to retain some profit within the company to allow for growth; undistributed profit is known as a *reserve*.

Working capital and capital employed

Capital is a term we normally associate with an owner's capital. Different kinds of capital are shown in the balance sheet of a sole proprietor in Fig. 8.5.

●QUESTIONS

1. Redraft the balance sheet of Modern Fashions Ltd (Fig. 8.4) *after* the dividends of £16 000 have been paid to the shareholders.
2. Again from Fig. 8.4, calculate: (a) owners' capital (remember to include reserves); (b) capital employed; (c) fixed capital; (d) circulating capital; (e) liabilities; (f) working capital.
3. A shareholder owns 4000 preference shares and 3000 ordinary shares in Modern Fashions Ltd. Calculate the dividends due to him or her as at 31 December.
4. In Fig. 8.5, to whom does the business owe: (a) £49 000; (b) £8000; (c) £2000? If all the creditors were paid in full, how much cash would remain?
5. In Fig. 8.5, the investments are sold for £4000. Redraft the balance sheet, showing the effect on both the circulating capital and current liabilities.

●THINGS TO DO

1. British Gas, British Telecom, the Trustee Savings Bank, BP and British Airways have all issued ordinary shares to the general public. Look up today's stock market quotation for each share. Can you account for the differences in the *face value* of those shares as against the *market value*?
2. Write to: (a) Young Enterprise, 48 Bryanston Square, London W1H 7LN; (b) Mini-Enterprise in Schools Project, Education Industry Unit, Institute of Education, University of Warwick, Westwood, Coventry CV4 7AL.
   Ask for information on the formation of a company in your class. As a group, would you feel able to participate in these schemes?

●SOURCES OF INFORMATION

1. British Gas PLC, Information Office, Rivermill House, 152 Grosvenor Road, London (SW1V 3JL), for *The Story of British Gas*.
2. Shell Education Service, Shell Mex House, Strand, London WC2R 0DX, for a copy of *Shell Education News*.
3. Training Packages Ltd, Unit 6, Bittacy Business Centre, Bittacy Hill, London NW7 1BA, for details of business games.
4. London Coffee Information Centre, 21 Berners Street, London W1P 4DD, for helpful educational materials.

Balance Sheet

Liabilities	£	Assets	£	£
Capital account	49,000	Freehold property	25,000	
Bank loan	8,000	Plant and machinery	10,000	
Creditors	2,000	Delivery vans	3,000	
				38,000
		Stock in trade	7,000	
		Investments	3,000	
		Debtors	6,300	
		Cash	4,500	
				21,000
	59,000			59,000

(i) Owner's capital 49,000
(ii) Capital employed (total of assets) 59,000
(iii) Fixed capital (property, plant, vans) 38,000
(iv) Circulating capital (stock, debtors investment, cash) 21,000
(v) Current liabilities (loans, creditors) 10,000
(vi) Working capital (circulating capital minus current liabilities) 11,000

Fig. 8.5 A sole proprietor's balance sheet

UNIT 8.3
Cash Flow, Stock, Profit and Turnover

Cash flow

In almost every business profitable trading is signified by a surplus of cash over and above the day-to-day expenses. The owner will be able to withdraw some of this profit in cash (called *drawings*) each month for his or her private use. In a loss-making concern, ready cash will not be available. The bills will accumulate, and the proprietor will have to borrow from the bank, or seek an agreement with his or her creditors, if the business is to survive. There will be little or nothing available for the proprietor.

So a satisfactory *cash flow* or *liquidity* situation is one where more money is coming in than is going out. Steady growth is possible, and the business prospers. An adverse *cash flow* or *liquidity* position would be one where expenses were greater than income. Unless rectified, such a position will ultimately lead to bankruptcy.

It is possible for a proprietor to have a problem with cash flow even when the business is doing well. For instance, large stocks of raw materials might have to be bought at the beginning of a month, but the manufactured goods may not be sold until the end of the month. In the meantime wages and other bills have to be paid. There is a lot of money flowing out of the business and none coming in. The proprietor will probably arrange an overdraft with the bank to finance the business until the goods are sold (profitably).

Stock

At the end of every financial year stock is valued (usually at purchase price) prior to the calculation of profit (or loss) for the year. The stock valuation at the end of the year becomes the stock in hand at the beginning of the following financial year. Adequate stock levels must be maintained to ensure customer choice or production flows.

Profit

At the end of each financial year it is necessary to make a formal calculation of the profit (or loss) for tax purposes. The company accountant will prepare a statement of profit and, with a balance sheet, submit what are known as *final accounts* to the tax inspector, who will assess tax liability.

Gross profit and net profit   Gross profit is the profit on buying and selling only, excluding expenses. Net profit is gross profit less expenses for the year. Fig. 8.6 shows a statement of *gross and net profit* for Modern Fashions Ltd, whose balance sheet appears as Fig. 8.4 in section 8.2.

Profit as a percentage of sales and purchases   Gross profit can be shown as a percentage of either sales or purchases. For example:

Sales in June	=	£1500
Purchases for June	=	£1000
Profit during June	=	£500

Therefore gross profit as a percentage of sales is:

$$\frac{500}{1500} \times 100 = 33\tfrac{1}{3}\%$$

And as a percentage of purchases is:

$$\frac{500}{1000} \times 100 = 50\%$$

It is more realistic to express profit as a percentage of *turnover* (total sales), because stock purchased will differ in cost during the year. Both gross and net profit may be expressed as a percentage of turnover, as can each item of expense, such as wages, rent and rates. Percentages are valuable for making the following comparisons:

1. one year's trading with another, within the same business;
2. one branch with another within the same group;
3. one business with another, especially where one business is doing better than another.

Such comparisons may reveal defects in the management of a business, which can then be rectified.

Rate of turnover of stock

Annual sales are sometimes referred to as *turnover*. The *rate of turnover* is the number of times per annum the average stock is sold. Stock levels do not vary greatly from one week to the next; as goods are sold, further orders are placed.

Profit or Loss: Modern Fashions Ltd

Stocks held at 1 January	=	£14 500
Purchases of stock during year	=	£180 000
∴ Total stock valuation for year	=	£194 500
Stocks held at 31 December	=	£15 000
∴ Cost price of stock actually sold	=	£179 500
Total sales of stock for year	=	£251 000*
Less cost price of stock actually sold	=	£179 500*
∴ Gross profit for year	=	£71 500

Gross profit for the year		=	£71 500
Expenses: Wages	£32 000		
Rates	£4500		
Light and heat	£10 000		£46 500
∴ Net profit for year		=	£25 000

Fig. 8.6 Statement of gross and net profit

* The difference between the two figures represents a mark-up of 40 per cent on cost. What is the percentage profit on sales?

$$\text{Rate of turnover} = \frac{\text{sales at cost}}{\text{average stock (at cost price)}}$$

Average stock is easily calculated. Sales at cost may be more difficult, and in practice are almost impossible to calculate where various prices are paid during the year for the same item of stock. Sales at cost are of course the sales figure less a (notional) percentage profit. For example:

Sales at selling price	=	£4800
Gross profit at $33\frac{1}{3}$% on selling price	=	£1600
Sales at cost price		£3200

If average stock level is £400, then rate of turnover = $3,200 \div 400 = 8$, which means that average stock is sold eight times per year. Conversely, sales at cost price = average stock × rate of turnover.

Statistical examples

Example 1 During a particular year, a business made a gross profit of 20 per cent on a turnover of £42 000 and a net profit of 9 per cent on turnover. The rate of stock turnover was 20. Calculate;

(a) The gross profit for the year.
(b) The average stock for the year.
(c) The net profit for the year.
(d) The expenses for the year.

(i) Sales at selling price = £42 000.
Gross profit on sales (20%) = £8400.
∴ Sales at cost price = £33 600
(ii) Average stock = sales at cost price ÷ rate of turnover.
∴ Average stock = £33 600 ÷ 20 = £1680.
(iii) Sales at selling price = £42 000.
∴ Net profit on sales (9%) = £3780.
(iv) Gross profit for year = £8400.
Net profit for year = £3780.
∴ Expenses for year = £4620.

Example 2 During June a trader purchases stock to the value of £1000 and expresses the profit made as $33\frac{1}{3}$ per cent on *selling* price. What is the actual profit (in £s)?

Let (notional) selling price = £100, then profit on each £100 = £$33\frac{1}{3}$, and cost price of goods must be £$66\frac{2}{3}$. We can express selling and cost price as a ratio:

(a) $100:66\frac{2}{3}$ or $3:2$

(b) $\dfrac{100}{66\frac{2}{3}}$ or $\dfrac{3}{2}$.

If we take the *actual* purchase price of £1000 and multiply by the ratio, £1000 × (100 ÷ $66\frac{2}{3}$) = £1500. So £1500 is the selling price, and the profit is £500.

Example 3 During January a business has a turnover of £5000. The mark-up is said to be 25 per cent on purchases. Calculate the cost price of the goods sold and the actual profit (NB mark-up × percentage profit).

Let the cost price = £100, then profit on each £100 = £25, and selling price of goods must be £125. ∴ Ratio of cost price to selling price is:

(a) $100:125$ or $4:5$

(b) $\dfrac{100}{125}$ or $\dfrac{4}{5}$.

If actual selling price = £5000 then purchase (cost) price = £5000 × (4 ÷ 5) = £4000, and actual profit is £1000.

●QUESTIONS

1. From Fig. 8.6, and using a calculator, express both gross and net profit as a percentage of: (a) purchases and (b) sales.
2. From Fig 8.6 and using a calculator, calculate the rate of turnover of stock in respect of Modern Fashions Ltd.
3. From *Example 1* assuming an opening stock of £1550 and a closing stock of £1810, construct a statement of gross and net profit for the business in question.
4. From *Example 2*, if the profit on *selling* price had been expressed at 20 per cent, what would have been the profit in £?
5. From *Example 3*, using the same mark-up, what would the average profit be on monthly purchases of £6000, assuming that all stock is actually sold?
6. A proprietor expresses his profit as 37 per cent (³⁄₈) on *selling price*. What will be his actual profit (in £) on goods purchased for £10 000?

●THINGS TO DO

1. If you know any shareholders (friends, parents, staff) ask them for copies of the annual reports and accounts, which they will receive from the companies they have shares in. Some of these are illustrated with graphs, bar charts and pie charts, usually in colour.
2. Your local town hall or building society will have brochures showing their sources of income and how that income is spent. Again this information will probably be in colour.
3. Organise a stocktaking of your stockroom at school or college. Calculate the cost of all the stock held in reserve.

9 MONEY AND BANKING

●UNIT 9.1
Decisions about Spending and Saving

Worth

What is anything worth? The answer is – whatever someone is prepared to pay for it. The famous painting by Leonardo da Vinci, *Virgin and Child*, in the National Gallery in Trafalgar Square, London is worth millions. The reproduction (Fig. 9.1), is worth 30p, the cost of the postcard. There is only one original, which is priceless; there are thousands of copies, which are virtually worthless.

Fig. 9.1 Leonardo's *Virgin and Child*

Choice

Very few people have an unlimited income. But all of us have basic needs (for survival) and plenty of *wants* (non-essentials): new clothes, books or records, a holiday, and so on. Everyone is faced with *choices*, to buy this rather than that, to purchase flowers for Mother's Day rather than go to the cinema, to save now in order to enjoy a holiday later.

Similar decisions have to be made in business. Businesses may have to choose to invest in up-to-date equipment, rather than employ more staff; to 'bank' (save) some of their profits now, rather than spend them, in case the business hits a bad patch later.

An economist would describe choice as *the application of scarce resources to a multiplicity of wants*, which is only like saying, 'You can't have your cake and eat it.' Even governments are faced with similar problems. Should we reduce income tax or spend more on employment-creating projects like road-building or the Health Service?

Saving and investment

Individuals save with a 'want' in mind. A better car or new furniture – these are short-term goals which we satisfy within the foreseeable future. Investment extends over a longer term and satisfies different wants. I invest in a new house because I need somewhere to live and my family is increasing. I invest in British Telecom shares hoping that I shall be able to sell them at a profit at some future date.

In the same way, businesses hold back profits in order to meet bills due in the future. They may also use surplus profit to invest in new premises or new equipment because the business is growing. Banks invest money left on deposit, and insurance companies invest clients' premiums. Money cannot be left idle; it must be made to work, either in earning interest or in increasing profits. A *capital investment* (e.g. new machinery) is made in the anticipation of greater efficiency and increased profits.

In the same way, governments invest in major industries of national importance which must be supported and maintained. They also invest in the education and health services, because high standards in these areas are essential to the well-being of a nation. Here the nation 'invests' to improve the quality of life – not to attract profits.

Fig. 9.2 A premium bond

Credit facilities

'Have now – pay later' is an alternative to 'Save now – buy later', a form of compulsory saving upon which you *pay*, rather than *receive*, interest. (See Unit 2, section 2.4.)

In business, credit facilities are common. Also common is *leasing*, a form of hiring goods on contract (like a fleet of cars) over an agreed period for a given sum. The goods never belong to the business; it merely hires their use.

Governments borrow money (think of Premium Bonds and National Savings certificates: see Fig. 9.2) and they also issue *government securities* upon which they pay interest. A government may buy (say) a submarine, paying interest on the capital sum involved.

● 62

Value, price and 'value for money'

We use *money values* to make choices and decisions, comparing the expenditure necessary to buy a pair of shoes against the enjoyment of an evening's entertainment. If a new bike costs £140, we know how much we have to save and how long it is likely to take.

Value expressed in cash terms means the *price* you have to pay for something. This is not necessarily the same as *value for money*, which is based on what people think something is worth. We all love a bargain, and our budgets can be upset by a tempting offer which we would not consider at normal cost, or in normal circumstances.

The cost of a house in the South of England is about twice the cost of a similar house in the North, while the cost of a new car is much the same wherever it is purchased. The semi-detached house in the South cannot be said to be value for money when compared with one north of Birmingham (see Fig. 9.3). House prices in the South increase because of the high *demand* for accommodation in a particular place. You cannot move a house elsewhere; you buy it where it stands, or not at all. Motor cars are mobile and *can* be moved from one part of the country to another, so the demand is equalised and price is constant.

●QUESTIONS

1. A Premium Bond I purchased in 1973 has not yet won any prizes. Why might I actually have lost money on this 'investment'?
2. We read in the newspapers that artists are often paid little for paintings that much later become valuable works of art. If your family had owned the Leonardo da Vinci painting (Fig. 9.1) originally, you would now be a multi-millionaire. Evaluate a decision to collect modern paintings *as an investment*.
3. Why do you think the house in the South costs so much more than the one north of Birmingham?
4. Copy out and complete the chart in Fig. 9.4. What form of savings seems the most attractive? From your point of view, is interest or ease of withdrawal more important?
5. You have saved £250. You can purchase: (a) a two-week holiday in the sun; (b) a new leather jacket; (c) a second-hand motor cycle, or (d) a correspondence course to gain promotion in your new job. What factors are likely to influence your choice?
6. Why will you have to pay more for a 1950 Morris Minor 1000 than you would for a 1980 Austin Mini 1000? What influences value? Which would be your choice and why?

Fig. 9.3 A house in the north of England for £60,000, or one in the south-east for £139,500

Method	Minimum deposit	How easy to withdraw?	Where to open an account	Opening hours	Rate of interest
NSB ordinary account					
NSB investment account					
Premium Savings Bonds					
Deposit account at bank					
Building society account					
National Savings Certificates					

Fig. 9.4 Different forms of savings

UNIT 9.2
Banks and Bank Accounts

High-street banking

Our high-street commercial banks grew out of the *joint stock banks* of the nineteenth century. These in turn developed because the earlier private banks had been unreliable.

The major high-street banks are Barclays, Lloyds, National Westminster, Midland and Trustee Savings Bank. In addition, the Yorkshire Bank and the Clydesdale Bank serve particular parts of Britain, and there are other smaller commercial banks such as Williams and Glyns. Banks exist to make profits and their main business is to accept customers' money in the form of deposits, and to lend this money carefully to other customers who need loans.

Types of bank account

Two main types of account are available:

1. A *deposit account* earns interest but does not usually offer a cheque-book or cash card. Maintained at no cost to the customer, it is sometimes called a *savings account*.
2. A *current account* is operated free of charge unless you overdraw; a cheque-book, cheque card and cash card are usually offered to current account customers. Interest *may* be available.

Either of the above accounts can be held by a single person, by two (or more) people jointly or by a business (usually in a business name like Duoparts Ltd or Smith & Smith). All those authorised to withdraw money, or sign cheques, must give a *specimen signature* to the bank involved.

A *budget account* is really a special kind of current account. First you discuss all your large payments with your bank manager (mortgage, gas, electricity, rates, telephone, insurance, etc.). These are totalled and an annual sum is obtained. You agree to pay one-twelfth of that sum plus interest into your budget account each month. The bank will then pay the bills received (or you can pay by cheque) when the amounts become due.

Deposits

Paying-in slips (see Fig. 9.5) are completed by the account holder and passed over the counter together with the cheques and coin to be credited to your account. The cashier will stamp both the giro in-payment and the counterfoil. The bank keeps the in-payment credit slips; you retain the counterfoil. Before close of business each night all in-payments are entered on the computer, and the balance of your account is increased by the amount paid in.

Business can be transacted at any bank in any part of the country. There may be a small charge if you use a bank other than your own (for example, Barclays rather than the Midland), and you may be asked for identification for some transactions.

Withdrawals

A withdrawal from any kind of account is looked at carefully. The cheque gives full details of the bank and branch, the account number and the size of withdrawal or payment (Fig. 9.6). If the withdrawal is for a large amount, the cashier will *call up* your account balance on the computer, just to check that you have the necessary funds.

In the case of cash withdrawals, deposit account holders usually have to attend at the branch at which the account is registered and use the approved withdrawal slip. Current account holders can withdraw any amount at their own bank; if they have a cheque card, they can also withdraw up to £100 at any branch of their own bank free of charge, or at other banks, where a small handling charge is made. Current account holders may also be issued with a *cash card* with which they can withdraw (up to) an agreed amount from service-tills set in the street walls of some banks. Finally, both deposit and current account holders can arrange for banking services to be available at a named

The printed figures include

A the code number of the bank and branch
B the serial number of the cheque
C the account number of the drawer
D the amount of the cheque which is later typed in line using a type-writer with a special type to be read by a computer.

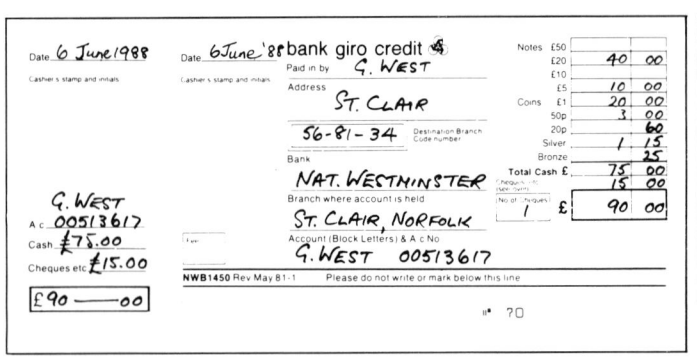

Fig. 9.5 An in-payment

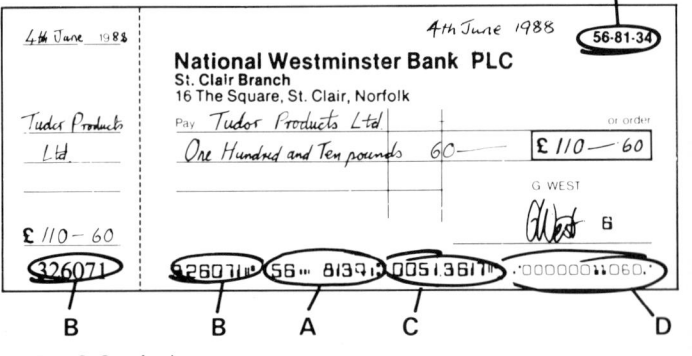

Fig. 9.6 A cheque

branch (say at Scarborough over holiday periods), or at a foreign bank (say Crédit Lyonnais, Paris, to provide funds for a business trip). Such arrangements can cover a short period or can be permanent.

Personal identification number (PIN) – this is used in association with cash dispensers and service-tills. Each card-holder is given an individual number which is electronically imprinted on the card. When the card is inserted in the machine, the cardholder uses the PIN as a means of identification. Enter the wrong PIN and the machine will retain your card.

What the banks do with your money

Banks have learned that only about 10 per cent of their deposits – that is the total of balances on both current and deposit accounts – is needed in cash at any one time. While one person is withdrawing money at one window, someone else is usually paying in the day's takings at the next.

So 90 per cent of all deposits is available to the bank to grant people loans (to buy a new car, to insulate the house or to finance a holiday). These are short-term personal loans, repayable over months rather than years. Equally, a bank manager will also agree a mortgage to cover the purchase of a house. This is a long-term loan, repaid by monthly instalments over anything up to 25 years. (For the difference between loans and overdrafts, see Unit 8, section 8.1).

Banks also extend loans and agree overdrafts for business use (to cover the cost of new machinery, to finance a fleet of vans for deliveries, to provide start-up capital to an individual going into business for the first time, etc. See Unit 8, section 8.1.). Again, these arrangements are short-term, but banks will also finance the purchase of business premises, on a mortgage basis.

The larger banks also lend money to governments of other countries and finance both government and private projects overseas.

All money loaned by the banks earns them interest at varying levels. The greater the risk to the bank, or the longer the loan period, the greater the rate of interest. Rates are negotiable with the manager involved.

Bank statements

From time to time your bank will issue a *statement* (see Fig. 9.7) which details all in-payments, all withdrawals, interest charges and any special bank charges. Most business people arrange to receive their bank statements monthly and check them against their own records to ensure that no mistakes are made.

●SOURCES OF INFORMATION

1. Banking Information Service, 10 Lombard Street, London EC3V 9AT
2. Midland Bank PLC, Griffin House, PO Box 2, Silver Street, Sheffield S1 3GG, for *Resource Pack for Schools and Colleges*.
3. National Westminster Bank PLC, Recruitment and Personnel, 14 Moorgate, London EC2R 6DA
4. National Westminster Bank PLC, Public Affairs Department, 41 Lothbury, London EC2P 2BP
5. Yellow Pages – see under 'banks'.

●THINGS TO DO

1. From your local high-street banks, collect information on banking for students. Which bank makes the most attractive offer? Divide into groups and compare your findings.
2. Make a survey of banks in your town centre which provide service-till facilities. Which banks are involved? Are service-tills provided by other organisations?

●QUESTIONS

1. Calculate the balance on G. West's account following the presentation of the cheque shown in Fig. 9.6.
2. Which bank does G. West use? At which bank is his account held? What is the code number?
3. Is the account a deposit or a current account? What is the account number?
4. In Fig. 9.7, what do the initials CD and DD stand for? Explain these terms.
5. Following the in-payment for £90 (Fig. 9.5), how much more can G. West withdraw before he becomes overdrawn?
6. Explain how the holder of a cheque card might use that card in a strange town when buying, for example, a pre-recorded videotape.
7. Describe how the holder of a cash card would obtain money from a service-till. What is a PIN?

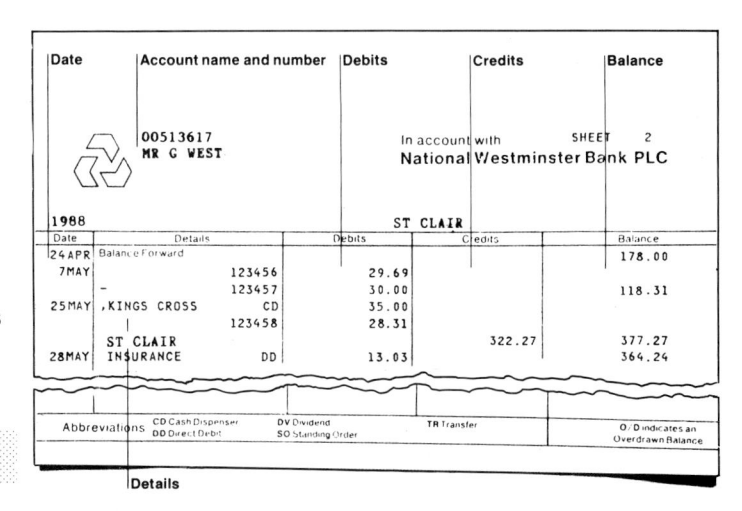

Date	Account name and number	Debits	Credits	Balance
	00513617 MR G WEST		In account with National Westminster Bank PLC	SHEET 2
1988			ST CLAIR	
Date	Details	Debits	Credits	Balance
24 APR	Balance Forward			178.00
7 MAY	-	123456 29.69		
		123457 30.00		118.31
25 MAY	KINGS CROSS CD	35.00		
		123458 28.31		
	ST CLAIR		322.27	377.27
28 MAY	INSURANCE DD	13.03		364.24

Abbreviations: CD Cash Dispenser DV Dividend TR Transfer O/D indicates an Overdrawn Balance
DD Direct Debit SO Standing Order

Details

Fig. 9.7 A bank statement

UNIT 9.3
Other Banking Services

Individuals and banks

Cash transfers The most common banking service is to transfer cash values from one person to another, from one business to another and from one bank to another, both in Britain and abroad. In the majority of cases this is done by drawing (writing out) a cheque (see Fig. 9.8). A *cheque* is an instruction to your bank to take a given amount from your account and transfer that sum to the account of a person named by you and shown on the cheque. At your instruction, a bank will also transfer given sums of money abroad to any account in any bank of your choice.

Safe keeping At all times your branch will guarantee the safety of your money on deposit, even after a robbery. Banks also provide a *safe-deposit service* for any valuables or papers, which are stored in a strong-room or safe-deposit box. Wall safe facilities, to deposit cash takings after the bank has closed, are also available to approved customers.

Advice Managers are always happy to offer advice to their customers on financial matters. Banks will draw up a will and carry out your instructions contained in that will on your death. Stocks and shares can be bought and sold through a bank, and a bank will act for you in the purchase and sale of property. Banks will provide foreign currency for your holiday – just tell the cashier how much, what country and when you are leaving. Similarly, the bank will arrange insurance, collect dividends on your investments, lend you money or act as a *referee* (e.g. to guarantee your reliability for employment, credit facilities or a mortgage application).

Standing orders and direct debits One especially valuable service is the payment of bills regularly and punctually by *standing order*. A standing order usually involves a *fixed amount* of money at regular intervals (annually, each quarter, or once a month).

You can also instruct your bank to accept a demand for *varying amounts* from a named creditor. This is known as a *direct debit*. For example, quarterly electricity, gas and telephone bills are for *varying amounts*.

You can cancel a direct debit or a standing order at any time. Both arrangements are also widely used by business organisations. (See Unit 5, section 5.2.)

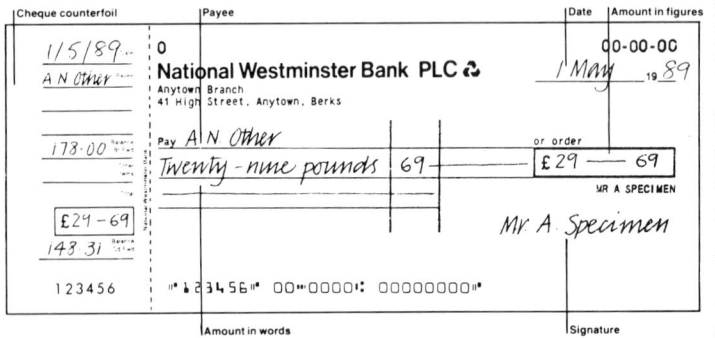

Fig. 9.8 Writing out a cheque

Businesses and banks

All those services described above as available to individuals are also available to sole traders, partnerships and limited companies, although wills are not usually required by limited companies. However, industry and commerce are more likely than individuals to do business abroad, as exporters or importers, perhaps both.

Overseas trade This topic is explained in detail in Unit 16. Whether the goods go by sea or air, various documents are necessary. Insurance is needed to cover the goods in transit, foreign currency is required to finance the deal, and suitable transport has to be arranged. A firm's bank can offer the necessary services or introduce a shipping agent who will act on the firm's behalf. The bank or the agent will give advice on the country with which the firm is dealing, and overseas agents will be contacted to look after the firm's interests. Until the transaction is settled, finance may be required; a bank loan is often available to smooth the deal to a successful conclusion.

Raising capital Again, this is dealt with in detail elsewhere (Unit 8, section 8.1). The services of a company's bank are always available to sell an issue of shares, to raise large loans for particular ventures or for the acquisition of shares in a take-over bid.

Factoring Most firms offer credit facilities to their trade customers and may have to wait some time for their money. Some clients may be so unwilling to pay that the process of collecting debts becomes very expensive, especially to a small business. Such businesses can take advantage of a *factoring service* provided by the banks, especially the merchant banks (these are described in Unit 10, section 10.1). Through this service, a firm can either sell all its debts to the bank, which will purchase at, for instance, 80 per cent of their value, or ask the bank to collect certain *bad debts* for an agency fee of 10 per cent of the amount actually collected. The firm can then use the money released without further delay and leave costly collection in the hands of experts.

Other services Banks are happy to distribute wage and salary credits, arrange audits, draw up final accounts, offer advice on tax matters, or put business customers in touch with accountants who will act on behalf of the firm. Legal matters are more specialised, but the banks also maintain legal departments which will act for business customers in the registration and transfer of documents, for example.

There are few financial services which are not offered by banks. They will either act directly in your interests or put you in touch with someone who will. These services are not free – charges are made in keeping with the service offered and the trouble taken on your behalf.

The banking ombudsman

An *ombudsman* is an independent *referee* (someone who solves disputes between two people or organisations). In the case of the *banking ombudsman*, he or she will consider complaints made by the general public on matters relating to banks and banking services. The banks themselves finance the scheme, but the complaints procedure is conducted fairly and impartially. The ombudsman has the power to make awards to customers in cases where individual banks have acted against the interests of their clients.

● SOURCES OF INFORMATION

1. Any high-street bank, for a students' guide to banking.
2. National Westminster Bank PLC, Market Intelligence Department, 41 Lothbury, London EC2P 2BP, for *The British Banking System* booklet.
3. *Small Business Digest*, National Westminster Bank PLC, 116 Fenchurch Street, London EC3M 5AN
4. Association of British Factors, Hind Court, 147 Fleet Street, London EC4A 2BU

● THINGS TO DO

1. Divide into groups and choose one person in each group to write a polite letter to different banks in your area asking for information on their night-safe facilities and requesting details of cost. Compare the replies and report back.
2. The Atlas Engineering Company is offering you a job in its offices. You have been a deposit account holder at the local branch of the National Westminster Bank for ten years. You have also completed a period of work experience at this branch. Write a letter to the manager of the branch to ask if she is willing to write a reference on your behalf.
3. Write out a cheque and counterfoil in favour of Atlas Engineering for the sum of £192.47. Sign the cheque and use today's date.

● QUESTIONS

1. What are the *two* main differences between a standing order and a direct debit?
2. If I wish to pay my rates by standing order, what details should I include on the application form?
3. In Fig. 9.8 how much did Mr Specimen have in his account *before* paying Mr Other?
4. In Fig. 9.9, what is G. West's account number at the National Westminster Bank?
5. In Fig. 9.10, how will the person involved check: (a) the payment of a standing order, and (b) the payment of a direct debit?

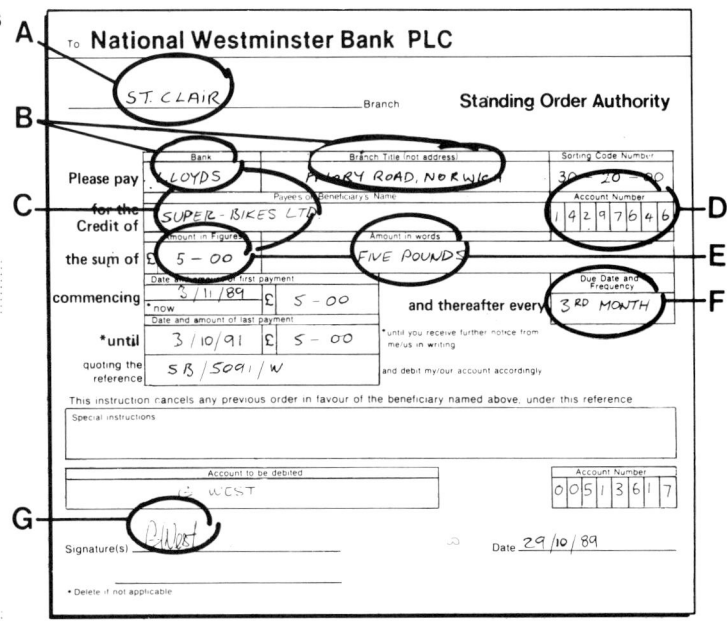

Fig. 9.9 A standing order
Key:
A – the branch of the National Westminster at which I bank
B – the bank to which the standing order is to be sent
C – the name of the account holder to be credited
D – the bank sorting code and Super Bikes' account number
E – the amount to be paid each month in words and figures
F – the date and frequency for each payment
G – my signature authorising the transfer

Fig. 9.10 Paying bills regularly and on time

UNIT 9.4
The Bankers' Clearing House

During the eighteenth century, banking in England was virtually confined to the City of London. Within this compact square mile, all institutions were within walking distance of each other. If a customer deposited a cheque drawn on another bank, then a messenger was sent to that bank, with the cheque, to draw the value in cash.

Some years later, all the messengers began to meet together, at a central point and at a prearranged time, to exchange cheques. They would account at the end of each day only for the *difference* between the totals exchanged.

This was the early origin of the *Bankers Clearing House*. Nowadays about 12 million cheques are issued daily. About half that number pass through the head offices of the *clearing banks* (members of the Clearing House) every working day. Such large quantities need to be processed by computer, using the *sort code* shown at the bottom of each cheque (see Fig. 9.6 in section 9.2).

The cheque clearing system

In any one day a bank branch will receive many cheques:

1. Those drawn by its own customers on accounts held at that branch. An entry will be made debiting one account and crediting another; no further action will be necessary.
2. Those paid in by customers of, for example, Barclays in Sheffield drawn on other Barclays branches. The head office of each of the 'big four' banks maintains an internal clearing system for its own cheques, and these do not go to the Central Bankers' Clearing House.
3. Those paid in by customers of the branch, drawn on a branch of another bank, for example, the National Westminster in Dover. These cheques must be cleared via the Bankers Clearing House in London.

If the individual banks had to send someone to Sheffield and Dover to collect the cash represented by the cheques, it would be a costly operation. The sensible thing is for all cheques that need clearing to be sent to the head office of each bank in London, and for a central office in the City to be agreed where all cheques can be exchanged. The Central Bankers' Clearing House in London is maintained for this purpose, and all clearing banks are members.

A system of settlement is necessary to record the value of the cheques exchanged, and the cost of the process to be allocated between the participating banks. For this purpose, accounts are held at the Bank of England by all members of the Clearing House.

Procedure

Every day each head office receives from its branches all those cheques drawn:

1. on other banks in the same group;
2. on other banks in different groups.

Cheques drawn on its own branches are dealt with internally, but the head office then sorts the other cheques according to banks: National Westminster, Barclays, Lloyds, etc. Lists are made and totals are calculated. At the time arranged by the Clearing House, cheques are exchanged between groups. The cash totals involved are noted by the Clearing House staff.

Daily settlement

Once the exchange is complete, each clearing bank will be aware of the total value of cheques *passed* to other banks. It will be equally aware of the total value of cheques *received* from all the other banks. Deducting one total from the other will reveal how much is to be paid to, or received from, the Bank of England, at which the Clearing House accounts are maintained (Fig. 9.11). No money actually passes from one bank to another. 'Receiving' or 'paying' involves account book transfers only, which tend to balance out over a period.

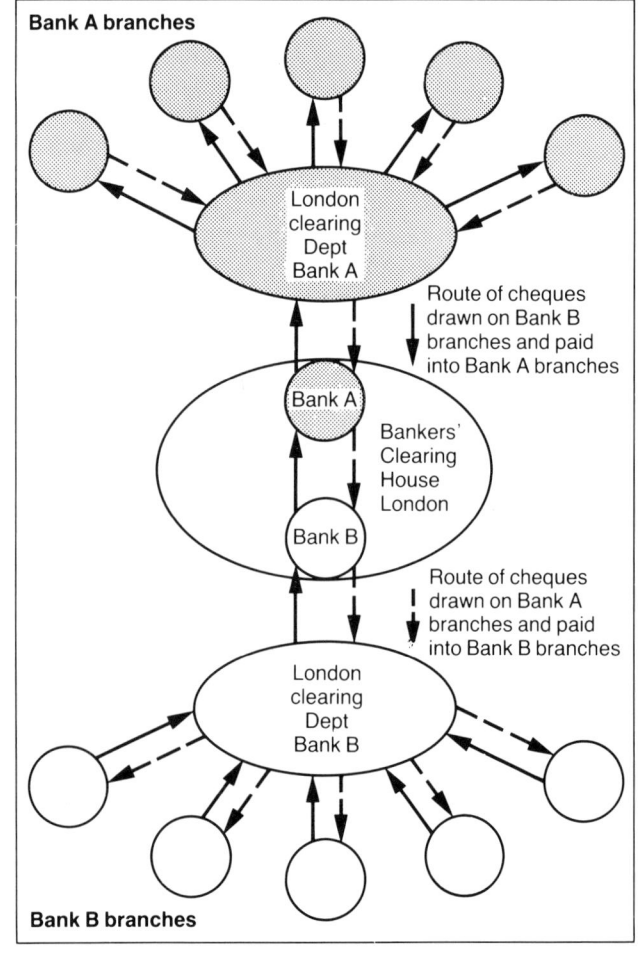

Fig. 9.11 Settlement through the Bankers' Clearing House, London

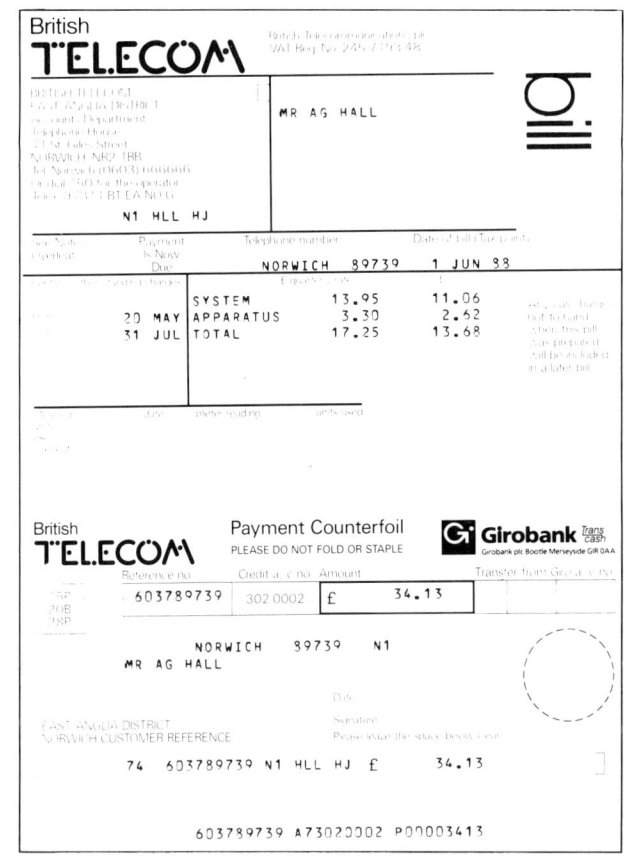

Fig. 9.12 Telephone bill credit transfer

CHAPS and BACS

Individual cheques take about three days to clear. But the *Clearing House Automated Payment System (CHAPS)* deals with cheques for large amounts. It provides a nationwide, *same-day* clearing service by the transfer of funds electronically from one bank to another.

Bankers' Automated Clearing Ltd (BACS) operates a similar service for *credit transfers* of the type seen at the bottom of gas and electricity bills or accounts issued by credit card companies (Fig. 9.12). Standing orders and direct debits are dealt with in the same way.

All this paper is 'cleared' through the Bankers Clearing House on a daily basis. An example is shown (Fig. 9.13) where Mr X, who banks at Lloyds in Southampton, pays £100 from his account there for credit against a hire purchase agreement held by a finance company in Derby. The credit transfer passes from the head office of Lloyds Bank, through the Bankers Clearing House, to the head office of the Midland Bank and on to their branch at Derby, where the transfer is credited to the account of the finance company involved.

●SOURCES OF INFORMATION

1 Banking Information Service, 10 Lombard Street, London EC3V 9AT, for Book 5 on the Bankers' Clearing House.
2 Bankers' Clearing House, 10 Lombard Street, London, EC3V 9AT
3 Bankers' Automated Clearing Ltd, 11 Bread Street, London EC4M 9BE
4 Any high-street bank, for leaflets.
5 Bank of England, Threadneedle Street, London EC2R 8AH for details of 'London Clear'.

●THINGS TO DO

1 Trace all the bank sorting codes for the banks in your high street. Do these codes resemble postcodes arranged by area?
2 Ask a friendly bank manager to talk to your group on cheque clearing locally.
3 Divide into groups. One member from each group should write to a Scottish and/or an Irish bank and ask what arrangements *they* make for clearing cheques.

●QUESTIONS

1 How many banks are members of the Bankers' Clearing House? What do the others do?
2 What are sorting codes, and why are they important? What other codes appear on a cheque? How are these codes used?
3 Why is the Bankers' Clearing House so anxious to clear cheques for large amounts? What advantage is gained by the customer?
4 Who or what maintains bank accounts for members of the Clearing House?
5 How often does the Clearing House *settle*, and what do you understand by this term?
6 In Fig. 9.12, who is: (a) paying £34.13, and (b) receiving £34.13 as a result of the giro credit?
7 In Fig. 9.13, at which bank does the finance company have its account, and where does Mr X bank?
8 List four different kinds of documents cleared through central clearing each day.
9 What do you understand by the term *electronic transfer*? What equipment is likely to be involved and why?

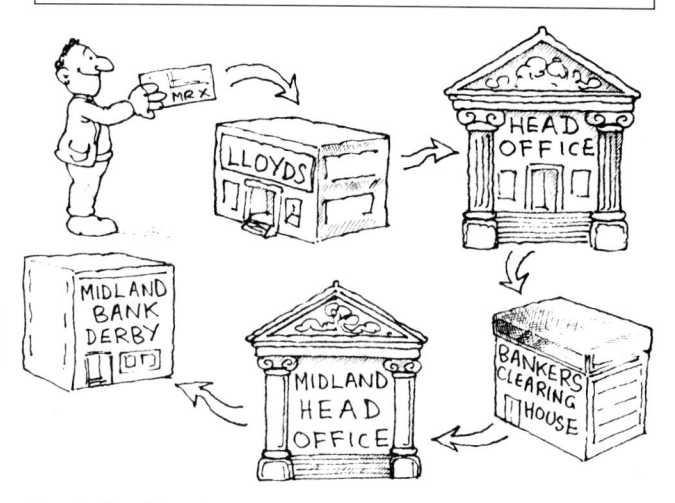

Fig. 9.13 How bank clearing works

UNIT 9.5
Building Societies and the Post Office

Building Societies

The first building society was establised in Birmingham about 1777. Early societies comprised of twenty or so people who made a weekly payment which was used to buy land and build houses. Each house was allocated to a member of the society by ballot or auction. Once every member had a home, the contributions ended and the society was wound up.

From about 1840 building societies began to accept money (deposits) from people who did not want houses, but who just needed a safe place for spare cash. In return they received a regular payment of interest. The accumulated deposits were then lent to other people for the purchase of a house; these people in turn paid mortgage interest to the society.

Current developments among building societies

The main function of building societies is to act as a home for savings and to provide loans for people buying their own homes. But an Act of Parliament passed in 1986 allows building societies to provide many more services to their customers. The larger societies currently find themselves with capital to spare, even after meeting the rapidly growing demand for funds to purchase homes at ever increasing values. As a result, the societies now offer services which we normally associate with a bank. They offer cheque accounts with cheque books and cheque guarantee cards and many offer interest on the balance (see Fig. 9.14). They can also buy and sell stocks and shares, provide travellers' cheques and insurance policies. Major building societies now grant personal loans for the purchase of goods rather than houses. The interest charged is in line with that applied by the banks, but does not qualify for tax relief in the same way as a mortgage interest.

Building societies compared with banks

In the early 1980s the banks began to offer mortgages on a large scale. But despite this competition, building societies account for 70% of all new mortgage loans. In terms of investment, cheque facilities, 24-hour cash availability, personal loans, etc. building societies are beginning to look very much like banks. Society offices are open for longer hours than banks: from 9am to 5pm on weekdays (bank hours are 9.30am to 3.30pm) and on Saturday mornings. The interest paid on their deposit accounts also compares favourably with that available at a high-street bank.

The high-street banks are public limited companies; they exist to make profits for their shareholders. Currently, most building societies belong to their depositors and do not make 'profits'. However, because of the change in the law several societies are considering becoming PLCs. Abbey National leads the way.

Fig. 9.14 Services now offered by building societies

Post Office banking services

There are some 20 000 post offices in Britain. About 1500 are *Crown offices*, staffed by Post Office employees. The rest are sub-offices run on an agency basis by sub-postmasters/mistresses, who combine the post-office counter with some other retail outlet (like grocery or stationery).

National Girobank

Girobank started in 1968 to allow the transfer of money from one part of Britain to another. Since 1968 the venture has developed into a full-grown banking service (see Fig. 9.15) with two million customers and Clearing House status. National Girobank uses all of the 20 000 post offices as branches, which are open 9am to 5pm and on Saturday mornings. Even tiny villages without normal banking facilities usually have a sub-post office and access to Girobank.

Girobank offers both current and deposit accounts, cheque guarantee and Visa credit cards, direct debits and standing orders, loans and foreign currency transactions, together with insurance cover called Superplan. For business firms and public authorities, National Girobank also offers rent/rates collection services, wage/salary/pension payments, cash transfers abroad, leasing finance and Transcash (the payment of bills by Giro transfer).

Girobank maintains cashpoints outside selected post offices. It is also part of a consortium known as Link which will service both building societies and banks like the Co-operative which do not maintain their own system. Cards will be interchangeable. Girobanking is free, provided you remain in credit.

At the time of writing, the Government intends to sell Girobank to the Alliance and Leicester Building Society.

Fig. 9.15 Girobank services

National savings

The Post Office acts as an agent for the National Savings Bank and will open accounts, accept deposits and effect withdrawals. Interest is paid on balances. The scheme is ideal for children and older people for whom the post office is more accessible than a bank.

Post offices also sell National Savings certificates, Premium Bonds and National Savings gift tokens. Encashment in these cases is by written application only. Many post offices will cash cheques drawn on any bank on presentation of a cheque guarantee card; a small charge is made for this service.

Government stock (see Unit 11, section 11.1) can be purchased at Crown offices. Again encashment is by written application to the Bonds and Stock Office in Blackpool.

Savings stamps

The Post Office sells savings stamps which can be used to meet the cost of television licences, telephone accounts, home help charges and water rates. No interest is paid on such deposits, but elderly people and those on a fixed income find the service helpful in meeting large annual bills.

Agency services

In none of these operations does the Post Office act on its own account. The availability and convenience afforded by post offices, large and small, make them ideal for doing business on behalf of the government and public utilities (like British Rail). For these agency services the Post Office makes a charge to the institution or government department involved. (see also Unit 14, section 14.1).

●SOURCES OF INFORMATION

1. Any building society – see Yellow Pages.
2. Building Societies' Association, 34 Park Street, London W1Y 3PE
3. Any Crown post office for savings facilities.
4. National Girobank, Freepost, Bootle, Merseyside G1R 0AA
5. Building Societies' Ombudsman, Grosvenor Gardens House, 35–37 Grosvenor Gardens, London SW1X 7AW

●THINGS TO DO

Research and compare the services offered to students by the institutions shown in Fig. 9.16. Which is the odd-one-out and why?

●QUESTIONS

1. Research and compare the interest given on the five savings accounts shown in Fig. 9.14. Does the rate differ? If so, why?
2. In what circumstances might you use a Visa card?
3. What rates of interest apply to National Savings Bank accounts? Is there more than one account? Compare these rates with those offered by building societies. How do you account for any differences you find?
4. What services are offered to Girobank clients which are not available to building society customers? Can you account for the differences in services offered?

Fig. 9.16 Five well-known financial institutions

UNIT 9.6
The Bank of England

History of the Bank

The Bank of England stands in Threadneedle Street in the heart of the City of London (Fig. 9.17). It was first created by Royal Charter in 1694, when a group of City merchants lent money to King William III to pay for a war against France. In return, the merchants were allowed to call themselves the Bank of England, to issue banknotes and to form a company with limited liability.

The wars with France (1797–1815), the rise of other banks and the need to control over-enthusiastic (would-be) bankers (many of whom went out of business) resulted in more and more authority for the Bank of England. Just before the Second World War (1939–45) the Bank's activities came under the control of the Chancellor of the Exchequer, through the Treasury. This status was formally recognised by the Bank of England Act 1946, which nationalised the Bank. Its Governor and directors, appointed by the Crown, together make up the Bank's governing body.

Functions of the Bank

The Bank of England has a number of functions:

1 It looks after the nation's money.
2 It supervises the work of other banks.
3 It advises the government of the day on economic policies.
4 It issues banknotes (but not coin).
5 It borrows money on behalf of the government – the National Debt.
6 It keeps in contact with similar banks and other governments abroad.
7 It is 'lender of last resort' (see below).

Fig. 9.17 The Bank of England in Threadneedle Street, London. (Note the lack of windows on the ground floor!)

Banker to the nation

The Bank of England has no private customers. But it keeps accounts for every government department into which taxes are paid and from which social security benefits, the cost of roads, wages for civil servants, etc. are met. Other 'customers' include most other banks operating in Britain, overseas central banks and some overseas governments. The Bank holds for safe keeping all Britain's stocks of foreign currency and the gold reserves.

Banker to the bankers

The Bank prints around 7½ million new banknotes (about the same number are burned) each day at its printing works in Essex. Some 10 000 million notes are currently in circulation. The average life of a banknote is 9–10 months.

The Bank regulates *interest rates*. This affects the percentage banks charge on loans and overdrafts, the rates applied to hire purchase agreements and the charges levied by credit card companies.

The Bank manages the *market rate of exchange* by which pounds sterling can be changed into other currencies, such as French francs, Japanese yen and US dollars. All our high-street banks maintain accounts at the Bank of England, through which inter-bank debts are settled, mainly arising from deals in the Bankers' Clearing House (see section 9.4).

The Bank regulates the activities of all other banks and all financial institutions in Britain. It ensures the safety of people's money by issuing regulations which have the force of law.

Banker to the government

The Bank borrows money for government use. It borrows from institutions in the City and from individuals (like you and me) – by the issue of National Savings certificates, by the issue of stocks and bonds through the government broker and by the issue of Treasury Bills which are 'sold' each day in the City. The Bank pays interest on these borrowings, when due, and records each transaction on behalf of the government. The vast amount of money raised over many years is called the *National Debt*.

The National Debt

The National Debt came into existence in 1694, when the Bank of England was founded. Since that time British governments have continued to borrow money both from people and from institutions. The early history of the National Debt resulted from the financing of wars: with France during Napoleonic times; with the American colonists who wanted independence from Britain; and during the First and Second World Wars.

Most modern loans are covered by *collateral* (e.g. a mortgage on home or business premises). But the

National Debt is not supported by any real assets and is covered only by the government's promise to repay at some future date. However, there are some government stocks which are *undated*, where there is no given date on which they will be repaid; most of these carry a very low rate of interest (Fig. 9.18).

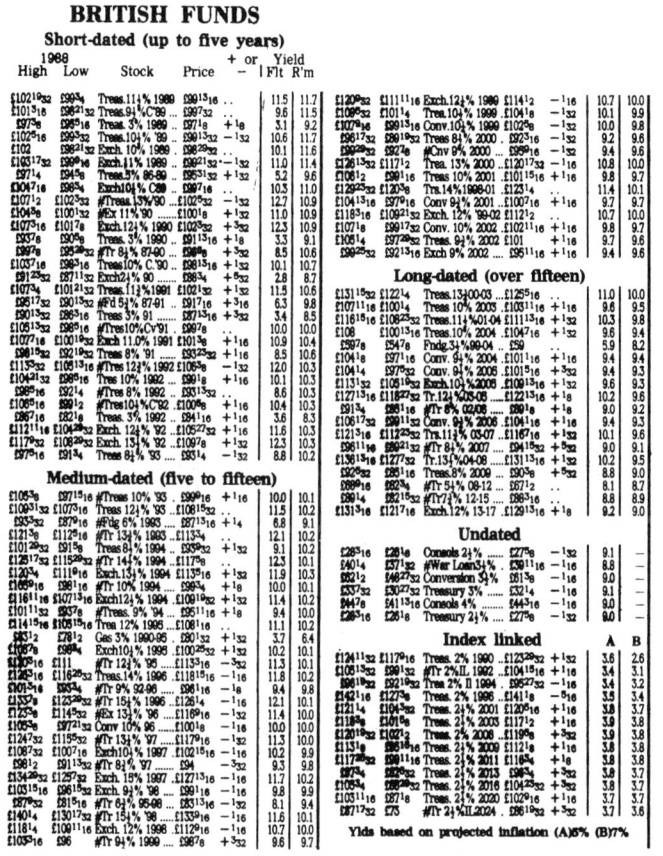

Fig. 9.18 Gilt-edged stock

The National Debt itself may never be repaid. As one group of loans becomes repayable, each government raises new money, as described below. Remember that the millions borrowed are owed to you and me, who are happily receiving interest. If we require the money, we can always sell the government bonds (known as *gilt-edged stock* or *gilts*) or cash in our savings certificates.

Source of the National Debt In Fig. 9.18, you will see examples of government stocks and bonds currently quoted in the newspaper. Others are added from time to time. These stocks can be bought and sold by investors just like any other debenture. You don't become a shareholder in Great Britain Ltd; your only satisfaction will be the receipt of interest.

Finally, the government borrows money for short periods (usually three months) by the sale of *Treasury bills*, which are offered to the highest bidders on Friday of each week. The bills are for fixed amounts (say £100 000) and carry interest. Profit is also made by buying the bills at a price slightly below the face value, knowing that you will be repaid in full when the bill matures. The rate of interest on Treasury bills is a strong indicator of current rates of interest. Banks usually follow this lead in their own lending policy.

National Debt Commissioners are a group of people responsible for the investment in government stock of all small savings at the Post Office. They also accept the duty to 'manage' the National Debt, buying and selling both stock and bills according to government needs.

● SOURCES OF INFORMATION

1 Bank of England, Information Division, Threadneedle Street, London EC2R 8AH
2 Bank of England, Museum and Research Section, Threadneedle Street, London EC2R 8AH
3 Bonds and Stock Office, Blackpool, Lancashire FY3 9YP
4 National Savings, Freepost, 4335, Bristol BS1 3YX
5 National Debt Office, Royex House, Aldermanbury Square, London EC2V 7HR

● THINGS TO DO

1 If you live in, or visit, London, the Bank of England organises tours. Write for details.
2 Write to the Bonds and Stock Office for further details of government stock.
3 Write to the National Debt Commissioners. Ask about their work and responsibilities.

● QUESTIONS

1 Why do you think that the Bank of England has no private customers like you and me? In your view, is it really a bank?
2 How many new banknotes are printed each year? How long does a note last? Do you think that the everyday use of money will decrease? What will take its place?
3 Look at Fig. 9.17. Why do you think that the Bank of England has no windows on the ground floor?
4 Using Fig. 9.18, calculate how much I will have to pay for £100 of Treasury stock at 14 per cent (1998–2001)? What does 14% and 1998–01 indicate?
5 In Fig. 9.18, what does *index linked* mean? What index is involved?
6 Why is it that Premium Bond holders receive no interest on their investment? How are they rewarded? Give examples.
7 The government issues Treasury bills partly to 'mop up' surplus funds and to restrict inflation. What effects do you think the issue of Treasury bills will have on the amount of finance available to industry and commerce? Will an increase in the cost of borrowing money have any effect upon a firm's: (a) profits; (b) selling price of goods manufactured; (c) decisions to expand the range of products on sale, and (d) Mortgage interest?

10 CREDIT

● UNIT 10.1
Merchant Bankers and the Money Markets

Merchant banks

Merchant banking is different from the high-street form of banking we have already looked at (Unit 9), because it grew out of international trade. Merchant banking developed at about the same time as stockbroking (Unit 11) and insurance (Unit 12). Wealthy merchants like Mayer Rothschild (born in Frankfurt, Germany in 1744) saw opportunities to finance international trade and to promote banking services in Europe. Rothschild had five sons, each of whom he set up in a different European capital, including London. This gave the Rothschilds a special importance to commerce in Western Europe.

The merchant banking firm of Rothschild can serve as a model for all the others, as they operate in the City and in Europe, providing capital and offering credit facilities for trading activities world-wide. Joint stock banks (the early form of commercial banks like Barclays and Lloyds) did not begin to flourish until after 1826 and then only outside London. So the Bank of England and the merchant banks had no competition in the financing of the profitable and developing international trade.

International banking

Foreign banks should not be confused with merchant banks. Just as our own high-street banks have branches in capitals and cities overseas, American, West German, Japanese and Arab banking interests (among others) maintain branches in London and other cities in Britain. Banking interests are international. While London sleeps, commercial firms are awake and actively trading in Tokyo and Brisbane. Money and capital are used to finance enterprises around the world 24 hours of every day, 365 days a year.

The foreign exchange market

If you are buying a crop of coffee beans from Brazil, wool from Australia or copper from Zambia, your purchase will have to be paid for in the currency of the country involved. Crates of wine from France will be paid for in francs, cars from Japan in yen and coffee from Brazil in cruzeiros.

In London and in all major capitals there are firms whose service to trade and commerce is to buy and sell the currencies of the world, all of which have a price (Fig. 10.1). If you want to sell pounds, then (at the time of writing) you will get about 11 French francs, about 200 Spanish pesetas, about 1.8 US dollars and so on. In the same way, if you have French francs and wish to buy Spanish pesetas, then you will receive about 19 pesetas for each franc offered for sale. Every currency is bought and sold every day; the international foreign exchange markets never close. Someone, somewhere, is at this moment buying foreign currency in millions to finance a cargo of wheat in transit from Canada to Europe.

THE POUND TODAY

$1.7572   Dm3.281

Trade-
weighted average 98.2

Australia	49¾p	2.0073
Austria	4¼p	23.04
Belgium	1½p	68.58
Canada	47¾p	2.0814
Denmark	7¾p	12.7191
France	9p	11.1494
Germany	30¼p	3.2810
Holland	27p	3.6988
Hongkong	7¼p	13.7360
Ireland	81¾p	1.2259
Italy (100)	4¼p	2395.96
Japan (10)	4¼p	228.17
Norway	8½p	11.8264
South Africa	23¾p	4.2137
Spain	½p	203.00
Sweden	9p	11.1283
Switzerland	35½p	2.7881
U.S.A.	57p	1.7572

TOURIST RATES

Austrian schilling	22.55
French franc	10.94
German mark	3.22
Greek drachma	269.00
Italian lira	2335.00
Maltese lira	0.582
Portuguese escudo	261.00
Spanish peseta	197.50
Swiss franc	2.73
U.S. dollar	1.7570
Yugoslavian dinar	8800.0

Fig. 10.1 Foreign exchange rates

Foreign exchange dealers are in constant telephone contact with clients and in continuous computer contact with all world currency markets. The decisions they make to buy or sell involve vast sums. Mistakes can be costly.

Deals may be *spot* (for delivery now at today's prices) or *forward* (for delivery at some future date, e.g. three months). There are gamblers who will buy or sell currency forward, anticipating a small rise or fall in prices, which will show a sizeable profit if the deal is large enough. Guess wrong and you are in deep trouble! (See also Unit 11, section 11.2.) Just as you obtain foreign currency for a holiday from your bank, a trader will probably finance an American deal by buying dollars through a merchant bank.

Acceptance houses

Most merchant banks have an attractive method of financing an import/export deal by the issue of a *bill of exchange* (see Fig. 10.2). This is a promise to pay a given sum of money (in any currency) at some future date. A *promise* to pay is not readily negotiable (i.e. cashable) anywhere, but *endorsement* of a bill of exchange by a merchant bank instantly guarantees that the issuers will honour their promise. So a bill *endorsed* (or *accepted*) in this way turns a worthless piece of paper into a 'cheque' guaranteed by the reputation of the *accepting house* (the merchant bank). The bill can then be used to finance a deal; the seller gets his or her money immediately; the buyer/issuer gets his or her goods, honours the promise to pay at the due date, and the merchant bank gets a commission for the service of endorsing the bill.

```
       B
       £8,240
                                          Keighley
       D                                  11th August, 1982

B  AT SIGHT OF THIS SOLA OF EXCHANGE PAY TO OUR ORDER THE SUM OF STERLING
   POUNDS EIGHT THOUSAND TWO HUNDRED AND FORTY ONLY FOR VALUE RECEIVED

   Drawn under Irrevocable Credit of Barclays Bank International PLC

   Pennine House, 45 Well Street, Bradford N. FDC/2/6789 dated 20th July, 1982


          C                             A
                                        For and on behalf of
       To: Barclays Bank International PLC    QUALITY WOOLENS LTD
           Pennine House,
           45, Well Street,
           Bradford


                                        ..................
                                        Director
```

Key:
A — signed by the drawer (Quality Woollens Ltd)
B — the amount in words and figures
C — addressed to the bank that will 'accept' the Bill
D — this Bill is payable at 'sight', i.e. immediately, but may be kept and negotiated on the Bill market

Fig. 10.2 A Bill of Exchange

Discounting bills of exchange Remember that bills of exchange are a promise to pay a sum of money on a particular future date. In other words, they have a value and can be sold for that value less a discount for having to wait for the money. A bill which changes hands in this manner is said to be *discounted*. There is a market for discounting bills made up of acceptance houses which specialise in this trade.

Raising capital: new issues

Merchant banks are expert in raising large sums of money from companies with spare funds to lend, possibly only for a short time – even overnight. They are also expert in raising large sums of money by the sale of new shares to institutions and the general public. In both cases much work is involved, but the commissions charged are large.

Underwriting In some cases, where it is not certain that a particular issue of shares can be sold, banking interests will, for an agreed commission, accept any shares remaining unsold, at the selling price, once the rest of the market has been satisfied. Such issues are said to be *underwritten*. The risk of being left with unsold shares has been covered, and the seller is guaranteed his or her money. The underwriter can sell the shares in small quantities when the market has recovered, and he or she has the commission as a bonus.

Underwriting of this kind was needed when the British government offered shares for sale in British Petroleum in autumn 1987. The general public did not want to buy all the shares; the remaining shares were bought in by the underwriters.

Take-overs and mergers

Capital raising and share promotion are often necessary when one limited company *takes over* (buys) another company, or where two or more companies *merge* (join) to form a new company. The situation is very similar to that of a new issue, described above. A merchant bank will lend its good name and expertise to the parties involved.

The money market

Although the money market may not *look* like a local produce market (farmers setting up a stall to sell their eggs and cheese), the basic idea is the same. Some people have goods to sell (i.e. the use of their money) and others wish to buy (i.e. borrow money).

The money market is made up of those people and companies, mainly in the City of London and overseas, who have money to lend, who wish to borrow, who finance deals, who service deals and who buy and sell money. At the core of this market are the banks: high-street, foreign and merchant.

●SOURCES OF INFORMATION

1 Lazard Bros & Co. Ltd, 21 Moorfields, London EC2Y
2 Kleinwort Benson PLC, 20 Fenchurch Street, London EC3P 3DB
3 Hambros Bank PLC, 41 Bishopgate, London EC2P 2AA
4 Moscow Narodny Bank PLC, 81 King William Street, London EC4P 4JS
5 Bank of China, 8–10 Mansion House Place, London EC4N 8BL

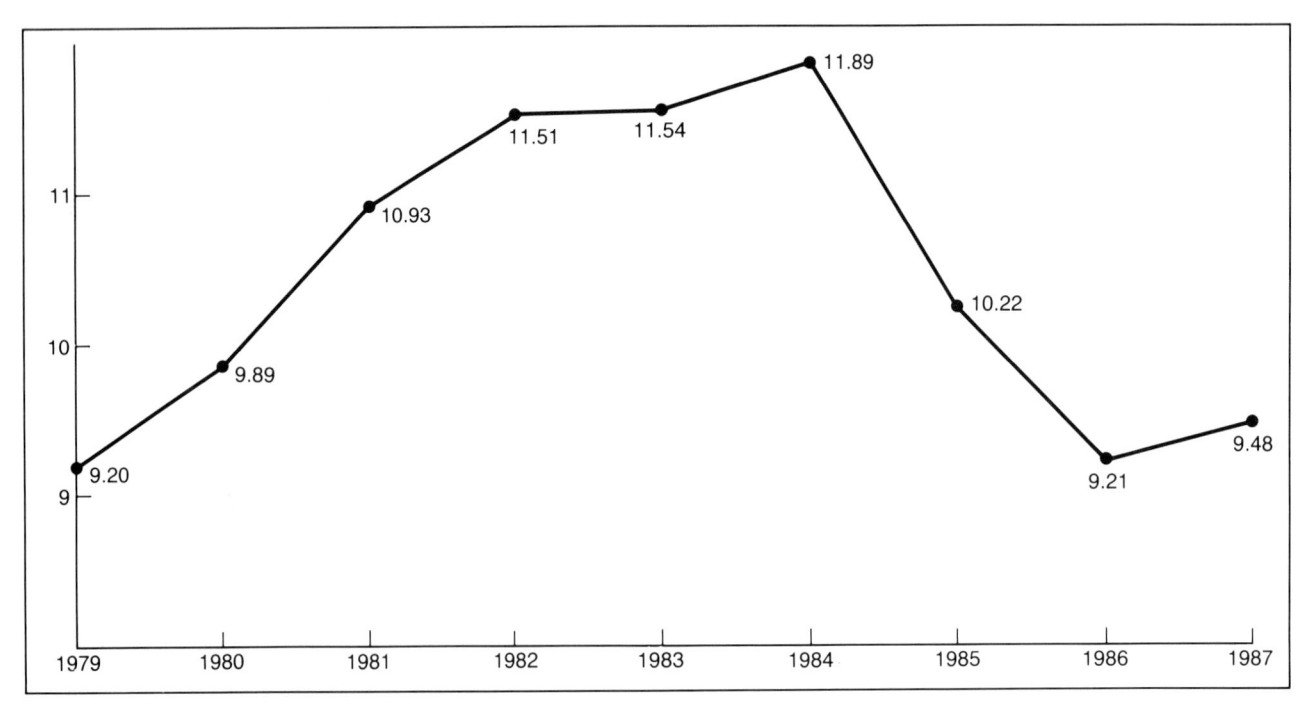

Fig. 10.3 Graph showing the value of the pound in French francs over the period 1979–87

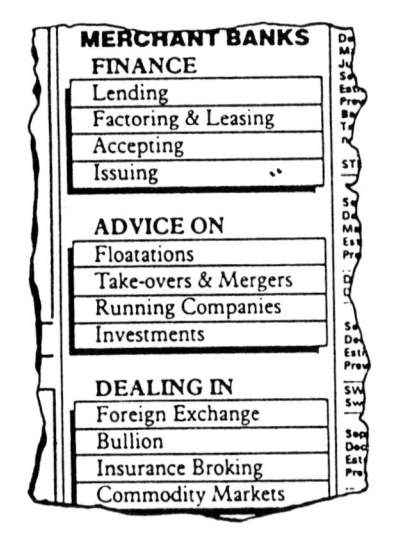

Fig. 10.4 Merchant bank services

●QUESTIONS

1. Using Fig. 10.1 imagine you are an Austrian merchant with 200 000 Schillings to be changed into French francs. Calculate how many you will get for your money.
2. In 1984 I exchanged £100 000 for French francs at the rate shown in Fig. 10.3. I changed all my francs back into £s sterling in 1986 at the rate shown. Calculate my profit on the deal.
3. In Fig. 10.4, what do you understand by the terms *advice on take-overs and mergers*, *dealing in bullion* and *flotations*?
4. In your view, what are the essential differences between a merchant bank and a joint stock (commercial high-street) bank? Give examples to illustrate your answers.
5. Research the term 'weighted average' shown in Fig. 10.1.

UNIT 10.2
Finance Houses and Credit Agreements

Credit

People often buy goods using credit facilities (Fig. 10.5). Cars and motor cycles, washing machines, TV and video equipment are favourites, but almost anything can be paid for on instalments. The credit system has many advantages:

1 The shopkeeper or dealer makes sales which would not otherwise be possible (because the buyer doesn't have enough cash now).
2 The seller gets his or her money from the finance house immediately, less a small commission.
3 The buyer gets the goods now, enjoys their use and doesn't have to find large sums all at once.
4 The buyer pays out of income over a period of time, perhaps as long as three years (but at a relatively high rate of interest).

Naturally, if you buy more than you can afford and run up huge debts, the consequences can be very serious. Also, if the period of repayment is too long, the goods (especially clothes) could be worn out and useless before you have finished the payments. Before agreeing to credit terms, borrowers should consider: (a) whether they can really afford the instalments; (b) how long they have to pay, and (c) what the *total* cost will be.

Fig. 10.5 Instant credit facilities

Fig. 10.6 The cost of borrowing money

Finance houses

Finance houses provide the capital to finance hire purchase (credit sales). Many finance houses already belong to the banks, and some are banks themselves:

Finance House	Owned by
Lombard North Central	National Westminster Bank
Mercantile Credit	Barclays Bank
Forward Trust	Midland Bank
United Dominions Trust	Trustee Savings Bank
North West Securities	Royal Bank of Scotland

Other finance houses borrow money at high rates of interest. They charge an even higher rate on money advanced to customers, though the real rate of interest is hidden by quoting a *hire charge* as an amount rather than a percentage of the money borrowed. The law now requires the real rate of interest APR to be shown in all agreements (see Fig. 10.6). In 1987–8 instalment trading totalled £20 billion.

APR (Annual Percentage Rate)

For mathematical reasons, any credit charge expressed as a rate per cent on the amount borrowed tends to be misleadingly low. The actual rate of interest can be as high as 35 per cent. For this reason the Consumer Credit Acts require that APR shall be stated on advertisements, documents and other material offering credit facilities to the general public. When signing any credit agreement, the APR *must* be drawn to the attention of the customer.

The charge for credit facilities is not negotiable. You either agree to pay or you don't get the goods. But beware of very high rates of interest which will increase the total cost out of proportion to the value of the goods you are buying.

Documentation

When a customer agrees to purchase goods on credit, most dealers (but not all) will require a deposit (say 10 per cent of the sale price). The deposit (if required) is deducted from the sale price, and a credit charge is added to the balance. The total shown is the amount to be repaid. After this total is divided by the number of payments, the customer is then told the amount of the monthly repayment. Here is an example:

A credit sale or hire purchase calculation

	£
Cost price of goods	1200
Less: Deposit	200
	1000
Add: Credit charge (10%)	100
Amount to be repaid	£1100

That is, 17 monthly payments of £61 and a final payment of – how much?

The document involved is either a hire purchase or a credit sale agreement. Both contain the description of the goods, the names of the buyer and seller, the calculation described above and the signatures of the two parties concerned. Once signed, a hire purchase or credit sale agreement is a contract between the finance house and the customer buying the goods. Under a hire purchase agreement the goods are not really yours until the final payment has been made. If the customer fails to pay, the finance house may be able to repossess the goods or go to court for the balance due.

Under a credit sale agreement, the goods become yours *immediately* the contract is signed. In this case the finance company has really given you a loan, and cannot (if you default) repossess the goods, but can still sue for its money. Note that in both a hire purchase agreement and a credit sale agreement your contract is with the finance company and not with the retailer.

Under 18

If you are under 18 you will need to persuade someone older to act as a guarantor. Usually a father or mother, a guarantor will be asked to countersign your contract and agree to meet the balance if you are unable to pay. Why do you think a guarantor is necessary? What is special about an eighteenth birthday?

Cooling-off period

The Acts of Parliament which control consumer credit recognise that people are sometimes 'carried away' by the prospect of owning a new television or replacing a kitchen on easy terms. They may also be too influenced by a representative's sales technique, and come to regret a hasty decision almost immediately. In such cases the law allows for a *cooling-off period* of a few days during which the agreement can be cancelled.

Hiring and leasing

Many families rent goods such as a television or video from companies like DER, Radio Rentals and Rediffusion. The goods never become yours, but under a consumer hire agreement the company installs the equipment for an agreed monthly rental. In these cases, the hiring company acts like a finance company.

In business, hiring is usually called *leasing*. An agreement is reached by which a finance company buys (say) machinery and leases it to the business customer. Like the television set, the equipment never becomes the property of the customer. He or she merely 'rents' these resources from the finance company and is able to charge the cost against tax.

Continuous credit

In most large shops you will see notices advertising 'immediate credit facilities'. The shop offers credit sales if you agree to pay a given sum every month. As long as you don't exceed your agreed limit you can have goods at any time, and you don't have to clear one debt before starting another. Your monthly repayments are fixed at the amount you feel you can afford, and the value of those repayments fixes your credit limit at so many times your monthly payment. A finance house may be involved; larger shops like Debenhams can finance their own continuous credit schemes (sometimes called a *reducing account*).

Consumer protection

Fairness in credit transactions is guaranteed by law. All individuals and companies extending credit must be registered and are issued with a licence to trade. The courts can alter any unfair credit contract. Misleading advertising is monitored by the Advertising Standards Authority, and the Director-General of Fair Trading acts as a watchdog through Trading Standards Officers at the town hall. The finance companies themselves must accept some responsibility for 'shady' deals and so will assist only reputable traders.

Credit reference agencies

These agencies exist to collect information on individuals and companies who may apply for credit. They file copies of county court records, newspaper articles, previous credit agreements, etc. They also store information on the type of area in which you live and the job you hold. They prepare a statement of your financial standing called a

Fig. 10.7 Vehicle leasing is now popular with large and small firms

credit rating, which they are ready to sell to any party willing to pay their agency fee.

The Consumer Credit Act requires such agencies to supply an individual with a copy of any file kept about them. If the consumer feels that this file is incorrect, they may request amendment. The agency must agree or put the case to the Director-General of Fair Trading for arbitration.

● SOURCES OF INFORMATION

1. United Dominions Trust Ltd, Freepost, Bristol B213 7BR
2. Lombard North Central PLC, Lombard House, Curzon Street, London W1A 1EU
3. North West Securities Ltd, Norfolk House, Wellesley Road, Croydon, Surrey
4. Dun & Bradstreet Ltd, 26–32 Clifton Street, London EC2P 2LY

● QUESTIONS

1. Using Fig. 10.6: (a) what is the upper amount that can be borrowed; (b) what APR is suggested?
2. What collateral does UK Loans require to cover the loan agreed? Why does UK Loans recommend cover and for which contingencies?
3. When you have written to, and received information from, the three finance houses given in Sources 1, 2 and 3 above, contrast their advertising material. Which is the most attractive and why?
4. Credit facilities are freely offered: credit agreements, charge cards, credit cards, bank loans, etc. What are the dangers for a society which relies heavily on credit cards? Give reasons for your answer.
5. Research the differences between the following credit arrangements: (a) hire purchase agreements; (b) credit sale agreements; (c) consumer hire agreements. Describe the basic differences and suggest circumstances in which each might be used by: (i) a private individual, and (ii) a business man or woman.

11 SHARE AND COMMODITY MARKETS

UNIT 11.1
Stocks and Shares

The Stock Exchange
The Stock Exchange building (called *the floor*) is now rarely used as a market-place for the buying and selling of shares. Most dealers conduct business from their various offices and deal by computer. Information about daily prices is fed to the video display units by a master computer maintained at the Stock Exchange. These prices are constantly updated as deals are completed and shares bought and sold.

Buying and selling
The purchaser must still buy through a *broker*. The broker will then contact a *market-maker*, who will quote a *bid–offer spread*. The offer price is the price at which the shares are offered for sale; and the bid price is that at which the market-maker is prepared to buy. The difference in price is the market-maker's profit. The broker charges the purchaser a commission for his or her services. Money and shares change hands on *settlement days* at the end of a two-week period called the *account*.

New issues
New issue shares are not bought through a broker, but directly from the merchant bank or issuing house that is handling the sale. Advertisements for new shares will appear in the national newspapers and individuals bid for any number of shares, filling in an application form and attaching a cheque for the necessary amount. Most privatisations (e.g. British Telecom, British Airways and Rolls-Royce) were sold to shareholders in this way.

Documents
Your broker will send you a *contract note* (Fig. 11.1) detailing the shares you have bought, the price paid, the total cost and the commission charged. Later you will receive a *share certificate* (Fig. 11.2) showing that you are the owner of 2,000 shares in Bailey Marine plc.

From the date you become a shareholder, the company, if it is profitable, will pay you dividends twice a year: an interim dividend about half-way through the company's financial year, and a final dividend at the end of each financial year. On each occasion you will receive a cheque for the amount due and a *dividend warrant* (Fig. 11.3) showing the dividend due on each share and the total amount due to you.

Cum divi – ex divi Dividends on shares are declared on a particular date but may not be paid until some time later. A sale of shares is said to be *cum divi* if the *purchaser* receives the dividend. Any sale where the sale is *ex divi* will indicate that the *seller* will receive the next dividend even though he or she has sold the shares.

FT (Financial Times) Index The FT Index is like a thermometer which reflects the temperature of the stock market. Each day, increases or decreases in the price of shares in thirty well-known limited companies are monitored. Any overall increase in the price of those shares is accepted as an indication that shares as a whole are rising in value, while an overall decrease is taken to show that share values generally are decreasing.

Thirty shares in our largest companies can give only a rough indication of the health, or otherwise, of the stock market. Other measures (such as the 100 Share Index) are used for individual sections of the market. The FT Index in London has its counterparts elsewhere: in New York the Dow Jones Index, in Hong Kong the Hang Seng Index, in Japan the Nikkei Dow Jones Index and in France the CAC General Index.

Stockmarket terms
A *bull* is a person who buys shares when the price is rising. A *bear* is a person who sells shares when the price is falling. A *stag* is a person who buys new issues. All hope to make a profit.

Unit trusts
Unit trusts are like clubs which buy and sell shares on behalf of the members. You purchase units at an agreed price, and the managers of the trust use your money to purchase shares of *their* choice. As a member of the trust, you don't own any shares yourself, but you can sell your units, at a profit if the shares have done well, any time you like. Trusts declare a dividend per unit which is paid to unit holders.

●SOURCES OF INFORMATION

1 Stock Exchange Distribution Centre, 120 Lavender Avenue, Mitcham, Surrey, for *An Introduction to the Stock Market.*
2 Yellow Pages, for names of Stock Exchange dealers.
3 Any main post office, for leaflets on government stocks.
4 Any bank, for leaflets on stock-market services for customers.
5 TSB Unit Trusts Ltd, Keens House, Andover, Hampshire SP10 1PG
6 The *Financial Times* and the financial pages of most newspapers, for daily stock-market prices and news.
7 Stock Exchange, Public Affairs Department, London EC2N 1HP, for *Buying and Selling Shares.*
8 Unit Trust Association, Park House, 16 Finsbury Circus, London EC2M 7JP

Fig. 11.1 A contract note

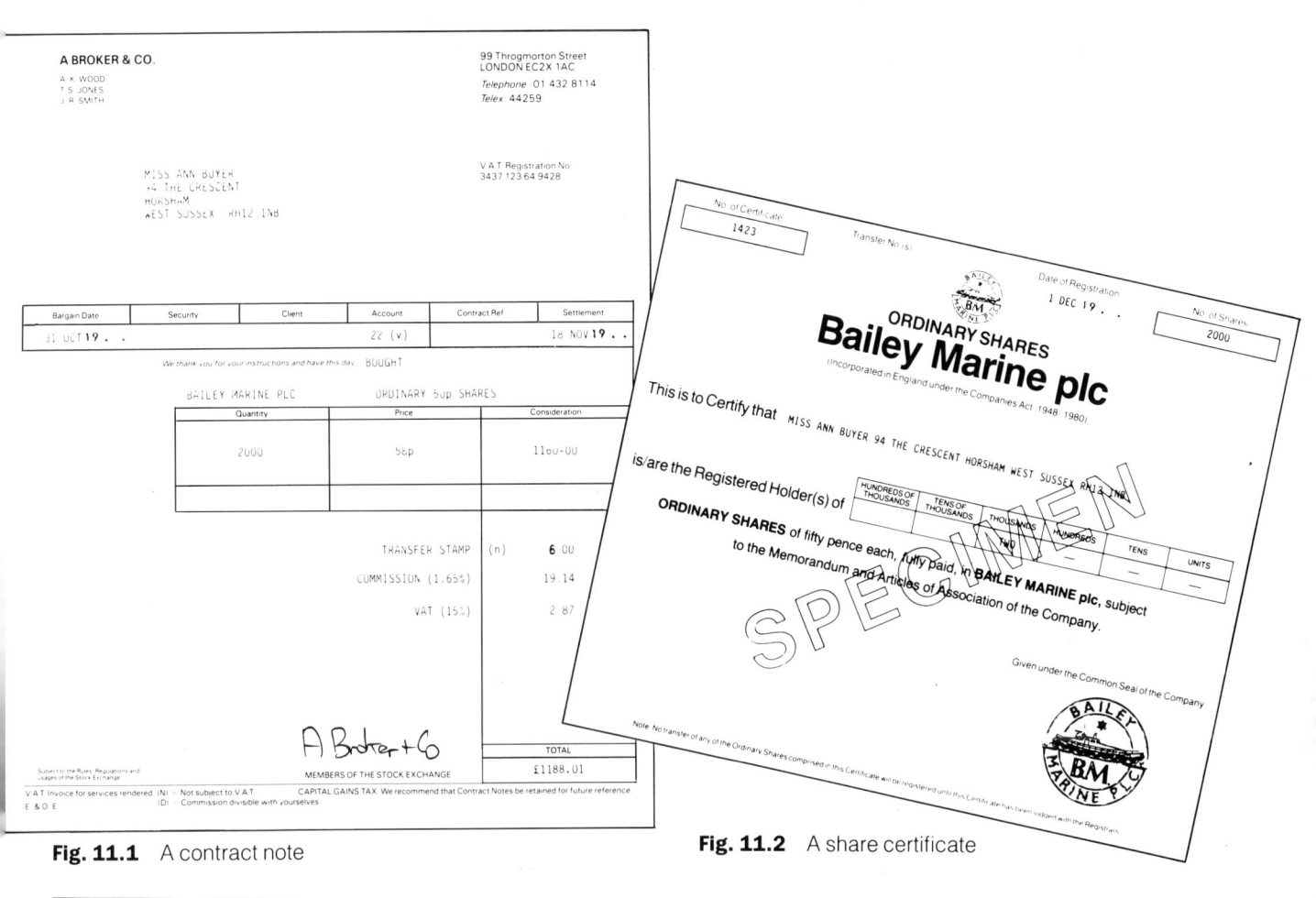

Fig. 11.2 A share certificate

Fig. 11.3 A dividend warrant

●QUESTIONS

For the following questions use Figs. 11.1, 11.2 and 11.3.

1. Who is the purchaser of the shares in Bailey Marine plc, and how many did she buy?
2. What is the *face value* of each Bailey Marine ordinary share?
3. What was the *purchase* price per share on 31 October? Was it *Com-divi* or *Ex-divi*?
4. What was the total cost of the purchase, including charges? Who receives the commission?
5. What is the name and address of the broker involved? How many partners are there?
6. How much per *share* was paid as a dividend on 21 January?
7. What was the *total* amount of dividend received for the half-year ending 31 December?
8. Assume the selling price per share quoted in today's financial pages to be 95p. If the holder sold her shares at that price, what would she receive?
9. How much profit would the holder have made, assuming such a sale?

●THINGS TO DO

1. Write polite letters to British Petroleum (extraction industry), Cadbury Schweppes (manufacturing industry), Marks & Spencer (distributive trades) and Grand Metropolitan (service industry) for copies of their annual reports. Keep a graph of share price fluctuations (quotes) each week over three months. Which share showed the greatest capital gain?
2. Form four investment clubs in your class. With an inheritance of £1000, each club invests its capital in shares, watches prices for suitable times to sell and buy and adds dividends as they are declared. Compare results at the end of three months. Which team has made the largest profit?

UNIT 11.2
Commodity Markets and Chartering

Commodity markets

When people are making things they require raw materials (*commodities*). In most cases they need to ensure a steady and regular supply well before the stock of materials is required. The producers of commodities are scattered across the world. The manufacturers are equally scattered, so it is sensible to establish a central market where buyers and sellers can meet to fix prices and do business. London is the world centre for commodity markets, dealing in copper, coffee, cocoa, cotton, wool, sugar, rubber, soya beans, tea, peppers and spices, jute, rice, ivory, barley, oats, rye, wheat, diamonds, furs and carpets. The *London Metal Exchange* (see Fig. 11.4) deals in zinc, tin, nickel, aluminium, silver, lead and copper.

The trading in each market and in each commodity is carried out by *brokers*, who may represent either buyer or seller. Bidding takes place over a frantic few minutes when everyone seems to be shouting at once. A note is made of all bargains agreed and this is confirmed later in writing.

Sampling and grading

Commodities are not physically present when buying and selling take place. In some cases there may be samples available, but an agreed system of grading is recognised, and sales are arranged accordingly. Goods may be purchased for delivery some time in the future: the cocoa beans bought may still be awaiting the harvester, while wool may still be growing on the backs of 2 million sheep.

A great deal is taken on trust and brokers fiercely protect their reputation for fair trading. Brokers receive a commission for the work they undertake on behalf of buyers and sellers, graded accordingly to the amount of business transacted.

Fig. 11.4 Ring trading at the London Metal Exchange

Futures market

It is relatively simple to fix the price of raw materials for immediate delivery (called a *spot* price). It is rather more difficult to determine what the price might be in, for instance, three months' time (called a *future* price). Coffee still growing may suddenly be struck by frost and the crop may be ruined. There could be an exceptional harvest in barley, and the price will fall. Manufacturers wishing to ensure a supply of raw materials must plan their requirements and buy forward for delivery on a given date. So dealing will be arranged using both spot and future prices; forward dealing tends to steady prices by equating supply and demand over a long period.

Dealing in futures

In any futures market there are people who will gamble against a rise or fall in prices. These individuals do not necessarily want or need the commodity involved, but use the futures market just to make profits. They need to know a great deal about the commodity prices. Such trading can be very costly if mistakes are made.

Futures are arranged as *options*. A *put option* is an option to sell, while a *call option* is an option to buy at an agreed price on some future date (say three months). An option costs money, and takes the following form.

On 1 April I purchase a call option to buy 1000 tons of metal at £100 per ton, for delivery in three months' time. That quantity is now mine *at the price agreed*, and I can sell my option at any time, to anyone who is interested, at any price I can get. My gamble is that the market price of my metal will gradually increase; and come the time to settle, the spot price could reach £150 per ton. My profit would then be 1000 tons × £50 = £50 000, less broker's commission.

Hedging Dealing in futures is a risky business. On some futures markets, prices will go up and down in an alarming fashion. A person wishing to take advantage of either a rise or a fall in prices can take a double option, both a *put* and a *call* option. This is termed *hedging*. If prices go down, the *call* option will be used; if prices go up, the *put* option will show a profit. However, a double option is doubly expensive, so prices must show a considerable rise or fall before the profit will exceed the costs involved.

The Baltic Exchange

The Baltic Exchange was originally concerned with the buying and selling of products from the Baltic countries. Commodity trading on the exchange still covers wheat and barley, pigmeat and beef, potatoes and soya beans. Deals are concluded during two short sessions each day.

However the main activity on this exchange now revolves around the chartering of ships to transport cargoes around the world.

Charter parties

Charter parties are contracts fixed on the Baltic Exchange for the hire of ships or aircraft. A *time charter* is for the use of a ship or aircraft for a particular length of time, while a *voyage charter* covers a particular voyage. Charters will be agreed in respect of both cargoes and/or passengers. *Tramp steamers* sail wherever there is a cargo. A *liner* (which will carry cargo and passengers) follows a particular route and observes a timetable.

Part charters will be negotiated by a broker on behalf of a merchant whose cargo will not fill a ship. A series of part charters will be necessary to provide a profit on a voyage.

Air charters are more expensive, but essential to holiday tour operators and in the transport of perishable goods (like strawberries from California). All modern aircraft carry cargo. Brokers must be aware just when and how to place air cargo to the best possible advantage.

Other functions of the Baltic Exchange

Sale, purchase and arbitration Some members of the Baltic Exchange conduct an active market in the sale and purchase of ships and aircraft anywhere in the world. The exchange also maintains a marine arbitration service with a world-wide reputation for the settlement of shipping disputes.

Invisible earnings In all its dealings in raw materials and shipping contracts, the City earns foreign currency to assist Britain's *balance of payments* (Unit 16, section 16.2).

Fig. 11.5 Ring trading at the Baltic Exchange

●SOURCES OF INFORMATION

1. Baltic Exchange, St Mary Axe, London EC3A 8BU
2. Metal Market & Exchange Co. Ltd, Plantation House, 31-34 Fenchurch Street, London EC3M 3AP
3. Coffee Terminal Market Association of London Ltd, Cereal House, Mark Lane, London EC3R 7AR

●THINGS TO DO

Organise a 'ring' to sell coffee using the process shown in Figs. 11.4 and 11.5 and described above: half to sell (in competition), half to buy (in competition). What do you think of this method of selling?

●QUESTIONS

1. Why do manufacturers need to buy raw materials 'forward'? What advantage is obtained?
2. Using Figs. 11.6, 11.7 and 11.8 what was the approximate price of: (a) copper in March; (b) coffee in November; (c) cocoa in June?
3. What is a *tonne*? Why do commodity markets deal in metric measures?
4. Using Fig. 11.8, I buy a *put* option involving 1000 tonnes of cocoa in September for delivery in December. What is my approximate profit or loss on the deal?

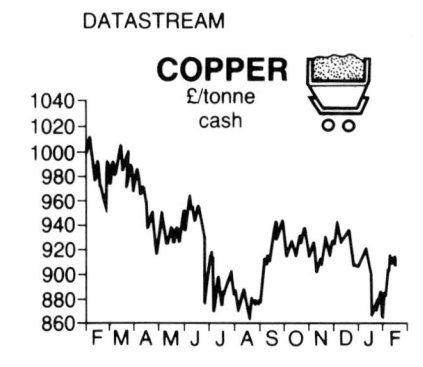

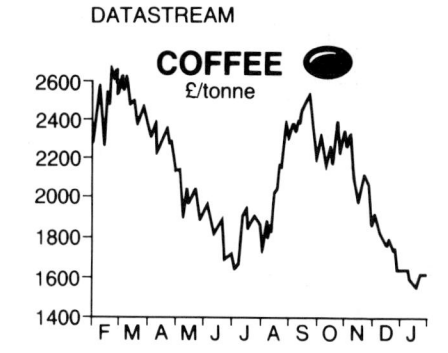

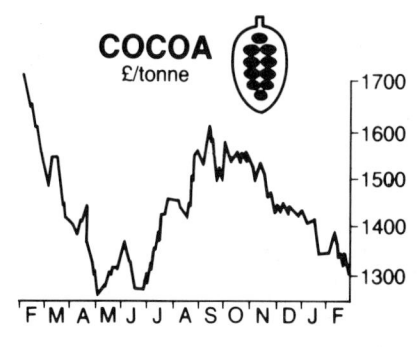

Fig. 11.6 Commodities: copper prices

Fig. 11.7 Commodities: coffee prices

Fig. 11.8 Commodities: cocoa prices

12 INSURANCE

UNIT 12.1
Personal Risk

The risk factor

We are all at risk. My house might burn down; we could be burgled; it is possible to have an accident in the car. Living in a flat, pipes could burst and the resulting flood could ruin decoration in the apartment below. Your holiday luggage might disappear while you're jetting to Corfu. Worst of all, a family bread-winner could die, leaving loved ones with no source of income.

In such cases people can ease the pain of financial loss by taking out an insurance policy either with an insurance company, like the Prudential, or with an underwriter at Lloyd's. The cheque received following a loss such as a fire will allow the insured to buy a new house and replace the contents.

The proposal form

To take out any insurance, it is first necessary to complete a *proposal form*, answering all the questions and leaving nothing out. The completed proposal form allows the insurance company to assess the level of risk. For example, if I am blind in one eye, then as a car driver I am a greater risk than a person who is fully sighted. Or, if your house is built on land which floods regularly, then the chance of damage, either to the house or to the contents, is greater than for a house on a hill.

It is essential to reveal all relevant information (called *material facts*) on the proposal form. If the company discovers something important that was not revealed, it is entitled to cancel any policy and leave the person concerned uninsured.

The premium

Having assessed the risk, the insurance company will set the *premium*, that is, the amount it will charge each year for the insurance cover. The size of the premium also depends on the size of the possible pay-out. A householder owning a house valued at £100 000 would expect to pay a larger premium than his or her neighbour whose bungalow is valued at £50 000. Similarly, if you (aged under 25) drive around London all day in a powerful sports car, having had two accidents in six months, your premium for motor insurance will be very costly. The motorist driving a Mini around Dundee with a clean licence will pay much less.

The policy

Once the proposal is accepted, the level of cover determined and the premium calculated, the insurance company will issue a *policy*. This is the contract between you (the insured) and the company (the insurer). The policy will say that, in return for the annual premium, the insurer agrees to cover the insured against any loss arising from (say) a fire, an accident or the death of the person involved.

Level of indemnity and betterment

A person insured is entitled to receive full compensation for any loss – no more and no less. This is called *indemnity*. I am not entitled to receive £5000 for the loss of a car worth £2000 merely because it is rarely out of the garage and I have polished it every day for five years. It sometimes happens that in repairing a car damaged in an accident the car will be in a better condition than it was before the accident (i.e. worth more). This is known as *betterment*, and the policyholder (the insured) may be required to contribute towards that increase in value.

Claims

Following an accident or loss, a policyholder must inform the insurance company, complete a claim form and describe the nature of the loss (e.g. goods stolen, fire damage, accident, etc.). The insurer can then assess the cost of the claim and might employ an *assessor* to view the damage and assess the cost of repair or renewal. Assessors are sometimes called *loss adjusters*.

'A day in the life of a loss adjuster'

'A recent fire in a toy supplier's warehouse was extinguished by the automatic sprinkler system but many of the goods stored there were damaged by water. Among the toys were 600 Paddington Bears. Adjusters assessing the compensation found that 150 which had been stacked with their heads protruding had suffered severe water damage. 450 were stored the other way round however, and were fully protected by their wellington boots. It was necessary only to wipe their boots clean to restore them to their perfect condition.' (Source: The Chartered Insurance Institute.)

Insurable interest

In every contract of insurance, the insured must have a financial interest in the person or thing to be insured and must suffer a financial loss if that person dies or the thing is destroyed or damaged. For example, my neighbour's caravan does not belong to me. If it were damaged, I would not suffer a loss. Therefore I have no insurable interest and cannot take out a valid contract of insurance on the caravan or the contents. However, if my neighbour is also my business partner, without whose skill my business would fail, I do have an insurable interest in his or her life. I would suffer a loss were he or she to have a heart attack. In these circumstances I can insure, and the contract would be valid.

Uninsurable risks

You cannot insure against a certainty (e.g. that it will rain some time during the year). But you can insure against rain spoiling a village fête on a particular day and the consequent loss of takings. Although you cannot insure against your business making a loss, if that loss is *caused* by the actions of someone who is insured against negligence you can claim on his or her insurance.

You cannot insure against something that is currently happening (like a fire) or something that has already happened (like theft). But you can insure against having twins even though you are already pregnant, provided you haven't been told of the presence of twins. The loss in this case is the cost of two children rather than one.

You cannot insure against fair wear and tear – rust, corrosion, fading curtains, etc. But you can insure against torn trousers caused by a fall.

The pooling of risk

Very many people take out fire insurance but only a few of those covered will actually have a fire. The premium collected from the many will be used to pay out the unfortunate few. In effect, we all insure each other, and the insurance company really acts as a collecting agent with profits as a reward. The company must, of course, get its sums right. Too low a premium and it will pay out more than it receives. Too high a premium and competitors gain all the business.

Most insurance companies are *tariff houses*. They charge the same premium for the same risks, but give reductions in premiums for any year free of claims, or introductory discounts for new business.

Life assurance

Note that this is assurance and not insurance. We must all die, unavoidably; but some people die at an early age and some at a late age. Through life assurance the insurers cover the risk of early death which possibly leaves relatives poorer than they would otherwise have been. This is a loss and can therefore be covered by a policy of assurance. Some policies (called *endowments*) are often used to cover a mortgage, which would be repaid entirely in case of premature death. With life cover, there is a risk, there is a loss, and there is an insurable interest; so the contract is valid even though the risk is inevitable.

Types of assurance policy

1 *Whole life* – the policyholder insures his or her life for (say) £50 000. Premiums are paid over the whole of the period, and the sum assured is paid on death.
2 *Endowment* – the agreed sum (say £100 000) is paid either at death or after an agreed period (the maturity date), whichever is sooner. Premiums are paid over the agreed period (say 20 or 25 years). Policies may be *with profits*, which attract a bonus each year.
3 *Term* – the policyholder's life is covered over an agreed term (e.g. 10, 15 or 20 years). Should the policyholder die during this period, the sum assured becomes payable. Premiums are paid over the agreed term.
4 *Annuity* – provides a guaranteed annual income for life, however long the person may live, in return for a fixed sum paid (say) on retirement. You gain if you live for a long time; you lose if you die early.

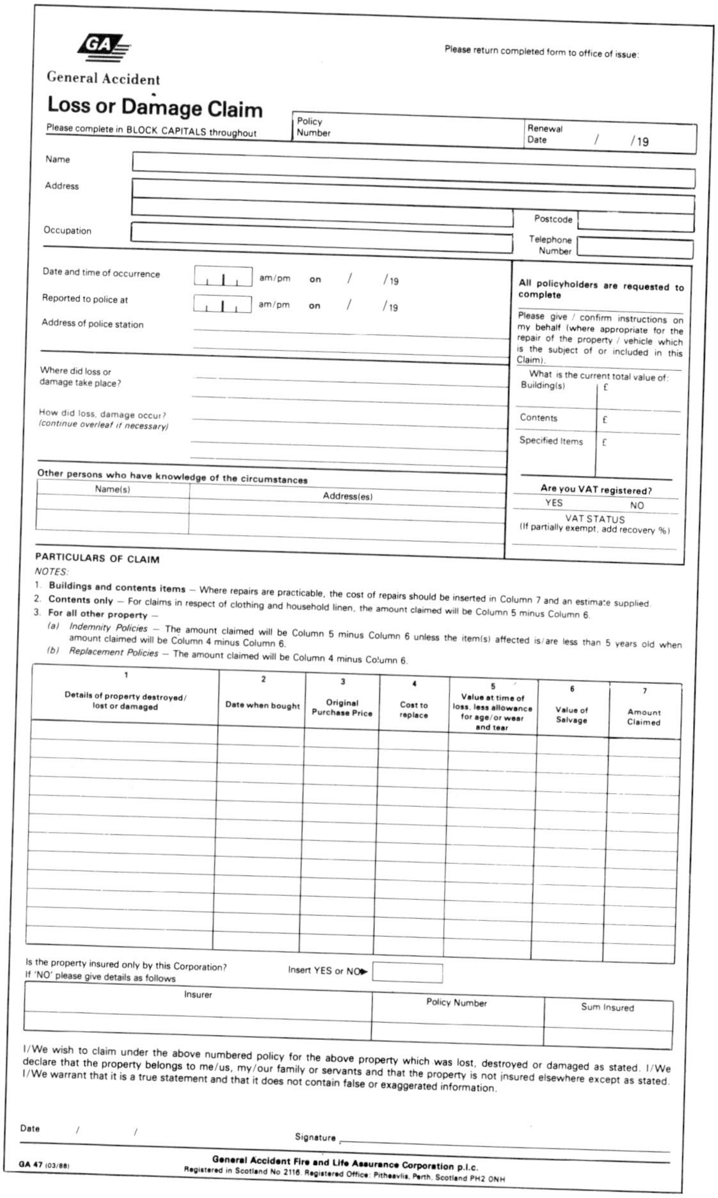

GA
General Accident

Please return completed form to office of issue:

Loss or Damage Claim

Please complete in BLOCK CAPITALS throughout

Policy Number

Renewal Date / /19

Name

Address

Postcode

Occupation

Telephone Number

Date and time of occurrence am/pm on / /19

Reported to police at am/pm on / /19

Address of police station

Where did loss or damage take place?

How did loss, damage occur? *(continue overleaf if necessary)*

All policyholders are requested to complete

Please give / confirm instructions on my behalf (where appropriate for the repair of the property / vehicle which is the subject of or included in this Claim).

What is the current total value of:

Building(s)	£
Contents	£
Specified Items	£

Other persons who have knowledge of the circumstances

Name(s)	Address(es)

Are you VAT registered?

YES NO

VAT STATUS
(If partially exempt, add recovery %)

PARTICULARS OF CLAIM

NOTES:

1. **Buildings and contents items** – Where repairs are practicable, the cost of repairs should be inserted in Column 7 and an estimate supplied.
2. **Contents only** – For claims in respect of clothing and household linen, the amount claimed will be Column 5 minus Column 6.
3. **For all other property** –
   (a) *Indemnity Policies* – The amount claimed will be Column 5 minus Column 6 unless the item(s) affected is/are less than 5 years old when amount claimed will be Column 4 minus Column 6.
   (b) *Replacement Policies* – The amount claimed will be Column 4 minus Column 6.

1 Details of property destroyed/lost or damaged	2 Date when bought	3 Original Purchase Price	4 Cost to replace	5 Value at time of loss, less allowance for age/or wear and tear	6 Value of Salvage	7 Amount Claimed

Is the property insured only by this Corporation? Insert YES or NO
If 'NO' please give details as follows

Insurer	Policy Number	Sum Insured

I/We wish to claim under the above numbered policy for the above property which was lost, destroyed or damaged as stated. I/We declare that the property belongs to me/us, my/our family or servants and that the property is not insured elsewhere except as stated. I/We warrant that it is a true statement and that it does not contain false or exaggerated information.

Date / /

Signature

GA 47 (03/88)

General Accident Fire and Life Assurance Corporation p.l.c.
Registered in Scotland No 2116. Registered Office: Pitheavlis, Perth, Scotland PH2 0NH

Fig. 12.1 A claim form

● SOURCES OF INFORMATION

1. Association of British Insurers, Aldermary House, Queen Street, London EC4N 1TT
2. Life Offices Association, Buckingham House 62–63 Queen Street, London EC4R 1AD
3. Yellow Pages – any well-known insurance company, e.g. Prudential, Sun Life, Friends Provident, etc.

● THINGS TO DO

1. Look at the sentences below. They are not in the correct order. Fill in the blanks by using *one* of the following words. No word may be used more than once.

premium	cover	policy	risk
insurance	insurance	agent	proposal
company	claims	insurer	betterment
indemnity			

(a) Mrs Brown writes a cheque for her first _____.
(b) Mrs Brown is given and completes a _____ form.
(c) The _____ _____ issues a contract which is called the _____.
(d) Mrs Brown goes to an _____ in the high street to seek advice.
(e) The company considers the _____ required and assesses the _____.
(f) Mr and Mrs Brown talk about the kind of __insurance__ they need.

Working in pairs, discuss the correct sequence of events and fill in the missing words, using the list given. Copy out Fig. 12.2 and, using the spaces in your diagram, write out the completed sentences in order. The first event in the sequence, sentence (f), has been done for you.

2. You and your family have just settled in Britain from abroad. You intend to start a business. Collect from a local insurance company all the various prospectuses relevant to your family and your business. Discuss your choice in class, with one from each group leading the discussion.

3. Invite the manager of a local building society to address your group on mortgage facilities. Compare the cost of: (a) a repayment mortgage; (b) an endowment mortgage; (c) a pension mortgage. What are the benefits of each on a property for which you require a mortgage of £50 000?

Fig. 12.2 Insurance: the sequence of events

UNIT 12.2
Business Insurance

Pooling risk

The idea of pooling risks started with *marine insurance*, covering ships and their cargo, possibly as long as 3000 years ago. It was introduced into Britain in the fourteenth and fifteenth centuries by the Lombards from Italy. Shipowners used to tour the City seeking rich merchants who would accept part of the risk of a forthcoming voyage. They did this by signing their names (*underwriting*) at the bottom of a document describing the ship and its cargo. The amount paid to the merchant underwriter was called the *premium*. If a ship and cargo were lost at sea, the shipowner made a claim on the underwriter(s) to cover the loss.

In the Great Fire of London (1666) so many people lost property that *fire insurance* became popular. Property owners paid premiums to underwriters for the security of cover against loss or damage. There came to be a great many voyages and properties requiring insurance, providing a pool of premiums from which claims could be met.

It is interesting that Roman soldiers had part of their pay put into a fund. If they were killed in battle, a death grant was given to their families. In the days of the corsairs, ships' captains used to contribute to a fund from which ransom could be paid for those unfortunate enough to be captured by pirates.

Business risks

Voyage insurance has now been extended to cover oil rigs, motor vehicles, aircraft, moon landings, satellite launches and all the personnel involved. Industry and commerce need insurance cover for premises, plant, machinery, motor vehicles, stock and fittings. Employees are covered by a policy of insurance both for retirement benefits and for injury or death during working hours. Industrial and commerical concerns are also just as liable to fire and theft as are individuals; any losses here are likely to be enormous.

Again, a proposal form is completed, the risk is assessed, the premium is determined, and a policy (the contract of insurance) is issued. If there is a loss then a claim is made. The concepts of indemnity, betterment and insurable interest (see unit 12.1) still apply.

Business interruption

Any major business disaster will usually stop sales or production. As well as covering losses arising from fire, for example, a sensible business man or woman will also cover loss of earnings or loss of profits, together with accruing expenses (such as rent and rates), interest to be paid on borrowed capital, the wage bill which accumulates even when there is no income and the cost of alternative accommodation in which the business can continue while repairs are in progress. All this cover is called *consequential loss*, an essential if the business is to survive the catastrophic consequences of a major fire.

Public liability

Though individuals can cover risks arising from negligence or carelessness (for example, golfers often insure against the risk of hitting another player or a passer-by), in business *public liability insurance* is essential. The general public visit different buildings, such as shops and restaurants. If there should be an accident on any of those premises, the proprietor could face enormous damages. Insurance will cover the risk.

Chemicals escaping from a factory and polluting land and water, a fire or explosion which damages someone else's property, product failure (e.g. steel girders not up to acceptable standards) causing damage or delay in (say) the building of a bridge: all these are *contingent risks* to be covered by public liability insurance, which provides indemnity against costs and damages following court action.

Motorists and airlines are insured against damage to things or people, including passengers. Such policies cover any incident in which it can be proved that carelessness or negligence has put individuals or possessions at risk and where there has been a consequent loss.

Some unusual liability claims

(The following examples are reproduced with kind permission of the Association of British Insurers.)

'A ship was being loaded in the docks. One of the containers dropped from the crane as it was being lifted onto the ship. The container went through the deck – and straight through the bottom of the ship! As a result, the ship sank. A claim made against the docks authority was paid by their engineering liability insurers.'

'A weld split open in a road tanker carrying syrup. The syrup poured out of the tanker and damaged another tanker. The company owning the tankers claimed against the welding company, whose insurers paid the bill.'

'Two workmen were removing a massive boiler from a dairy-product factory. The men had to winch the boiler round a corner and they were told *not* to secure the rope around one of the pillars supporting the factory. They did just that, and the building collapsed. As a result the dairy firm had to close down for several months. The insurers of the workmen's employers were presented with a bill for £500 000.'

Insurance companies

Insurance companies offer a range of policies covering all the major risks discussed in this and the previous section. They provide cover to both individuals and business, but market only their own policies, which are similar to, but not identical with, all those policies offered by their competitors.

Brokers

Brokers are companies or individuals in the insurance business giving advice on the range of policies on offer to suit the needs of individual clients. Brokers will often shop around to obtain the best possible cover at the lowest possible premiums. Their income is derived from commissions paid by insurance companies for the introduction and continuation of new business. They do not write policies themselves, nor do they charge their clients a fee.

Agents

Bank and building society managers, solicitors and car sales people are well placed to introduce to insurance companies clients seeking the benefits of insurance. These *agents* receive a commission for all business introduced.

Reinsurance and self-insurance

An insurance company may accept a risk so huge (like an oil tanker) that any claim for total loss would bankrupt the company. Then follows a process, a little like underwriting, as sections of the policy are offered to other companies. These companies will accept part of the risk for a share of the premium. This is called *reinsurance*.

Very large companies may decide to 'carry' some of their own insurance risks. As huge concerns, the cost of (say) losses from shoplifting can be averaged relatively cheaply over all their outlets: the actual losses are less costly than the cost of cover. This is *self-insurance*.

Actuaries

Actuaries are statisticians who are able to calculate the level of risk attached to all policies of insurance. The number of burglaries per 1000 of the population, the average loss following a fire, death rates for each age group: these are statistics which assist in the determination of a premium.

From the base premium calculated by an actuary, the insurance company may allow a deduction in the form of a bonus. Premiums on a life policy are lower if you don't smoke. You pay less on home insurance if your house is properly protected against fire and burglary. By contrast, a car insurance premium may be *increased* if you park your car overnight in the street rather than locking it in a garage.

Investment

The premiums paid by policyholders are invested by the insurance companies in property development, in stocks and shares, in the granting of mortgages and in loans to governments both in Britain and abroad (Fig. 12.3). It would be uneconomic to leave these vast sums of money idle. The interest earned by such investments averages £500 for every man, woman and child in Britain.

●SOURCES OF INFORMATION

1. British Insurance Brokers' Association, BIBA House, 14 Bevis Marks, London EC3A 7NT
2. Chartered Insurance Association, 20 Aldermanbury, London EC2V 7HY, for *Careers in Insurance* booklet.
3. Yellow Pages – look under Insurance Brokers.
4. Insurance Ombudsman, 31 Southampton Row, London WC1B 5HJ

For every pound which insurance companies invest, roughly:

34p is in industry and helps to build factories, machinery, offices and shops, providing jobs at home and earnings from abroad. When industry needs fresh capital the insurance companies put up their share.

29p has been used to provide mortgages and loans or to buy land and property for business, farmers and families to use.

26p has been lent to the British Government or to local councils helping them to pay for our social services, houses, schools, roads, aid to industry and other benefits.

11p Is kept close at hand for immediate needs such as claims from policyholders. Some of this is put in banks, who in turn lend it out again to industry, business and government.

Fig. 12.3 Insurance: company investments

● THINGS TO DO

1 Test yourself. Copy out the following self-test and tick the correct answer(s) in each case.
(a) People buying their own home, should take out:
 (i) contents insurance ☐
 (ii) life assurance ☐
 (iii) buildings insurance ☐
(b) If you require a guaranteed income on retirement you should purchase:
 (i) whole life assurance ☐
 (ii) an annuity ☐
 (iii) term assurance ☐
(c) The amount paid to effect insurance is called:
 (i) the policy ☐
 (ii) the risk ☐
 (iii) the premium ☐
(d) People who offer advice on the *range* of policies available are called:
 (i) brokers ☐
 (ii) jobbers ☐
 (iii) agents ☐
(e) A very large risk, parts of which are offered to other companies, is called:
 (i) claim ☐
 (ii) investment ☐
 (iii) reinsurance ☐
(f) The contract of insurance is called:
 (i) betterment ☐
 (ii) the policy ☐
 (iii) indemnity ☐
(g) The initial document containing details of the person or thing to be insured is called:
 (i) the proposal form ☐
 (ii) the cover note ☐
 (iii) the claim form ☐
(h) The person covered against loss and who has the insurable interest is called:
 (i) the insurer ☐
 (ii) the assured ☐
 (iii) the insured ☐
(i) Marine insurance covers:
 (i) ships ☐
 (ii) promenades ☐
 (iii) cargoes ☐
(j) The many premiums used to meet the claims of the unfortunate few are termed:
 (i) uninsurable risk ☐
 (ii) the pooling of risk ☐
 (iii) consequential loss ☐

2 Imagine you are starting up in a small manufacturing business. Consider what forms of insurance would be suitable for that business. Collect the relevant leaflets from a local insurance office. Calculate the annual cost of insurance in premiums. What did you include, and why?

3 A sole trader's premises and stock covered by an insurance policy in the sum of £150 000. Unfortunately, his shop and stock are totally destroyed by fire and, following discussions with a builder and his wholesale suppliers, he submits a claim for £200 000. Research what will happen next.

UNIT 12.3
Lloyd's of London

Lloyd's of London is a unique market-place. It is not a company and has no shareholders, but is a *society of underwriters*, all private individuals, organised in syndicates (groups), who are prepared to write a policy covering any kind of risk, however large or small. Each accepts *unlimited liability* (i.e. risks to any size).

Following the English Civil War (1642–6) merchants in London, already a centre of trade, began to underwrite insurances. They covered the various risks associated with trade, particularly overseas trade. About the same time, coffee drinking became popular, and City merchants met in coffee houses to do business. Lloyd's Coffee House opened in 1688 (Fig. 12.4). Edward Lloyd, the proprietor, encouraged ships' captains, merchants and shipowners to meet there to transact business. Lloyd's became recognised as the centre for marine insurance and was used by the wealthiest merchants.

In this period (1690–1720) many people risked fortunes on get-rich-quick schemes, many of which were just swindles. The government had to act to restrict these unreliable schemes, but Lloyd's gained in respectability and came to dominate the London insurance market (Fig. 12.5).

Organisation and control of Lloyd's

Members of Lloyd's (known as *names*) are private individuals accepting unlimited liability for any losses. Members employ underwriters, who themselves form groups known as syndicates, to transact business on their behalf. Membership of Lloyd's is open to both men and women, but the Council at Lloyd's must be satisfied that any applicant has enough funds to meet any losses should there be financial disaster.

Lloyd's is controlled though a Council and a Committee to which are elected both underwriting members from the 'floor' and outsiders who have City interests. Both Council and Committee meet regularly under an elected chairman. The Council decides policy and admits new underwriters. The Committee supervises day-to-day running and the insurance market generally.

The Lloyds Act 1982 is the controlling Act of Parliament.

Personnel

Lloyd's is now situated on Leadenhall Street in the heart of the City (see Fig. 12.6). The Underwriting Room (known as *the Room*) is a market-place for the 'writing' of insurance. People allowed to transact business are the underwriters and Lloyd's brokers, who negotiate the best deals for their clients world-wide.

A broker will move about the market, seeking the lowest rates he or she can find, accepting the best available quotation. Any enormous risk will be split between various syndicates, each of which will decide the

Fig. 12.5 Merchants outside Lloyd's, hearing of the Duke of Wellington's battles in Portugal in 1808

Fig. 12.4 Lloyd's coffee house as it would have been in the seventeenth century

number of 'shares' it is prepared to accept, underwriting the policy accordingly. When the policy is fully covered, the premium agreed will be split between the various syndicates according to the size of the share underwritten.

'Utmost good faith'

Throughout every insurance transaction, especially at Lloyd's, it is understood that all relevant facts will be disclosed and that nothing affecting assessment of the risk will be kept secret. *'Utmost good faith'* is essential between broker and underwriter, both of whom regard a verbal agreement as absolutely binding.

Lloyd's agents

Lloyd's maintains a network of 500-plus agencies throughout the world, operating within the business community. Agents send back to London news on shipping, aviation and similar matters. This information helps in the assessment of overseas risks, and provides a loss adjustment service in case of an overseas claim.

The information received in London is used to produce a daily newspaper, *Lloyd's List,* periodicals like *Lloyd's Log* and a Shipping Index, all of which contain information about the movement of ships, ship arrivals and departures. With a world-wide market, up-to-date information is essential in the assessment of risk (say) on a ship which may never dock in Britain.

Lloyd's Register of Shipping

The Register is produced by an independent organisation which collects information on the character and construction of all vessels afloat and needing insurance. All marine underwriters use the Register to assess risks associated with a particular ship and its cargo. *A1 at Lloyd's* is a classification which suggests a first-class vessel, seaworthy in every respect, which can be insured with confidence.

Invisible exports

Lloyd's, like the commercial and merchant banks, the Bank of England, the Stock Exchange and the commodity markets, is part of *the City* (see Fig. 12.6). These institutions provide services for Britain, but an enormous amount of their business is done for foreign clients and earns foreign currency. These earnings are known as *invisible exports* and greatly assist Britain's *balance of payments* (see Unit 16, section 16.2).

Insurance is a major earner in this respect (see Fig. 12.7). British companies and Lloyd's underwriters insure, for example, satellites orbiting the Earth, ships at sea, cargoes in transit, coffee beans growing in Brazil, consignments of uncut diamonds flown by jumbo jet from Amsterdam to Singapore, oil rigs and drilling platforms in every part of the world and the voices of opera stars appearing at La Scala, Milan.

All these were orginally the subject of a proposal, assessment of risk, calculation and payment of a premium and the issue of a policy, in exactly the same way that your family car may be insured by a local insurance company.

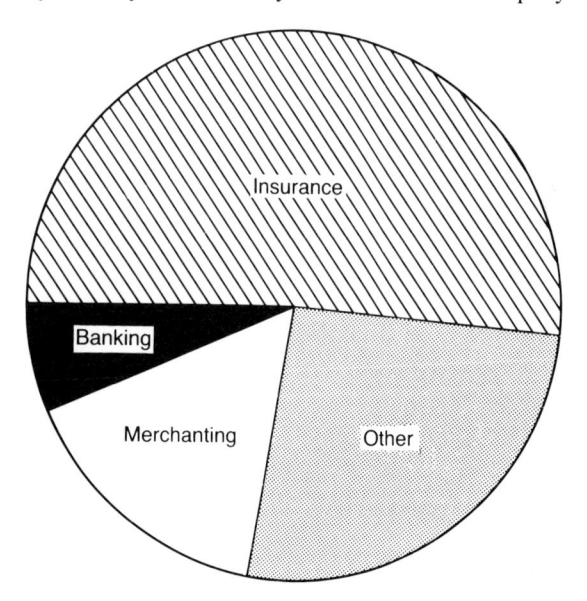

Fig. 12.7 Invisible earnings of British financial institutions

●THINGS TO DO

Write to all the institutions shown in Fig. 12.6 for source material. Compose a wall chart, using materials like those shown in Figs. 12.4 and 12.5, to illustrate the history of the City of London. Include its beginnings as a Roman fort, the Great Plague, the Great Fire and the Civil War, going up to the present day. Try also to include a commercial bank like the National Westminster and a merchant bank like Kleinwort Benson Ltd, 20 Fenchurch Street, London EC3.

Fig. 12.6 The City of London

[1] Mansion House
[2] Bank of England
[3] Stock Exchange
[4] Royal Exchange
[5] National Westminster Tower
[6] Baltic Exchange
[7] Lloyd's of London
[8] Lloyd's Register of Shipping
[9] Tower of London
[10] Monument
[11] HMS Belfast

13 TRANSPORT AND DISTRIBUTION

●UNIT 13.1
The Railway Network

An effective transport system, which allows people and goods to travel freely, is an important aid to trade and commerce. The transport of goods (or *freight*) is central to the process of *distribution* (see also Unit 3, section 3.1).

History
Steam railways were pioneered by private companies, from the 1830s onwards, to link major towns (e.g. Liverpool and Manchester). A maze of competing lines developed. These often served the same routes, with rolling stock of different sizes and tracks of different widths. Travel over any distance required a great deal of loading and unloading at junctions (like Clapham, Crewe and Watford) where the various lines met. As a result, rail travel was slow, unreliable and goods were often lost in transit.

In 1921 the large number of independent railways were merged into four groups: London, Midland & Scottish (LMS), London & North-Eastern (LNER), Great Western (GWR) and Southern (SR). These groupings were still private companies, but all were nationalised in 1947 when British Railways (now called British Rail) took over all assets and ran the rail network as a public corporation.

1 **Southern England and South London**

2 **South Midlands, West of England, South Wales and West London**

3 **East and West Midlands, North Wales, Northwest England, Scotland via West Coast and Northwest London**

4 **East and Northeast England, Scotland via East Coast and North London**

5 **East Anglia, Essex, Northeast and East London**

6 **Republic of Ireland**

7 **Northern Ireland**

8 **British Rail Europe**

Fig. 13.1 British Rail's regional groupings

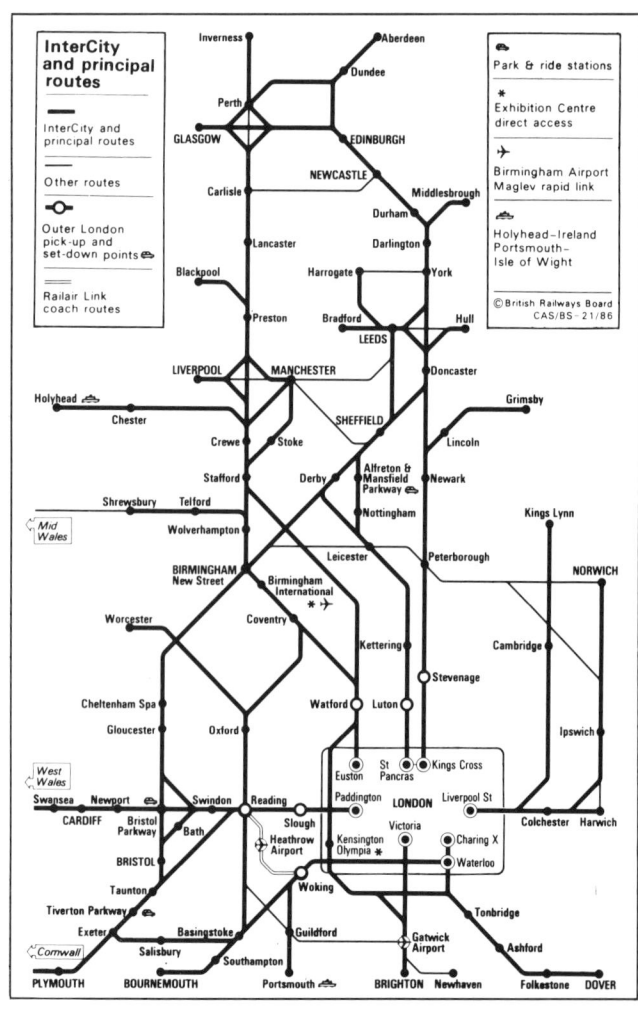

Fig. 13.2 Inter-City network and principal rail routes

Fig. 13.3 Container rail traffic reduces the time needed to move bulky goods

The present regional groupings are shown in Fig. 13.1. In 1963 many uneconomic branch lines were closed, the labour force was reduced, and British Rail assumed its present Inter-City network (see Fig. 13.2). Huge areas of Britain were left without rail services and had to rely on buses and road transport. Only major cities and major ports now enjoy both passenger and freight transport by rail.

Containerisation

Because trains cannot deliver door to door the loading and unloading problem remains. This, as well as the demands of international trade, has led to the development of *containers* (see Fig. 13.3) which can be transported by road, rail and container ship. They are packed at source and are not opened again until they arrive at their destination. The effect of containerisation is to reduce damage in transit, misdirection, handling costs and pilfering. Also, the transfer of loads from road and rail to container ships, and vice versa, is considerably eased.

Railway traffic

Inter-City trains and Freightliner services are able to move traffic quickly between major cities and British Rail is still a major carrier of passengers. But its freight, other than letters and parcels, is limited to the bulk movement of cars, coal, china clay, milk, grain, cement and steel, much of which is the uneconomic end of freight transport. Vast investment is needed to electrify the whole network, all of which must be maintained by British Rail, the cost being passed on to customers.

Problems and competition

Profitability is a major operating problem. Overheads are high. Neither passenger nor freight traffic is increasing relative to competitive methods of transport. The workforce is vast, and inter-union disputes do not assist efficiency. There are peak demands, such as commuter services from the South-East into and out of London, which leave rolling stock idle over long periods of each day and at weekends. The railways face competition from road transport: coaches which offer cheaper fares and from private cars. On long distance routes air travel, although expensive, is much quicker and therefore appeals to business people.

For the freight service, future competition will come from pipelines, currently carrying oil, gas and water, which can be adapted to carry any fluids or solids that can be made to flow such as coal dust which is used by the power-stations.

Advantages of rail transport

Once the goods are on rail, they can be moved quickly and without the congestion normally associated with roads. Railway terminals exist in the centre of towns which, unlike airports, are easily reached. Passenger and freight traffic begins and ends at a station with its special loading facilities. British Rail has its own transport for onwards delivery and collection to and from customers. Modern passenger trains are comfortable, provide refreshment facilities and call at major stations on the way. The ability to pick up and set down is much greater than with either air or road transport. All diesel and electric locomotives can pull huge trains, and the average cost per mile will decrease as electrification proceeds. Environmentalists (Greens) point out that moving large loads by rail does far less damage to the surrounding environment than heavy road transport does.

The future of rail transport

Our system is slow by comparison with the French and Japanese railways, where speeds of between 150 and 200 mph are achieved. It is only a matter of time before BR offers the same service, and London to Glasgow will become a two-hour ride, rivalling the journey by air. City centre to city centre, the railways will then have a clear advantage.

The Channel tunnel, providing an on-rail service, will allow a direct link between Britain and Europe without the loading and unloading difficulties currently experienced (Fig. 13.4). Speed and convenience will make the railways more attractive for both passenger and freight transport.

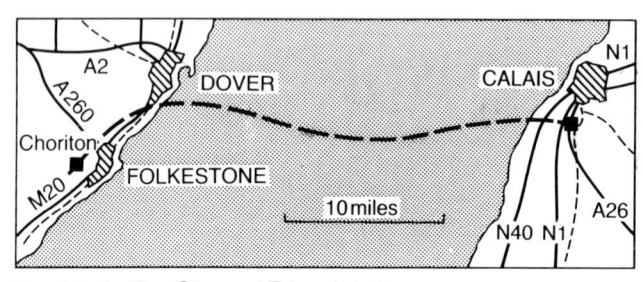

Fig. 13.4 The Channel Tunnel route

● SOURCES OF INFORMATION

1. Telephone directory, for British Rail's area/regional headquarters in your area.
2. British Rail Headquarters, 222 Marylebone Road, London NW1 6JJ
3. British Rail Europe, Paddington Station, London W2 1HF
4. Eurotunnel Share Information Office, PO Box 501, Bristol BS99 1ET
5. French Railways Ltd, 179 Piccadilly, London W1V 9DB
6. Belgian National Railways, 22 Sackville Street, London W1X 1DE
7. British Gas, for details of pipelines.

● THINGS TO DO

1. With help from your teacher, research and discover the original railway system in your area. With visual material, this can provide a subject for an assignment.
2. Visit a container depot in your area to see packing, handling and dispatch.
3. From your home base, research the cost and times of a journey using (a) train, and (b) bus to Aberdeen, London or Plymouth. What are the advantages of each method? Are there any disadvantages?
4. Using Figs. 13.2 and 13.5, research a rail journey from Bristol to Norwich. Detail the route you would take, the London terminals used, the underground journey linking the terminals and the approximate time of the journey.
5. You are travelling from Belfast to Nottingham for a trade fair. Plan your journey using Figs. 13.1 and 13.2. Contrast the cost and times by ferry/train and by air.

● QUESTIONS

1. What do you understand by *steam railways*? Why was there a move from steam first to diesel and then to electric trains?
2. What part does the rail network play in the distribution of the Royal Mail?
3. How does containerisation aid the transport of goods, and what advantages do containers offer to carriers?
4. What form of Channel tunnel is being built? What effect will this project have on: (a) air transport; (b) sea transport; (c) road transport; (d) rail transport?

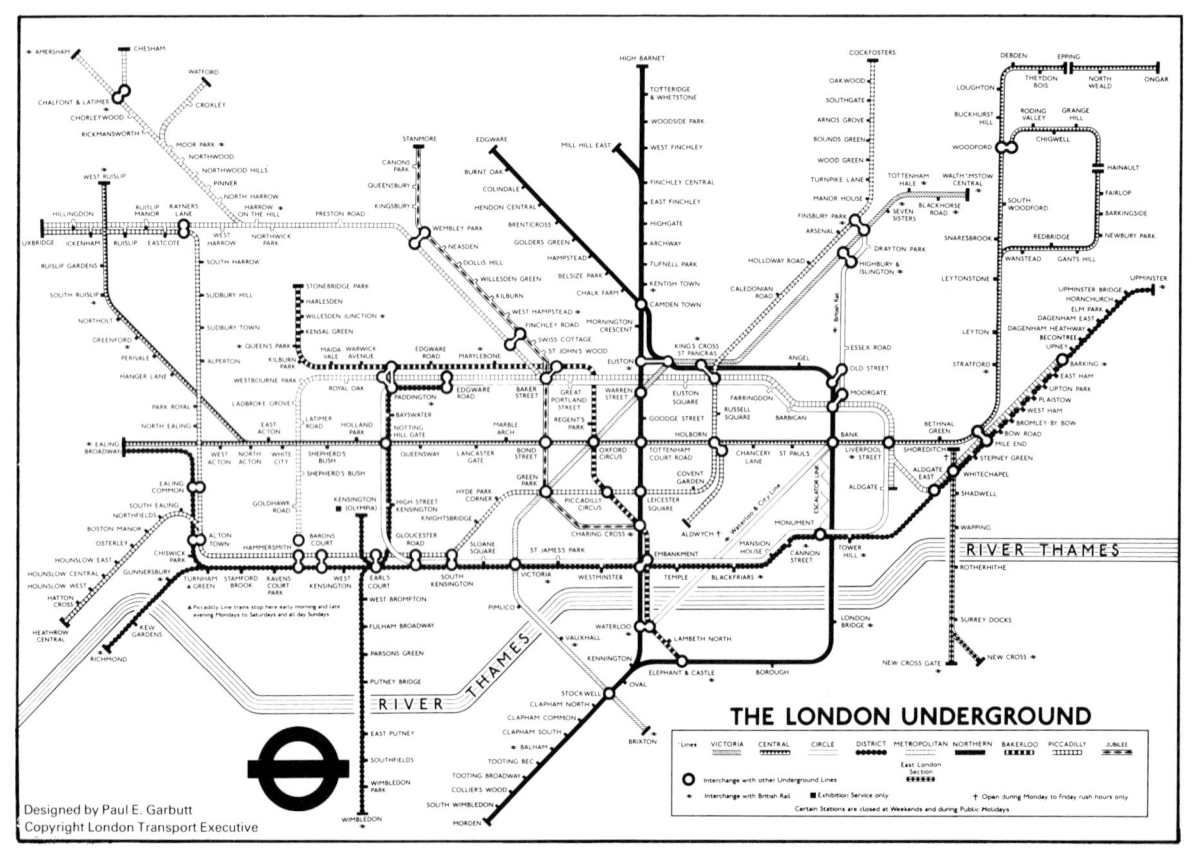

Fig. 13.5 Map of the London Underground

UNIT 13.2
Road Systems and Freight Ferries

In Britain the road network is free to users, although vehicle owners pay road fund tax. There are points, like the Dartford Tunnel and the Severn Bridge, where *tolls* (charges) must be paid. But, unlike those in France, Spain and Italy (where a fee is charged according to type of vehicle and distance travelled), motorways in Britain are free. All vehicles registered in Britain must display a road fund licence and carry motor vehicle insurance, whether travelling at home or abroad. Road haulage now provides the major share of freight movements in Britain and Europe.

Classification of roads

Roads are classified according to size and importance (see Fig. 13.6). Motorways are prefixed M (e.g. M4 – London to Swansea), and trunk roads finished to motorway standard have an M suffix (e.g. A1M – Doncaster By-pass). Main roads, carry an A prefix (e.g. A38 – Bristol to Exeter). Subsidiary, mainly country, roads are prefixed B (e.g. B1393 – Epping to Harlow).

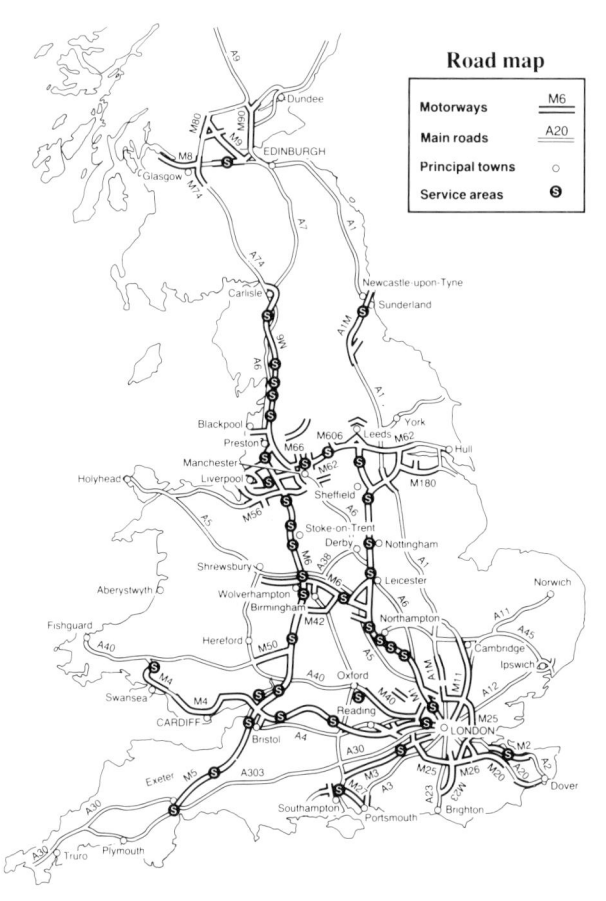

Fig. 13.6 Motorways and main roads in Britain

Advantages of road transport

1. All highways are maintained at public expense, although partly paid for by the road fund tax on vehicle owners.
2. Delivery can be made door to door, offering express 24-hour services.
3. Loading and unloading are unnecessary between start and completion of journeys.
4. Juggernauts (giant lorries) can carry huge loads over vast distances. Only one or two drivers/delivery people are involved in each journey.
5. Depots are maintained in all large cities where return loads are available.
6. Individual vehicles do not have to observe timetables or stop on the way. They are not restricted by shipping lanes, international flight paths or variations in widths of rail tracks.
7. People like to have the convenience of personal transport. They can use their own car, van or lorry when and how they need or want to.

Disadvantages of road transport

Roads are often congested, road works cause delays, and there are speed restrictions – all making road transport slow at times. The law limits the distances and time individual lorry drivers can stay behind the wheel. As a form of passenger transport, cars can be wasteful – all the car drivers in a traffic jam could fit into one train or a few buses, saving both time and fuel. Heavy lorries passing through towns and villages are dangerous and can damage roads and buildings. Lead in petrol can cause brain damage. Diesel fumes are unpleasant.

Passenger traffic

The development of motorways has encouraged the expansion of cheap passenger-carrying services over long distances in comfortable buses travelling at high speeds. Journey times and costs compare favourably with rail and air services. Bus stations are located in the centre of towns, their facilities leased from local authorities. So coach companies do not have to maintain expensive sites, buildings or offices, while the motorway service stations are available for refreshment halts. Although vast numbers of passengers travel by rail and air, the number of passenger journeys by road (by coach and private car) is increasing and will continue to increase, encouraged by continuous improvements in our road network.

Freight and delivery traffic

Many businesses provide their own transport for local deliveries. There are also firms which specialise in short-distance delivery, offering a service costed on the basis of weight or bulk and distance. Larger businesses, with branches in many towns, maintain their own medium- and long-distance fleets to deliver goods from factory or warehouse to their outlets. Such transport displays the name of the company and a logo as a means of identification and advertising.

Private firms (some only one-person businesses) offer similar services. They work either on a continuous contract basis or by offering this service for haulage business wherever it can be found. In this category are the specialised hauliers with refrigerated vans or tankers carrying dangerous loads over large distances.

All lorries need a special licence, which must be displayed on the windscreen in addition to the road tax disc. Drivers are required to pass a Heavy Goods Vehicle (HGV) driving test.

Long-distance haulage

Long-distance road haulage is specialised and international in character. We have all travelled behind those enormous articulated lorries, from all over Europe, with a *TIR* (Transport International Routier) emblem on the back. These lorries are sealed by Customs and must not be opened before reaching their destinations. All exports from Britain, and all imports into Britain, which travel by road, use one or other of the European ferries (see Fig. 13.7).

Containers are widely used, and international journeys of 2000 miles or more are not unusual. Several national frontiers will be crossed in the course of such journeys. The loads are covered by a large volume of paperwork (manifests, Customs declarations, health authority clearances, etc.) which is similar for all international cargoes.

The major part of each journey is covered on motorways. The driving (non-stop) is done by teams, and the regulations covering such movements are fixed by international agreement. Computerised equipment in each cab records distance travelled, speeds maintained, frequency and length of stops and changes of driver. The drivers are a special breed, akin to seamen, often multilingual and away from home for long periods of time. They carry every kind of cargo imaginable, but often specialise on particular routes or in particular goods.

Adding value

All forms of freight transport take goods and raw materials from the point of production, manufacture or storage to the point at which the customer is prepared to accept delivery and at which they are prepared to pay. So transport *adds value* to a consignment by the process of *distribution* (see Unit 3, section 3.1). For example, rolls of newsprint have only limited value in the warehouse of the paper mill. But they gain in value through being transported to the printing works, where newspapers will be produced for sale

●THINGS TO DO

1. Obtain freight rates and schedules from all the major European ferries. Compare costs and terms on the various crossings.
2. Organise a lorry census at a busy road junction in your area. Where do the loads come from?
3. Research progress on the Eurotunnel. What provision will be made for container lorries? Is freight from Birmingham to Lyons (France) likely to use the tunnel or continue to use channel ferries?

●SOURCES OF INFORMATION

1. Freight Transport Association, Hermes House, St John's Road, Tunbridge Wells, Kent TN4 9UZ
2. Yellow Pages – see under 'freight services'.
3. Transport and General Workers' Union, Transport House, Smith Square, London SW1P 3JB
4. Department of Transport, 2 Marsham Street, London SW1P 4JY
5. Friends of the Earth, 26–28 Underwood Street, London N1 7JQ, for leaflets on transport systems and the environment.
6. Any road atlas of Britain showing motorways and service stations.
7. Any road atlas of Europe.
8. Any AA centre, for the AA's *Guide to Motoring Abroad*.
9. An AA or RAC member's manual.

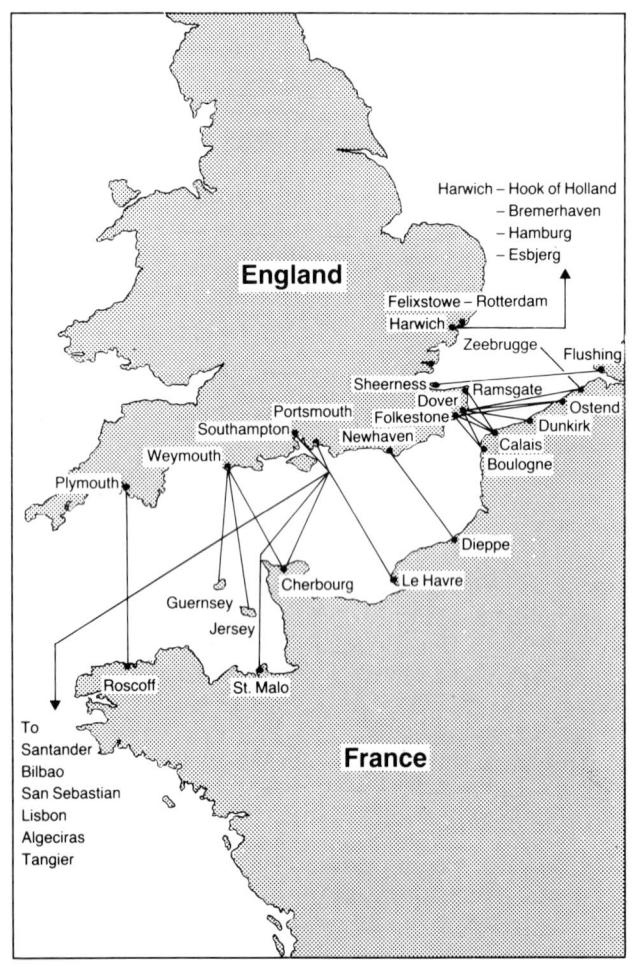

Fig. 13.7 Main European cross-Channel ferry routes

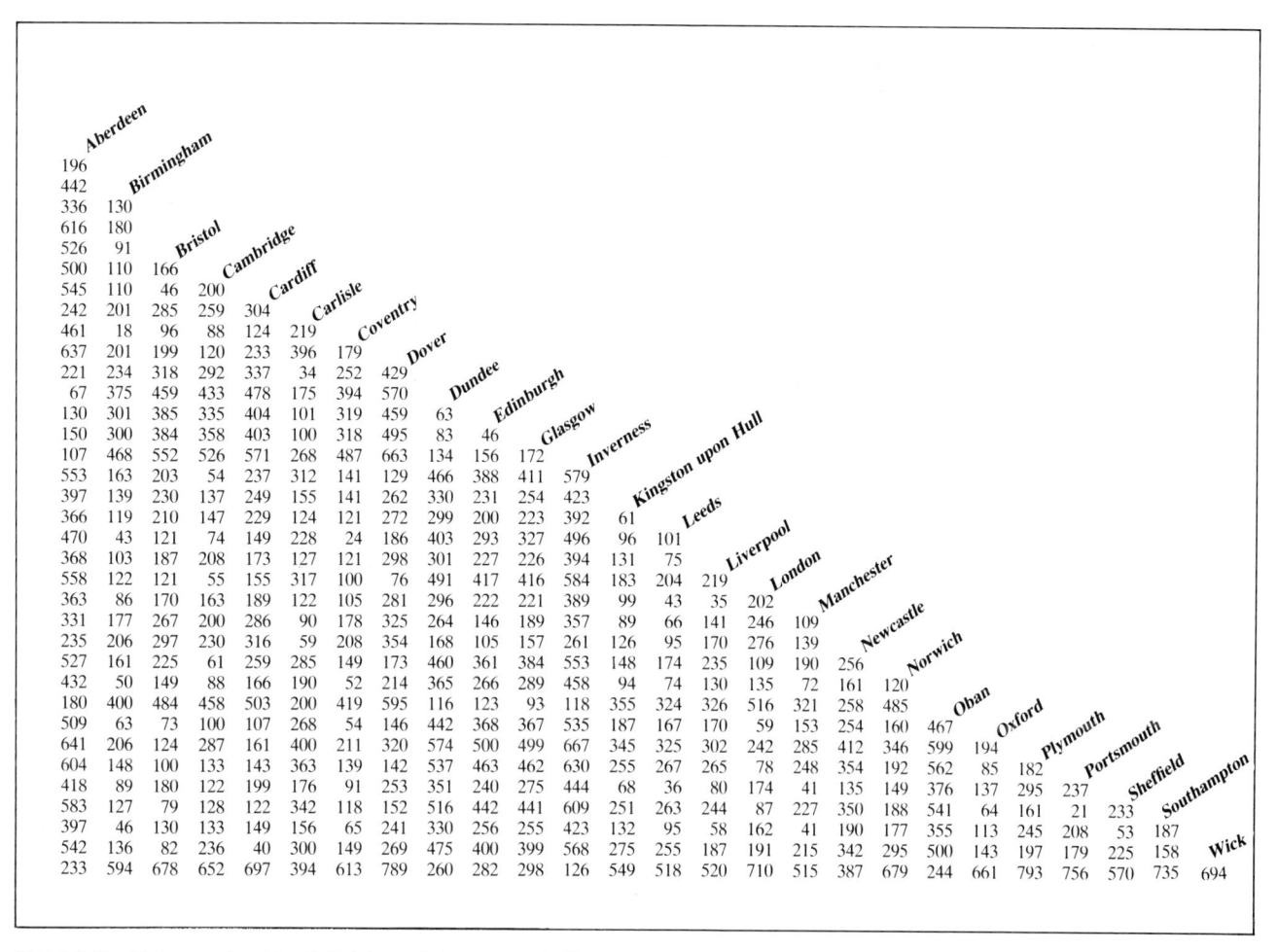

Fig. 13.8 Mileage chart for Britain's main towns and cities

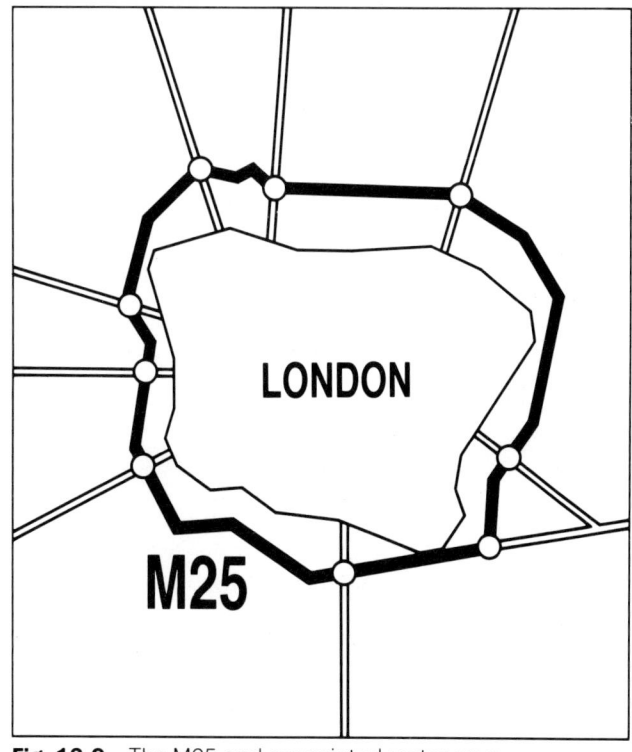

	Aberdeen	Birmingham	Bristol	Cambridge	Cardiff	Carlisle	Coventry	Dover	Dundee	Edinburgh	Glasgow	Inverness	Kingston upon Hull	Leeds	Liverpool	London	Manchester	Newcastle	Norwich	Oban	Oxford	Plymouth	Portsmouth	Sheffield	Southampton	Wick
196
442	130
336	180
616	91	166
526	110	46	200
500	110	285	259	304
545	201	96	88	124	219
242	18	199	120	233	396	179
461	201	318	292	337	34	252	429
637	234	459	433	478	175	394	570
221	375	385	335	404	101	319	459	63
67	301	384	358	403	100	318	495	83	46
130	300	552	526	571	268	487	663	134	156	172
150	468	203	54	237	312	141	129	466	388	411	579
107	163	230	137	249	155	141	262	330	231	254	423	61
553	139	210	147	229	124	121	272	299	200	223	392	96	101
397	119	121	74	149	228	24	186	403	293	327	496	101	75
366	43	187	208	173	127	121	298	301	227	226	394	131	204	219
470	103	121	55	155	317	100	76	491	417	416	584	183	43	35	202
368	122	170	163	189	122	105	281	296	222	221	389	99	141	246	109
558	86	267	200	286	90	178	325	264	146	189	357	89	95	170	276	139
363	177	297	230	316	59	208	354	168	105	157	261	126	174	235	109	190	256
331	206	225	61	259	285	149	173	460	361	384	553	148	74	130	135	72	161	120
235	161	149	88	166	190	52	214	365	266	289	458	94	167	516	321	258	485
527	50	484	458	503	200	419	595	116	123	93	118	355	324	59	153	254	160	467
432	400	73	100	107	268	54	146	442	368	367	535	187	325	302	242	285	412	346	599	194
180	63	124	287	161	400	211	320	574	500	499	667	345	267	265	78	248	354	192	562	85	182
509	206	100	133	143	363	139	142	537	463	462	630	255	36	80	174	41	135	149	376	137	295	237
641	148	180	122	199	176	91	253	351	240	275	444	68	263	244	87	227	350	188	541	64	161	21	233
604	89	79	128	122	342	118	152	516	442	441	609	251	95	58	162	41	190	177	355	113	245	208	53	187
418	127	130	133	149	156	65	241	330	256	255	423	132	255	187	191	215	342	295	500	143	197	179	225	158
583	46	82	236	40	300	149	269	475	400	399	568	275	549	518	520	710	515	387	679	244	661	793	756	570	735	694
397	136
542
233	594	678	652	697	394	613	789	260	282	298	126

Fig. 13.9 The M25 and associated motorways

●QUESTIONS

1. You are sending a lorry from Leeds to catch the 18.00 Dover–Calais ferry. Reporting time is one hour before departure. Assuming an average speed of 30 mph, use Fig. 13.8 to calculate at what time the load should leave Leeds.

2. You run a small haulage company in the Midlands. You have accepted the following contracts for one week: (a) a load from Edinburgh delivered to Walsall (b) a load from Swansea delivered to Worcester (c) a load from Birmingham delivered to Glasgow (d) a load from Coventry delivered to Bristol. Consult a road atlas and decide in which order the jobs should be done so that you drive as few miles as possible.

3. Plan a journey from Exeter to Newcastle-on-Tyne using motorways (shown in Fig. 13.6). (a) What roads would you use? (b) What is the distance and travelling time overall? (Use Fig. 13.8 and assume an average speed of 40 mph.)

4. Copy out Fig. 13.9. from your road atlas, list the motorways linking with the M25. Where does each motorway go to?

UNIT 13.3
Waterways, Shipping and Ports

Canals and rivers
Until the eighteenth century Britain had no proper road system. Once the Industrial Revolution (1780–1820) was under way, it became important to move raw materials to the towns and mills, and finished goods to the ports. In England canals were dug connecting the rivers Thames, Severn, Trent and Mersey, while the Manchester Ship Canal (1894) linked that city to the seaport of Liverpool. In Scotland the rivers Clyde (Glasgow) and the Forth (Edinburgh) were also joined by canal.

Canal transport, being slow and awkward, has declined. Northern canal boats are wider than those used in the South. With the development of speedier traffic using roads and railways, the canals, with their locks and tunnels, gradually deteriorated through lack of maintenance. Canal traffic is now confined to bulk carriers of raw material on a limited commercial network (Figs. 13.10 and 13.11). Many boats have been sold off for private or holdiay use.

Coastal routes
At the same time goods were moved along coastal routes by ships using ports situated on tidal estuaries like London, Bristol, Glasgow, Leith, Liverpool, Hull and Newcastle. Until the road network began to emerge; canals and coastal shipping provided the only reliable means of transport, linking the centres of industry to major ports and international trade. Unlike canal transport, the coastal trade is still widely used.

International waterways
By contrast, continental use of inland waterways and canals is growing. European rivers are navigable for long distances inland. The River Rhine is linked by canals to the Danube, allowing access from the North Sea by river and canal to the Black Sea. European waterways carry considerable traffic at speed and over long distances. In Canada and the United States, deep-sea shipping is able to reach large inland areas via the St Lawrence River and the Great Lakes. The Suez and Panama canals cross continents linking oceans for sea-going shipping.

Ports and harbours
Today's huge ships require deep anchorage and cannot afford to be left 'high and dry' on tidal rivers. Many of Britain's ports and harbours, like the network of docks in London, stand on tidal rivers. Once-famous dockland areas, now out of use, are being developed for housing, ship museums, shopping centres, marinas and leisure interests. By contrast, deep-water developments at Southampton, Milford Haven and Harwich show the pattern of modernisation in shipping, along the lines of the Rotterdam docks and harbour complex in Holland.

Fig. 13.10 Canal traffic

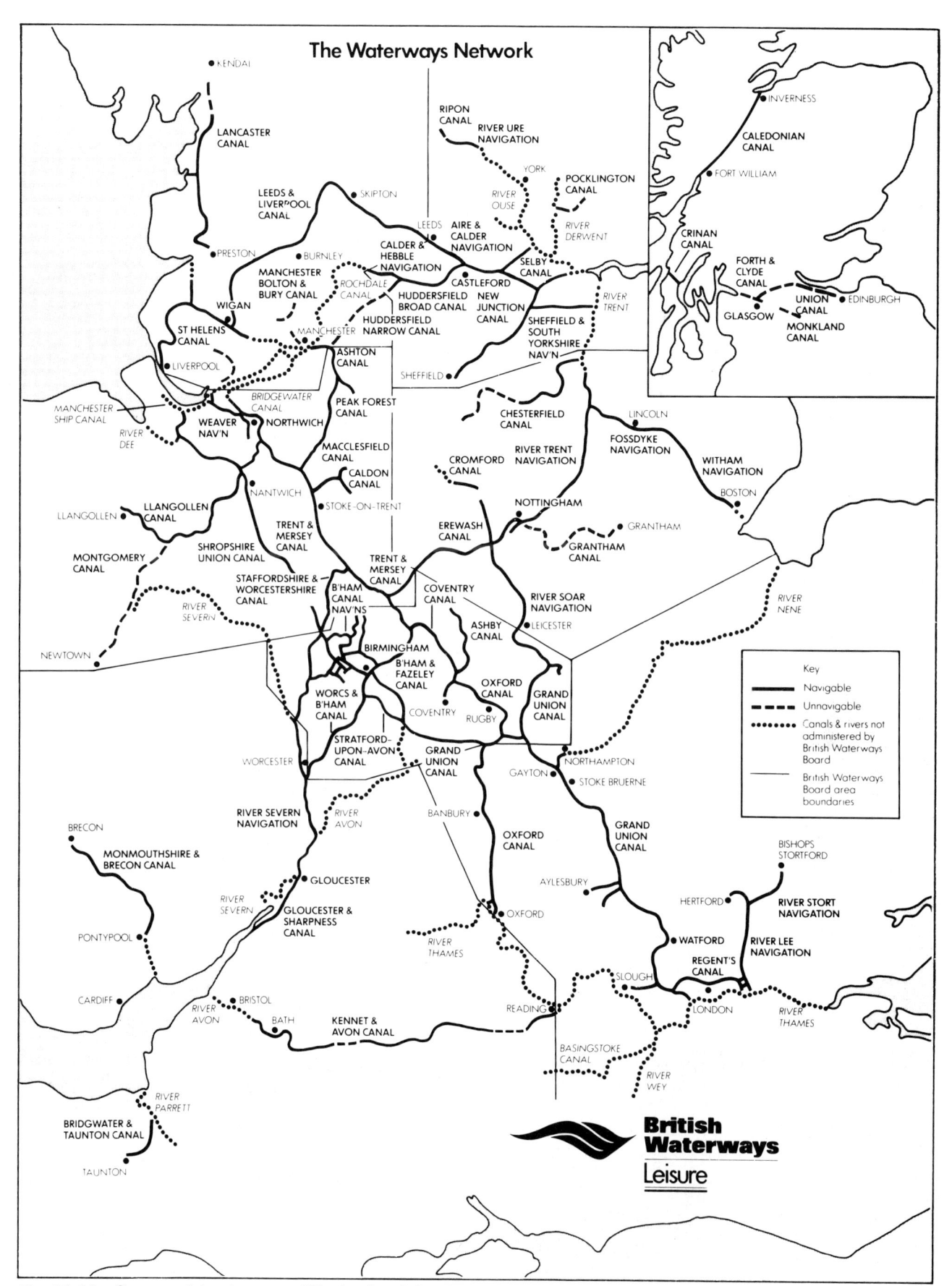

Fig. 13.11 Commercial waterways of England and Scotland

During its peak in the early 1980s, North Sea oil produced boom conditions for many ports like Aberdeen and Hound Point on the Firth of Forth. The needs of road transport to and from Europe have steadily increased the importance of Dover, Harwich, Portsmouth and Southampton, all of which employ roll-on/roll-off (known as *RORO*) ferries for freight transport.

Sea transport

Britain is an island. All our bulky cargo is brought in and sent out by ship. Ports on the western side of Britain (Glasgow, Milford Haven, Liverpool and Bristol) serve the Americas, the Caribbean, Africa, the Far East and Australia. Departures from harbours to the East (Edinburgh, Newcastle, Hull and Harwich) trade with the Baltic, Scandinavia and Northern Europe. Shipping from the Channel ports serves France, Belgium, Holland and Spain. Southampton sends ships to all four corners of the world.

Passenger liners, cargo ships, tramps, tankers, hovercraft and ferries maintain the supply routes for our industrial and commercial interests. When you shop this weekend your trolley will probably contain goods which originated half-way across the world.

Duties, levies and taxes

When goods are shipped into Britain, excise duties, European Community levies and value added tax may be charged. These costs are met by the importer and can be a heavy financial burden, especially in the case of raw materials. The capital tied up in these deals cannot be regained until the goods are sold.

Freeports

To avoid this problem Britain has designated six *Freeports*: Belfast, Prestwick, Birmingham, Southampton, Liverpool and Cardiff. Here goods can be stored, raw materials processed, imports repacked, relabelled or sorted and possibly re-exported (the *entrepôt trade*) without incurring duties, levies or VAT. The Birmingham and Prestwick Freeports are based on airports to service goods imported by air.

Liverpool Freeport Liverpool Freeport at Sefton covers 600 acres (Fig. 13.12) and is surrounded by a wire fence 10 feet high. Warehouses, processing plants and storage facilities are situated together with major docks and harbours for all kinds and sizes of ships. The Freeport is an industrial village controlled by HM Customs and

Fig. 13.12 Liverpool Freeport in Sefton

Excise; for purposes of duties and levies it is classified as being *outside* the United Kingdom. Duties are charged, levies are applied and VAT is demanded only when goods pass through Customs at the gates. If goods are re-exported to countries other than within the EC, no duties, levies or taxes are required.

The advantage of Freeports   Cash, normally tied up in taxes, is released for more important uses. Security is so tightly controlled within the Freeports that insurance premiums are reduced. Costs are minimised, and goods can be handled more competitively. *Re-exporting* (a major part of Britain's overseas trade) is much easier and free of many restrictions.

SOURCES OF INFORMATION

1. British Waterways Board, Melberry House, Melberry Terrace, London NW1 6JX
2. British Waterways Board, Penn Place, Rickmansworth, Hertsfordshire WD3 1EU
3. National Waterways Transport Association, 43 Brackley, Queens Road, Weybridge, Surrey KT13 0BL
4. National Union of Seamen, Maritime House, Old Town, London SW4
5. HM Customs and Excise, Dorset House, Stanford Street, London SE1 9PS
6. Freeport Manager, Mersey Docks & Harbour Co, Pier Head, Liverpool L3 1BZ.
7. The Manager, Birmingham Freeport, Birmingham International Airport, Birmingham B26 3QJ

THINGS TO DO

1. Using Fig. 13.11 write politely to the water authority closest to your school or college. Ask: (a) what kind of cargo uses the particular piece of water;   (b) what major firms are served by the waterway involved;   (c) whether the traffic along the waterway is increasing or decreasing.
2. The canal/river system shown in Figs. 13.10 and 13.11 represents what remains of 4250 miles of navigable waterways which existed in 1800. From your research in **1**, why do you think these fragments remain? What is the total length still in use? Do you feel that there is any future for the inland waterways?
3. Contact the port nearest to your school or college. Enquire about coastal transport. What ports are used for these freight movements, and what kind of cargo is involved?
4. Contact your nearest Freeport like the one shown in Fig. 13.12 for some information about the firms engaged in that zone. Working in groups, contact one of the firms involved to find out about the processes undertaken by that firm within the Freeport. What eventually happens to the goods?
5. Obtain the name of a shipping company: write for brochures and ask for details of the ports used, the cargoes involved, destinations, etc. Your local newsagent may be willing to obtain a copy of *Lloyd's List*, which you will find helpful.

Your class may wish to share the above assignments. Each group can then report back to the class. Use wall charts and diagrams to illustrate your findings.

UNIT 13.4
Air Transport

History and development

Air transport is the 'youngest' of all the transport services. The first powered flight by the Wright brothers was in 1903 (Fig. 13.13). The first crossing of the Atlantic was in 1919, the same year as the first regular British Air Service for passengers between London and Paris. The First and Second World Wars (1914–18 and 1939–45) produced rapid advances in powered flight. But the greatest development in both passenger and freight aircraft services took place over the thirty years between 1945 and 1975. The hundred years between 1903 and 2003 are likely to rank as a century of outstanding achievement, both in air and in space travel.

Advantages of air transport

Once an aircraft is clear of the runway, use of the skyways is absolutely free. At heights of about 7½ miles, air friction is virtually non-existent, so aircraft can cruise over long distances at a surprisingly low cost per passenger mile. Speeds are higher than 500 mph, and can be as much as 1400 mph (Fig. 13.14) – making air travel fast and convenient, but only over distances of more than 200 miles.

However, to the time in the air must be added the time taken to reach the airport and return to the city of destination. So, short hops by air may be no faster overall than by train. It is in *intercontinental* travel that the aircraft has no real competition for passengers and even some freight.

All modern aircraft will carry freight, but costs are so high that carriage is confined to post and parcels, perishables and goods of high value. Aircraft can also reach parts of the world not accessible by any other means of transport (in Australia for example).

Fig. 13.13 Wilbur Wright gets off the ground in 1903

Fig. 13.14 Concorde – capable of travelling at 1400 m.p.h.

Disadvantages of air transport

Congestion to and from airports, with delays on the ground, are not uncommon. Air travel is also affected by bad weather, particularly fogs, which can result in the *stacking* of aircraft queuing to land at busy airports. The cost of the aircraft themselves runs to millions of pounds; fuel is expensive and consumed in great quantities. Insurance rates are heavy while landing charges are constantly increasing, especially at international airports like London Heathrow, New York Kennedy and Paris Charles de Gaulle. Noise at take-off and landing is considerable, so most airports have to be sited away from densely populated areas.

However, *Stolports*, catering for aircraft requiring short take-off and landing facilities, are now planned for city centres. A Stolport has been sited at London's new City Airport in the docklands. Similar services are provided by helicopters, which need only a pad and not a runway.

State airlines and independents

Many countries like to 'show the flag' by having a state airline. El Al (Israel), Qantas (Australia), Aer Lingus (Eire), Alitalia (Italy) and Aeroflot (USSR) are examples. British Airways was Britain's state airline; although now privatised, it still uses the Union Flag as a logo.

Pan Am and TWA (USA) are probably the best known international independents, while Dan Air, Air Europe and British Midland Airways are well known to the British holidaymaker looking for charter flights to the sun.

Smaller 'working' aircraft

Crop-spraying, services to and from North Sea oil rigs, police helicopters, Post Office Datapost and private aircraft maintained by multinational corporations are all examples of smaller aircraft working for their keep. Such planes either provide a passenger service or ferry freight on a charter basis. Aircraft can be chartered, just like ships, at the Baltic Exchange (see Unit 11, section 11.2), for either a time or a voyage charter. Privately owned aircraft are rare in Britain. In the United States, where distances to be covered are much greater, small landing-fields and individually owned small craft are much more common.

Control of airlines and traffic

Civil Aviation Authority (CAA) The multitude of aircraft in the sky at any one time demands some controlling authority to impose regulations. The flying public expect high safety standards. The CAA licenses aircraft and personnel in Britain. It regulates both state and independent airlines, as well as all civil airports throughout Britain.

Air traffic control Aircraft in the air, about to take-off or preparing to land, are regulated by a network of air traffic control centres, situated at major airports. These centres decide on height, speed and manoeuvres of all aircraft in their area. Aircraft movements are monitored on the ground by radio and radar. The aircraft themselves carry equipment (the *black box*) which records all changes of speed and direction as well as contacts with other aircraft and air traffic control. Black boxes are built to survive a crash and can be an important source of information about a plane that has crashed.

●SOURCES OF INFORMATION

1. British Airways, Bealine House, Douglas House, PO Box 7, Ruislip, Middx
2. British Airways PLC, Cargocentre, Heathrow Airport, Hounslow, London.
3. British Airports Authority, 2 Buckingham Gate, London SW1E 6JL
4. Civil Aviation Authority, CAA House, 43–59 Kingsway, London WC2B 6TE

●QUESTIONS

1. Which airline and route have the lowest cost per mile in the table below? Can you suggest why this price is cheapest?
2. The journeys given in the table are *scheduled* services, i.e. they run to a timetable. Study the weekend newspapers: can you locate lower fares for the same journeys? Are these scheduled services? If not, what are they called? What conditions attach to such bookings?
3. Find out and give meanings for the terms:
   (a) *standby*; (b) *shuttle services*; (c) *apex fares*; (d) *super apex*. What is involved in each?

●THINGS TO DO

Copy out the following table. Then go to your local travel agent and ask for help in completing your table. Calculate answers for the 'cost per mile' column.

Airline	Journey	Miles	Single fare 'economy class'	Cost per mile
Swissair	Heathrow–Zurich			
Qantas	Manchester–Sydney			
British Airways	Gatwick–Glasgow			
Aer Lingus	Dublin–Edinburgh		*	

* Irish pounds do not have the same value as £ sterling. How do you convert from one to the other?

14 COMMUNICATIONS

●UNIT 14.1
The Post Office

History and organisation

The Post Office has its origins in the royal postal service used by British kings and queens from the 1400s. The service was opened to the public in 1635. Telecommunications were added in 1870, parcels in 1883 and Girobank in 1968. The modern Post Office was nationalised by the Post Office Act 1969, after more than 300 years as a government service. The telecommunications section was transferred to a new corporation, British Telecom, by the British Telecommunication Act 1981 and was privatised two years later.

The Post Office is now organised in four sections:

1 Royal Mail letters;
2 Royal Mail parcels;
3 Counters (mainly agency services);
4 Girobank (marked for privatisation).

The offices themselves are classified as *head post offices* (each responsible for services within a district), *Crown post offices* (staffed by salaried officers) and *sub-post offices* (usually attached to a shop like a confectioner or newsagent).

Royal Mail

The Royal Mail offers a general service for letters, packets and parcels in terms of collection and delivery nation-wide. Within this sector there are specialised services such as *Datapost* (an express courier delivery), *Intelpost* (a facsimile delivery), *registered post* (for valuables, including signature on receipt), *recorded delivery* (signature on receipt), *special delivery*, *Freepost* (the receiver pays in bulk for all replies) and *Post Office (PO) box numbers* (mainly for business use).

Letters and parcels

The Post Office enjoys a near-monopoly of the collection and delivery of letters in Britain. There are exceptions – for example, charities may deliver Christmas cards. Very urgent mail can be delivered by courier (you will have noticed the couriers on motor bikes) as long as the charge is at least £1 (at the time of writing). Mail may be delivered by private firms to an aircraft for delivery abroad.

Despite these exceptions, the Post Office carries by far the greatest quantity, about 12 billion letters every year, which is about 42 million every working day. There are two levels of service: first and second class. Where possible first-class mail is delivered on the following day. second-class mail costs less and is suitable for non-urgent items.

Parcels The Post Office does not have a monopoly of parcel post. It competes with private carriers (like Parceline, much of whose work is connected with the delivery of mail-order items). Again, there is a first- and a second-class service, catering for 205 million parcels each year.

Transport

About half the mail travels by road and half by rail. There are special railway coaches, added to normal trains, fitted as mobile sorting offices. The Royal Mail maintains a fleet of easily recognisable red lorries and vans, each of which carries the Post Office logo. Aircraft have been added for the Datapost service, to ensure overnight delivery from one end of Britain to the other.

Aircraft networks are maintained from Speke (Liverpool) and East Midlands (Derby) airports, which connect with all other major airports in Britain and Northern Ireland (see Fig. 14.1). Almost all overseas mail travels by *air mail*, usually on scheduled, passenger-carrying flights.

Postcodes and mechanisation

With today's huge volume of mail, 24 million addresses in Britain and the need to compete with other carriers, old-fashioned hand-sorting methods have given way to mechanised/electronic sorting, computerisation and *postcodes*. Each postcode is a simplified address. The first one or two letters are the area code, the following figures indicate the district and the sector, and the final two letters identify the road or street (Fig. 14.2). Blue dots on your envelope allow the computerised sorting machinery to read the postcode.

Agency services

Agency services are maintained at head, Crown and some sub-post offices, depending on location and size. They include:

1 Payment of social security benefits and pensions.
2 The sale of National Savings certificates, Premium Bonds and gift tokens, together with the National Savings Bank in-payments and withdrawals.
3 Television and CB radio licences and savings stamps.
4 Payments for telephone bills (free of charge) and some other bills (e.g. electricity and gas) for a nominal charge.
5 Road fund tax licence renewals.
6 British visitors' passports and similar documents.
7 Dog and game licences.
8 Sale of Railcards, issue of milk tokens, film developing and printing.
9 Various application forms and brochures on services.
10 *Cheque cashing* The Post Office will now cash personal cheques up to a maximum of £50 on presentation of a cheque guarantee card. A small charge is made for the service.

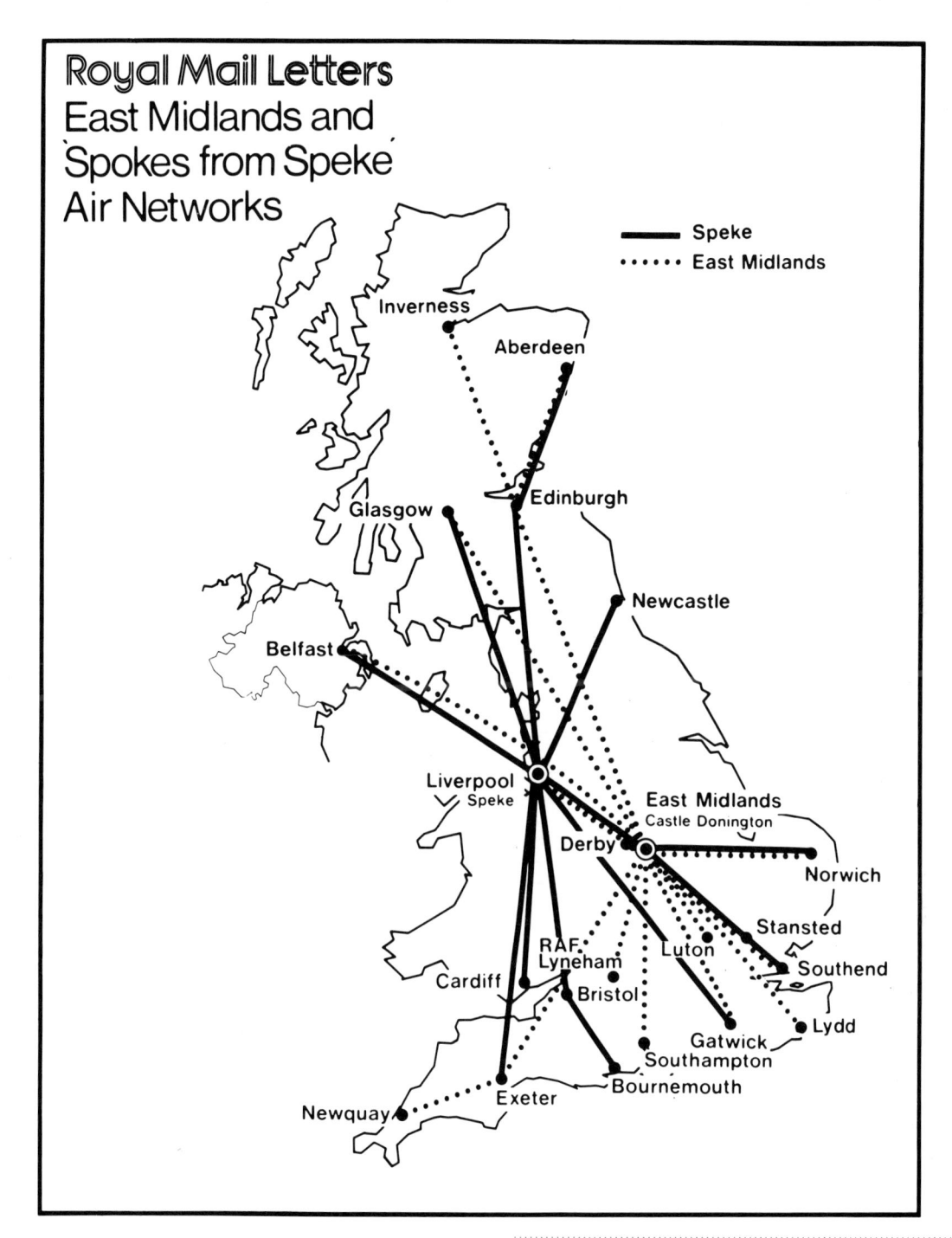

Fig. 14.1 Royal Mail air networks

For those services which are free to the public, the Post Office is paid a commission based on the volume of trade.

National Girobank

The Girobank is dealt with in Unit 9, section 9.5.

Post Office Users' National Council (POUNC)

This body has a watchdog or ombudsman-type role. Complaints can be made and all price increases must be referred to it. Members of POUNC are appointed by the Secretary of State for Trade and Industry.

●SOURCES OF INFORMATION

1. Post Office Headquarters, Briefing and Research Unit (G64), 33 Grosvenor Place, London SW1X 1PX
2. Post Office Users' National Council, Waterloo Bridge House, Waterloo Road, London SE1 8UA
3. Post Office Schools Officer, Room 127, 22–25 Finsbury Square, London EC2A 1PH
4. Post Office Customer Information, Room 143, 33 Grosvenor Place, London SW1X 1EE
5. Post Office Public Relations Department, 33 Grosvenor Place, London SW1X 1PX
6. *Thompsons Local Directory*, for postcodes.
7. The Post Office Guide.

Your postcode – the vital link

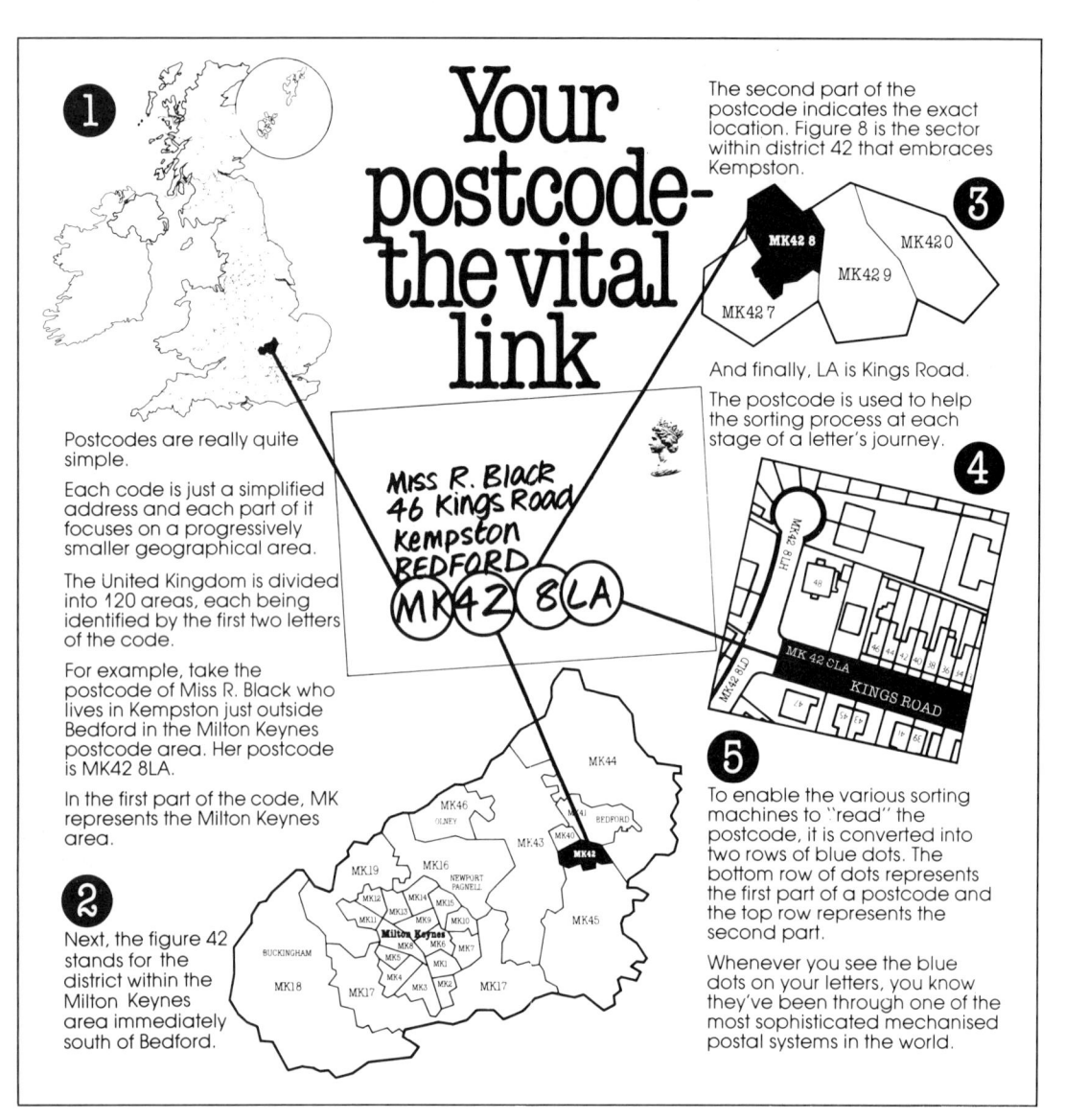

1 Postcodes are really quite simple.

Each code is just a simplified address and each part of it focuses on a progressively smaller geographical area.

The United Kingdom is divided into 120 areas, each being identified by the first two letters of the code.

For example, take the postcode of Miss R. Black who lives in Kempston just outside Bedford in the Milton Keynes postcode area. Her postcode is MK42 8LA.

In the first part of the code, MK represents the Milton Keynes area.

2 Next, the figure 42 stands for the district within the Milton Keynes area immediately south of Bedford.

3 The second part of the postcode indicates the exact location. Figure 8 is the sector within district 42 that embraces Kempston.

4 And finally, LA is Kings Road.

The postcode is used to help the sorting process at each stage of a letter's journey.

5 To enable the various sorting machines to "read" the postcode, it is converted into two rows of blue dots. The bottom row of dots represents the first part of a postcode and the top row represents the second part.

Whenever you see the blue dots on your letters, you know they've been through one of the most sophisticated mechanised postal systems in the world.

Fig. 14.2 Making sense of your postcode

● THINGS TO DO

1. Visit a head post office and ask about services to collectors of stamps and coins. Report back to your group.
2. Collect all the free Post Office brochures available. Design a wall chart to illustrate the Post Office services available to industry and commerce.
3. Research the cost of, and the process for, operating the following services: (a) registration of a letter, (b) recorded delivery, (c) Datapost, (d) bill payments, (e) Intelpost, (f) poste restante, (g) Freepost, (h) PO box numbers.
4. Research your own postcode (see Fig. 14.2). Split it down to its parts. Illustrate the use of each part.
5. Ask at your local town hall whether there are any shops in your area licensed to sell *game*. Visit the shop. What is game?
6. Research the current status of Girobank.

● QUESTIONS

1. How much is: (a) first-class, and (b) second-class letter post or package post? What weight can be sent for these amounts? What is the additional cost of (a) recorded delivery, (b) special delivery and (c) registered post? What are the advantages of each?
2. What new services have in recent years been introduced by the Post Office suitable for use by: (a) the general public, and (b) industry and commerce?
3. What postal services are in general use by commercial firms in your area? Design a questionnaire to research the answers of (say) four such firms with which your school or college has work experience links. Ask if representatives of your group can interview a member of staff.
4. Do you feel that there is a service not offered by the Post Office to the general public that would be of benefit to commercial organisations? Give reasons for your answer.

UNIT 14·2
Telecommunications

British Telecom
Formerly part of the Post Office, British Telecom was privatised in 1984. It is now owned by shareholders and is part of the private sector of industry. When it was part of the Post Office, Telecom had a *monopoly* of telephone communication (i.e. there were no competing suppliers). This is not now the case, and competition comes from Mercury Communications (see below).

The telephone system
The Post Office handles written communication, both for private individuals and for the business sector. BT in the same way maintains a network of 21 million subscribers linked by the telephone lines, radio signals and satellites. Customers make more than 50 million calls every day both in Britain and to 200 other countries abroad. Many countries can be dialled direct using *subscriber trunk dialling* (STD) or *international subscriber dialling* (ISD).

Satellites
Telecommunications satellites are launched by rocket and placed in permanent orbit around the Earth. They pick up energy from the Sun using solar panels and contain sophisticated microcomputer elements, which can be switched on and off by signals from dish aerials on Earth. Overcoming the curvature of the Earth, radio signals travelling in a straight line can be beamed up to the satellite and directed back to a second dish receiver on the ground. Both sound and pictures are transmitted in this way.

Satellite services to and from Britain are provided by stations at Goonhilly Down (Cornwall), Madely (Hereford) and the London Teleport. Telstar, the first active communications satellite, was launched in 1962 to transmit television pictures across the Atlantic.

Telecommunication services
British Telecom provides many services for business users. Written messages, pictures, photographs, facsimile copies of documents, plans and drawings can be transmitted from one subscriber to another anywhere in the world, using special equipment. This consists of duplicating equipment activated by electronic impulse transmitted over telephone links. By this method good-quality copies can be transmitted instantly to one receiver or a network of subscribers.

International television links are maintained and transmitted by satellite. Share prices from Wall Street in New York (say) can be instantly available to share dealers in the City of London. Television conferences can be arranged linking people in several countries by sound and vision.

Fig. 14.3 Telecom Tower in London

Prestel, Ceefax and Oracle
These are *teletext* sevices which use the normal domestic television system to relay commercial and leisure information to subscribers owning suitably adapted sets. You may be able to 'page' Ceefax and Oracle in your own home on a suitably adapted set so as to become familiar with the information available. Ceefax and Oracle are free services (operated by the BBC and Independent Television companies respectively) offering information like a newspaper.

Prestel is different in that it is at present primarily an information service for business users, enabling them to contact other subscribers offering commercial services in which they are interested. A charge is made for each 'page' consulted, and customers are sent a quarterly bill, like a normal telephone account.

Using Prestel, you can order theatre tickets and book a holiday or a business flight to Brazil. Eventually, householders using Prestel will be able to order groceries, choose clothes from a television mail-order catalogue or send a visual birthday card to an aunt in Australia, receiving a bill each month similar to the ones sent by credit card companies. Ultimately, by dialling in your bank account number, that account will automatically be debited with the amount of your purchase.

Fig. 14.4 Mercury's London Docklands satellite station for receiving transatlantic calls

Commerical radio links and cellular phones

These radio links are provided by British Telecom. They allow individuals (for example, taxi drivers, sales representatives) to be linked by radio pager with their base. A *page* can be a 'bleep' or a speaker system. Cellular phones (an in-car service) are gaining in popularity among business people on the move (see Unit 1, section 1.4, on *cellular phones*).

Mercury Communications

Mercury is an independent telecommunications company in direct competition with British Telecom. It provides an alternative service for business users only, mainly in London and around Birmingham (Fig. 14.5).

Mercury uses some BT lines and satellite links, but has laid its own cables of hair-thin glass fibres alongside railway lines to main towns. The system provides all the services offered by BT.

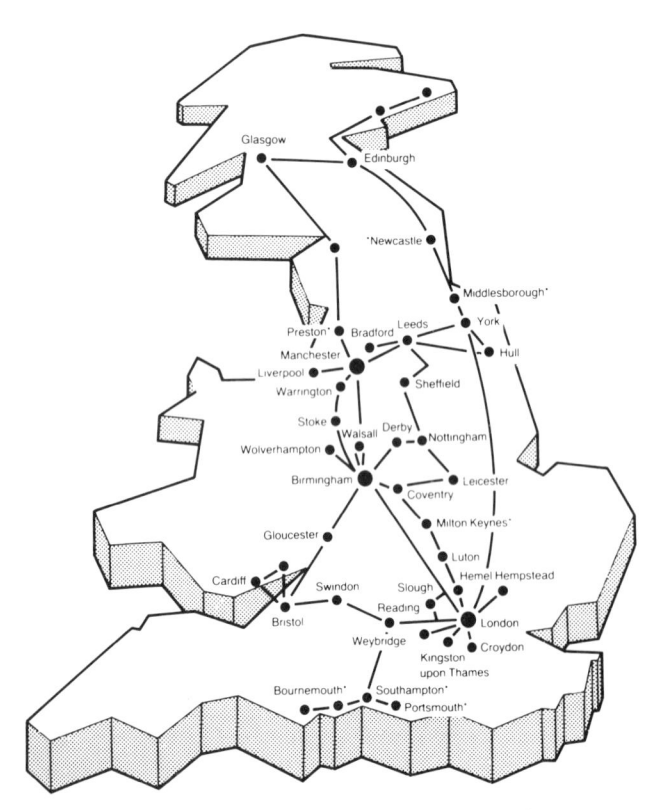

Fig. 14.5 The present Mercury telecommunications network

●SOURCES OF INFORMATION

1 British Telecom Education Service, BT Centre, Floor B4, 81 Moorgate Street, London EC1A 7AJ
2 British Telecom Education Service, PO Box 10, Wetherby, West Yorks LS23 7EL
3 Telecom Technology Showcase, 135 Victoria Street, London EC4V 4AT

4 British Telecom Museums in Oxford and Norwich – see Yellow Pages.
5 Goonhilly Satellite Earth Station, Helston, Cornwall TR12 6LQ
6 Mercury Communications, 90 Long Acre, London WC2E 9RA

●THINGS TO DO

1 'Page' Oracle and Ceefax. Make a list of the main subject pages available. Compare the information and give reasons for any differences you identify.
2 Arrange a demonstration of Prestel. Find out how a business person might use the information and services available.
3 Write to the addresses above for details of: (a) Post Fax; (b) Telex-Plus; (c) Datel; (d) Telemessages; (e) Intelfax; (f) Intelpost/Bureaufax. How would each be used in a modern office?
4 Have a look for the following in the front pages of your local phone book (a) Recipeline; (b) Challengeline; (c) Discline; (d) Sportsline; (e) Timeline; (f) Weatherline. Do you feel that these services are of real use to the general public? Give reasons for your answers.

●QUESTIONS

1 Using your local phone book, research the times for *peak*, *standard*, and *cheap* telephone calls. Using this information, what *three* factors influence the cost of a telephone call?
2 What are the ISD (international subscriber dialling) codes for: (a) Brussels (Belgium); (b) Bombay (India); (c) Dallas (Texas, USA); (d) Oslo (Norway)?
3 You have a customer in Tasmania (Australia) who asks that you telephone her at 9.00 a.m. local time (i.e. in Tasmania). Using Fig. 14.6, at what time would you have to telephone from London to meet her request?
4 Again using Fig. 14.6, you fly from London Heathrow to New York on a Concorde flight which takes off at 10.00 a.m. GMT taking three hours for the journey. At what time will you land at Kennedy Airport?

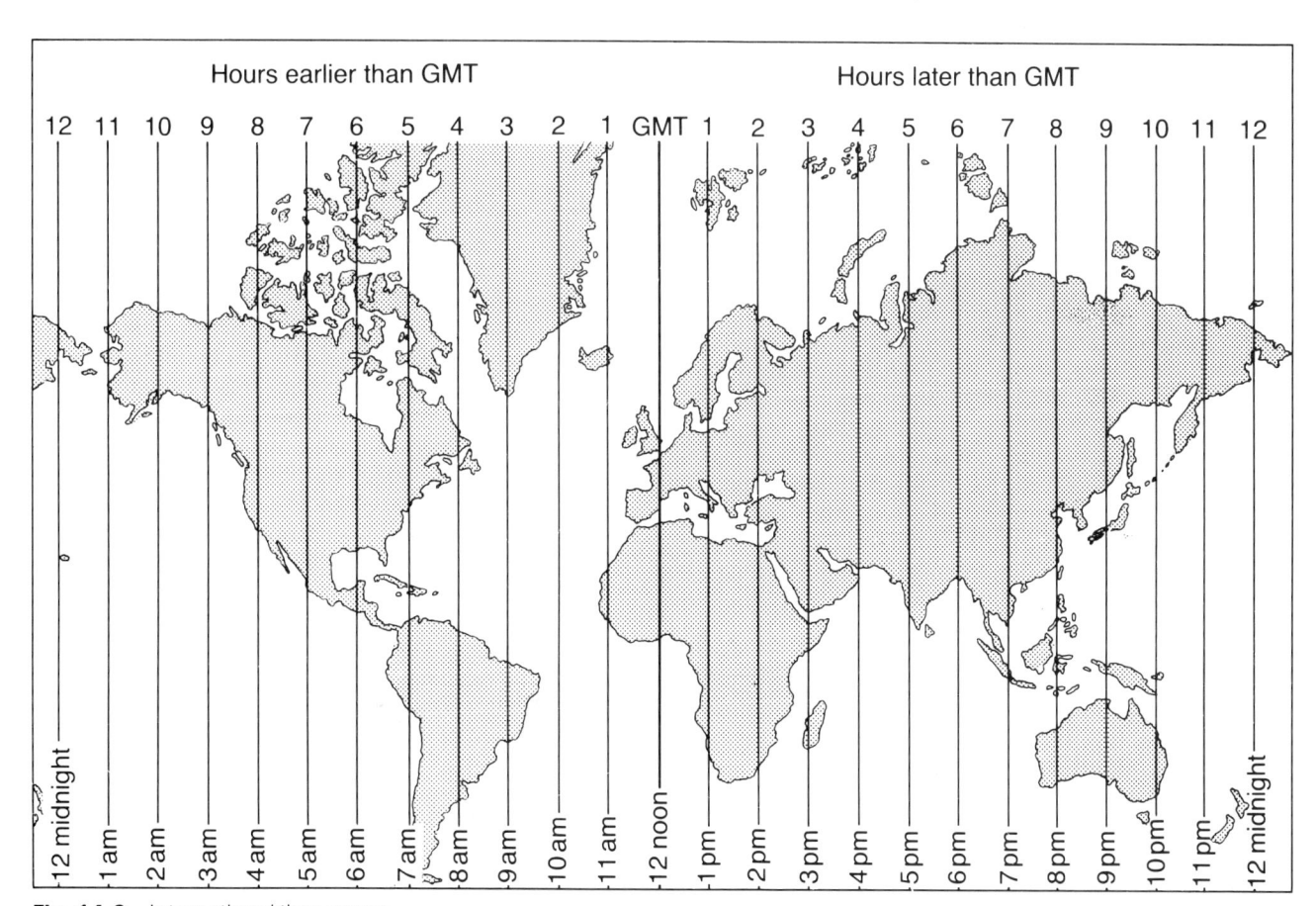

Fig. 14.6 International time zones

15 CONSUMER PROTECTION

UNIT 15.1
The Buying Public

The need for protection

We speak of the 'general public' as though it were an organized body of people who always make sensible consumer decisions, armed with the full facts about possible alternatives, quality, relative prices and their rights. Nothing could be further from the truth. We are all members of the 'general public': individual customers and shoppers looking for a bargain. We are often badly informed and hardly ever organised as a group.

The business world, on the other hand, *is* organised. In any case where a consumer makes a complaint, businesses are well aware of the law as it affects buying and selling, and they have lawyers on hand. Members of the general public are therefore often unable or unwilling to press a claim for compensation.

Codes of practice and voluntary protection

But all this does not mean that members of the public are unprotected. Most traders will act quickly to satisfy a customer who has a real complaint. Trade organisations often have a *code of fair practice*. If you wish to belong to that organisation, you must observe its code. One such trade organisation is the National House Building Council, which has minimum standards of workmanship in house-building. Agents of this Council inspect houses while they are being built. A builder who is a member can then give a purchaser a ten-year guarantee against defects, which will be put right without cost to the owner.

Many manufacturers try hard to protect consumers' rights. It is in the manufacturer's interest to have satisfied customers – they return and buy again. (See also *guarantees and warranties*, below.) Because manufacturers *brand* their goods, the public can shop with confidence in a name which is nationally advertised and well known.

Many carpets, for example, carry a manufacturer's label giving details of the materials from which the carpet is made and advice as to use (e.g. bedroom quality or hard-wearing, suitable for a lounge). Most foods carry 'sell by' date stamps, so shoppers can confirm that food is fresh.

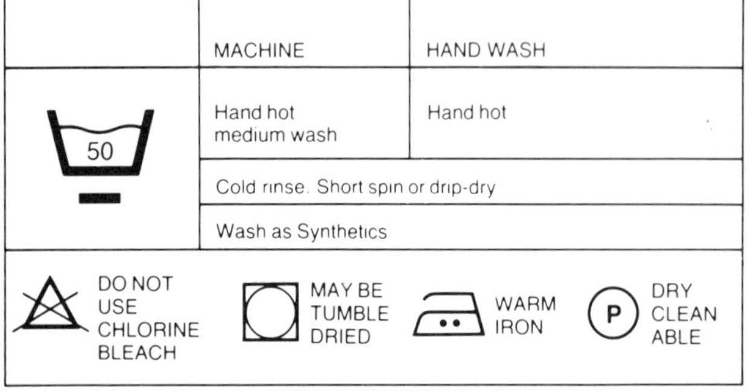

	MACHINE	HAND WASH	
50	Hand hot medium wash	Hand hot	
	Cold rinse. Short spin or drip-dry		
	Wash as Synthetics		
DO NOT USE CHLORINE BLEACH	MAY BE TUMBLE DRIED	WARM IRON	P DRY CLEAN ABLE

Fig. 15.1 Fabric label giving washing instructions

Clothes, blankets, sheets and curtains are sold with washing instructions (Fig. 15.1), while other products have carefully worded advice as to use, especially medicines, soap powders and cosmetics. All clothes and some shoes carry labels on the materials used (e.g. '30 per cent cotton, 70 per cent polyester', or 'leather sole, synthetic upper'); these allow shoppers to judge quality and durability prior to purchase.

Protection by law

Despite the voluntary protection just discussed, the public needs some *legal* protection. Many laws now govern the sale of goods and outline the shopper's rights against the seller in case of dispute. Cases in the courts are often reported in the newspapers. These laws, known as *consumer protection legislation*, include the following acts.

The Sale of Goods Act 1893 requires that goods offered are: (1) of marketable quality; (2) as described, and (3) fit for the purpose for which they are sold. This means that shoddy goods should not appear on the market. If you clearly rely on the experience and expertise of the salesperson, you will have a claim against the seller if an article turns out to be unfit for the purpose for which it is bought.

The following Acts brought the original Sale of Goods Act up to date: *The Supply of Goods (Implied Terms) Act 1973*; *The Sale of Goods Act 1979*, and *The Supply of Goods and Services Act 1982*. If a customer makes known the *use* to which goods are to be put, the goods must be reasonably suitable for that purpose.

The Trade Descriptions Acts 1968–1972 legislate against a supplier who offers misleading information or a false description in the sale of a product. For example, holiday firms have had to pay compensation for misleading their clients when hotels have been unfinished or lacking the amenities described in the holiday brochure. Manufacturers now need to be more careful in labelling their products and in giving advice: a well-known cosmetics company was prosecuted for misrepresenting one of its products. A motor dealer was prosecuted for describing a second-hand car as a 'good little runner'. The car was later found to have serious defects, and the purchaser maintained that he had been misled by the enthusiasm of the salesman; the contract was declared void (not valid), and the firm was fined.

Goods manufactured abroad usually have the country of origin clearly indicated.

The Food and Drugs Act 1955 specifies what may or may not be added to food and the circumstances under which food and drugs may be manufactured and sold. The use of essences, colouring and artificial additives is strictly controlled, while some artificial sweeteners are not now used because they were found to be harmful. A customer can reasonably complain if he or she finds dirt or other matter in food, and the public health inspector will help with any complaints. In certain cases compensation may be claimed.

Even though drug companies are careful with their research, one drug – Thalidomide – caused the birth of deformed children after it had been prescribed to pregnant women as a mild tranquilliser. Subsequent court action led to agreed damages of millions of pounds.

Weights and measures

Local authority inspectors are authorised to sample products, mainly for correct measure. These inspectors regulary inspect and test shopkeepers' scales and publicans' measures. They can also take samples of goods for analysis and report. A prosecution would be the responsibility of the local authority.

In one famous case, following a complaint by a member of the public that he had received less than a pint of beer, the High Court held that a pint consisted of liquid and froth. Provided both filled the glass to the mark, the correct measure had been sold. On all *prepacked* foods the weight must be shown – a clear help in shopping.

Dangerous substances

All dangerous substances (e.g. bleach) must be properly labelled, and warnings as to use must be displayed on the package. Packaging (cartons, bottles, etc.) must also be leak-proof and child-proof. Government regulations, having the force of law, cover the use of foam fillings used in furnishing, particularly those manufactured for children.

European Community regulations

Food regulations of the European Community are more rigid than those in Britain. When these regulations are fully adopted here, as they will have to be, artificial essences and colouring in foods will be banned.

Consumer Credit Acts

Legal protection is provided on goods and services covered by any agreement to supply on credit terms. For more details, see Unit 10, section 10.2.

'Caveat emptor'

In general the law requires that the buyer takes every care when purchasing. *Caveat emptor* ('let the buyer beware') is the legal term used. You should use common sense when buying goods or services. If you don't, you may lose your right to replacement or compensation.

Guarantees and warranties

For our purpose the difference between a guarantee and a warranty may be ignored. All of us will have bought goods, particularly electrical goods, where a written guarantee is given (see Fig. 15.2). The purchaser usually has to fill in his or her name and address, together with details of date and place of purchase, and post it to the manufacturer.

Before 1973 it was not always realised that the completion of a guarantee or the acceptance of a warranty could often *reduce* a buyer's legal rights. The Supply of Goods Act 1973 now ensures that the signing of a guarantee card does not reduce the customer's rights; cards now often give extra protection over and above that provided by law. Those sections of a guarantee which attempt to reduce a customer's rights are null and void (not valid).

●SOURCES OF INFORMATION

1. Health and Safety Executive, St Hugh's House, Stanley Precinct, Bootle, Merseyside L20 3QY
2. National House Building Council, 58 Portland Place, London W1N 4BU
3. Advertising Standards Authority, 15–17 Ridgemount Street, London WC1E 7AW
4. Any town hall – contact the trading standards department.
5. Open University, Parsifal College, 527 Finchley Road, London NW3 7BQ, for learning materials on consumer protection.

Miele
GUARANTEE

This appliance is of excellent quality and construction. We will correct, free of charge, any defects in material or workmanship for a period of one year, subject to the terms of our Guarantee shown below.

CONDITIONS AND TERMS OF THE GUARANTEE

This Guarantee provides benefits which are additional to, and do not affect, your other legal rights.

Miele will repair free of charge any appliance supplied by Miele and located in the United Kingdom or repair or replace any part or parts thereof which are shown to the satisfaction of Miele to be defective due to faulty materials or workmanship within 12 months from the date of purchase (or 6 months where domestic appliances have in Miele's opinion been used for commercial purposes). Any part or parts removed will become the property of Miele.

THIS GUARANTEE SHALL NOT COVER ANY FAULT OR DEFECT CAUSED BY:

(a) faulty installation arising e.g. from failure to observe the instructions of Miele;
(b) careless operating, handling or misuse, e.g. using unsuitable detergents, lack of maintenance;
(c) external sources e.g. transit damage, weather; or,
(d) repairs or alterations carried out by parties other than Miele or an authorised agent.

This Guarantee shall not apply to nor cover any other claims whatsoever. It will in particular (but without limiting the generality of the foregoing) not cover any claims for conversion or modification or for the costs of repairs carried out by any third party without the prior consent of Miele. Before free service under this Guarantee can be provided the purchaser will be required to substantiate the date of purchase.

If replacement parts are fitted to any appliance this will not extend the period under this Guarantee.

Fig. 15.2 A manufacturer's guarantee

●THINGS TO DO

1. In a supermarket, look for 'sell by' dates, sometimes shown as 'best before' dates. Do you feel that this information is of use to the public? In your view what protection does such labelling offer to the public?
2. All the clothes in your home will have washing instructions (Fig. 15.1). As a class, examine as many examples as possible to discover how clear such instructions are. Do you feel the symbols could be simplified even further to assist people in the understanding of printed instructions?
3. Most families have a collection of warranties or guarantees (Fig. 15.2) given on purchase, especially for electrical goods. Examine some. What protection do you think warranties and guarantees offer? Are the instructions as to claims clear and easily understood.
4. Identify the tags shown in Fig. 15.3 and say what form of consumer protection each represents.
5. Make a study of the methods used to display weights and measures (say at a petrol station, a grocery or a DIY store). Consider the use of metric measure alongside standard British (Imperial) measure (pounds, pints, feet, etc.). Do you find the lack of standard display confusing? If so, what would your group suggest to an MP as the next Act of Parliament regulating this display?

Fig. 15.3

UNIT 15.2
Consumer Protection in Action

First of all the general public must be prepared to protect themselves. The law requires that they take the utmost care (*caveat emptor*, see section 15.1) before agreeing to any purchase. Even so, it is recognised that people need the protection of the law, they need someone to enforce the law, they need organisations which will give assistance when difficulties arise and they need the government to give a lead in setting standards of honesty in business.

Fair trading

It is now firmly established that the remedy for defective goods is with the supplier, not the manufacturer. Similarly with a service rendered: repairs, house painting, laundry work, dry cleaning and hairdressing are all covered by the various Acts described (see section 15.1). In the case of shoddy work, the remedy lies with the person who performed the service and not with the manufacturer of the paint or hair lotion used – though there may also be a good case for action against both.

The Director-General of Fair Trading

The Director-General heads the *Office of Fair Trading*. This body has responsibility for advising the government on matters of consumer protection and on business practices which work against the interests of the general public. For example, the Director-General has investigated advertising methods and the validity of warranties and guarantees. In both cases the findings led to a change in the law. The Director-General has also investigated the protection offered by hire purchase agreements and has the duty to superintend the working of the Consumer Credit Acts.

Trading standards officers

Although the Director-General has a staff to assist, the monitoring of the consumer protection Acts is managed through *trading standards officers* based in the town hall. Weights and measures and sampling have already been mentioned. Officers also investigate complaints about defective goods, shoddy work and polluted food, arranging tests on materials and substances thought not to be of the standard suggested. Prosecution for any offence may well follow.

Ombudsmen and advice centres

Several commercial groupings like banks and insurance companies have set up a complaints procedure through which customers can settle disputes. These referees are called *ombudsmen*, a Scandinavian term for individuals who act as 'watchdogs' to ensure fair play.

Consumer advice centres are also run by local authorities. They offer objective advice on the availability of goods and current prices.

The British Standards Institute

The *British Standards Institute* (BSI) is a voluntary body which sets minimum manufacturing standards for producers of a wide variety of goods. Flameproof materials and crash-helmets are obvious examples where minimum standards of safety are set in the public interest. Companies which observe the codes of practice agreed with the BSI are allowed to display the BSI's *kite mark* as a guarantee of quality, safety and performance.

The BSI maintains contacts with similar organisations in the European Community in an attempt to establish international standards.

The Consumers' Association

This voluntary organisation constantly tests different ranges of products (from washing-machines and hi-fi to breathalysers). It seeks to expose faults, list advantages and disadvantages and determine a best buy at a given price. The results of these tests are publicised through press and TV and also published in *Which?*, the Consumers' Association's Magazine, which is sent to Association members (Fig. 15.4).

Professional and trade organisations

Many trades and professions agree voluntary codes for their members to set a standard to ensure fair trading (see section 15.1). For example, the Independent Broadcasting Authority, the Retail Standards Authority, the Association of British Travel Agents, the British Toy Manufacturers' Association and the Association of Estate Agents all set codes of practice which members are expected to follow.

Government agencies maintain 'watchdog' committees to which the general public can complain: e.g. British Rail has the Transport Users' Consultative Council; the Post Office has the Post Office Users' Council; and the electricity boards have the Electricity Consultative Council.

Radio, television and newspapers

All three mass media run consumer protection services for their audience or readers, for example *That's Life* and *Watchdog* on BBC TV or *4 What It's Worth* on Channel 4. Some of these programmes and articles expose the tricks practised by 'con-artists' to cheat people of their money. Others draw public attention to shoddy goods and how to spot them; or they advise people of their rights and the available methods of seeking fair treatment.

Most newspapers and magazines belong to the *Mail-Order Protection Scheme*. This scheme protects readers from dishonest advertisers and from dissatisfaction with the goods they offer for sale.

Remedies and how to obtain them

If you have a complaint, go and see the supplier. In most cases the retailer will exchange the article or arrange for repair. In the case of a service, most firms will be ready to put things right, because they rely upon a reputation for honesty and good work.

Where satisfaction cannot be obtained you might first try the Trading Standards Offices or the Public Health Department (contaminated food or drink) at the *town hall*. They might also help where you feel that you have been misled by advertising, faulty labelling or a shopkeeper's advice.

If this is unsuccessful, your next call might be a *Citizens' Advice Bureau*. Your local office will be listed in the telephone directory. CABs offer free advice on consumer affairs and, if all else fails, may direct you to a solicitor and arrange for legal aid.

Justice and the courts

Seeking compensation through the courts can be a costly business, and the judgement of a court may not necessarily be in your favour. *Small claims courts*, attached to the county court, provide an informal atmosphere in which disputes can be settled quickly and

CD players

Players picked out in coloured bands are recommended in the Buying Guide, p185.	target price £	size hxwxd cm	track access	displays	programming	repeat	other features	error correction	shock resistance	player	remote control	noise of operation
Denon DCD-600	250	10x43x32	EJ	HLMNO	15 PQRS	UV	aceh					
Fisher AD-M67 [6]	180	9x34x35	CE	K	16 PR	UV	e					
Hitachi DA-009	250	8x43x28	ACDFJ	HKLMNO	24 PRST	UVX	acehj					
JVC XL-V250	190	8x44x29	FJ	H	15 PR	UV	eh					
Kenwood DP-860	200	9x42x26	AEJ	H	20 PQR	UV	aeh					
Marantz CD-273	190	8x32x33	CI	HKLN	20 QR	UV						
Onkyo DX-130	230	9x44x36	F	HLMN	16 PQR	UV	e					
Philips CD207 [6]	170	7x28x25	IJ	H	20 QR	UV	fhj					
Philips CD371	170	8x32x33	I	HK	20 QR	UV	eh					
Philips CD373	240	8x32x33	CDI	HK	20 QRY	UV	abcehj					
Pioneer PD-4050	180	8x42x33	GJ		16 P	UV	e					
Sharp DX-150H	180	8x33x30	F[1]J	H	20 PR	UV	e					
Sony CDP-M20	180	8x36x31	GJ	HKLN	16 PQRT	UVW	eh					
Technics SL-P111 [7]	180	8x43x27	FJ	HLMN	20 PQR	UV	e					
Technics SL-P220 [8]	230	8x43x29	FJ	HLMNO	20 PQRS[4]	UV	abcehj					
Yamaha CDX-700 [6]	300	11x44x39	ACDFJ	HKLNO	24 PQRT	UVWX	aehj					
MULTI-DISC PLAYERS												
Pioneer PD-M50	280	8x42x32	A[4]GJ	HM	32 PTZ	UV	acdfhj					
Sharp DX-C6010	350	11x43x32	AF [1]	HLN	32 PQRT	UV	acdfhp					
Sony CDP-C5M	350	11x36x42	EJ	HKLM	32 PRT	UVW	adehj					
MINI PORTABLES												
Sanyo CP12	260	3x13x13	G	HL	16 P	UVW	a[2]fhjkmn		[5]		[5]	
Sony D100	300	3x13x13	G	HLN	21 TP	UWX	a[3]thjk[3]mn		[5]		[5]	
Technics SL-XP5	250	4x13x13	F	HLO	18 PQ	UV	fhjm		[5]			
Toshiba XR-9437 [6]	250	5x14x16	E	HL	16 P	UV	fhjkln		[5]			

All the players tested are made in Japan except the Marantz and Philips models (Belgium).

Key to features

Track access
All models have 'next' and 'previous' track selection.
- A = direct access keypad
- C = index point access from 'stop'
- D = index point access from 'play'
- J = pause cueing (see text)
- E = one-speed fast search with sound
- F = two-speed fast search with sound – speeds up automatically
- G = two-speed fast search with sound in play, without in pause
- I = three-speed fast search, two with sound, speeds up automatically

Displays
All models show number of the track playing. Others include:
- H = elapsed time of track being played
- K = display of index points
- L = total disc time left
- M = total track time left
- N = total programme time left
- O = 'calendar' type display permanently shows track numbers in memory

Programming
- P = track can be programmed more than once
- Q = programme review in 'play'
- R = programme review in 'stop' or 'pause'

- S = corrections can be made during play
- T = random play
- Y = favourite track selection FTS – see text
- Z = can sample each track while building up programme

Repeat
- U = whole disc
- V = programmed tracks
- W = track being played
- X = A-B repeat (see text)

Other features
- a = remote control unit
- b = volume adjustable by remote control
- c = programming by remote control
- e = drawer can be 'nudged' closed
- f = drawer must be closed by hand
- h = headphone socket
- j = headphone volume variable
- k = can run on ordinary batteries as well as supplied battery pack
- l = FM/AM radio and digital clock
- m = carrying case
- n = in-ear type phones supplied
- p = single disc tray as well as six-disc holder

KEY TO RATINGS	▨	▧	☐	▨	■
	best	←		→	worst

[1] Fast search in pause mode only
[2] Remote control linked by cable
[3] With optional accessory
[4] Using remote control
[5] Rating of portables not directly comparable to other players
[6] Being discontinued but should still be in shops
[7] To be replaced by similar SLP200
[8] To be replaced by similar SLP250

Similar models
These are models similar to those we've tested but with a different cabinet width (see 'Size') or features like remote control.
JVC XL-V 450 £230: like XL-V250 with remote control
Kenwood DP-460 £170: like DP-860 without remote control
Philips CD471 £180: like CD371 but 42cm wide
Philips CD472 £200: like CD371 but 42cm wide and remote control
Philips CD473 £250: like CD373 but 42cm wide
Pioneer PD-5050 £200: like PD-4050 but has headphone socket, extra display and programming features
Pioneer PD-M60 £350: like PD-M50 but has single disc tray and extra display features
Sony CDP-M30 £200: like CDP-M20 with remote control
Technics SL-P320 £250: like SL-P220 with features A, O.

Fig. 15.4 Survey of compact disc players in the Consumers' Association's magazine *Which?*

● 114

cheaply. Such courts do not insist on complicated paperwork, and it is not necessary to be represented by a solicitor. The presiding registrar acts as a referee, offering common-sense remedies. A real effort is made to reach an amicable agreement.

An action in the county court or High Court is not recommended unless the amount involved is substantial and you have the money to meet the costs, which could be considerable. This kind of case is best left to the larger firms and limited companies, unless you qualify for legal aid.

● SOURCES OF INFORMATION

1 Consumers' Association, Freepost, PO Box 44, Hertford SG14 1SH, and 2 Marylebone Road, London NW1 4DX
2 Office of Fair Trading, Government Buildings, Bromyard Avenue, London W3, or Field House, 15–25 Breams Buildings, London EC4A 1PR
3 Your town hall for public health officers.
4 The Ombudsman, Church House, Great Smith Street, London SW1P 3B
5 Health and Safety Executive, Regina House, 259–69 Old Marylebone Road, London NW1 5RR
6 British Standards Institution, 2 Park Street, London W1A 2BS
7 National Federation of Consumer Groups, 70–76 Alcester Road South, Birmingham B14 7PT
8 NACAB (National Association of Citizens' Advice Bureaux), 115–123 Pentonville Road, London N1 9LZ

● THINGS TO DO

1 Invite a trading standards officer to address your group, or arrange a visit to the town hall to see them.
2 You have bought a pair of 'walking boots' advertised in a newspaper as 'strong and reliable in all weathers'. They fell apart the first time you wore them in the rain. Describe what action you would take.
3 You take a pair of blue trousers to be dry-cleaned and they come back several sizes smaller and bright green. The firm points to the label which says, 'Hand wash only.' What do you do now? Would your answer be different if you had consulted the dry-cleaning manager (before leaving the trousers) on the best way of removing an ink stain and she said 'Leave it to me. They will come back as good as new'?
4 Obtain several issues of *Which?* magazine. Do you feel that the analysis given of a particular product is helpful and aids choice? If not, what additional advice would you like to see included?
5 Working in groups, write to all the national daily newspapers and ask whether the paper has any policy to ensure that the products advertised are good value for money. Ask how they try to protect their readers from unscrupulous advertisers.
6 Look at the trade organisations shown in Fig. 15.5. What kind of firm does each represent? What is contained in their codes of practice? Do you feel that these codes protect *your* interests?

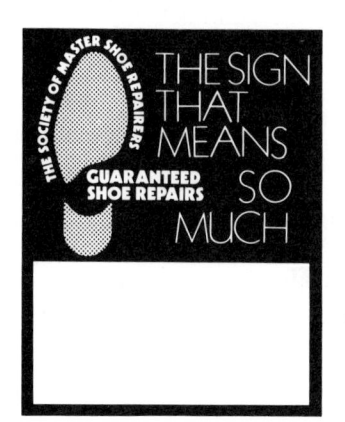

Fig. 15.5 Trade associations draw up codes of conduct

16 INTERNATIONAL TRADE

UNIT 16.1
The European Community

The European Community (also called the *Common Market*) was established on 25 March 1957, when six countries ('the Six') signed the *Treaty of Rome*: France, West Germany, Italy, Belgium, the Netherlands and Luxembourg. The Treaty allows for economic co-operation between the countries involved and in 1992 aims for increased political unity, common currency (the ECU) and a central Bank.

Britain, Denmark and the Irish Republic became full members in 1973; in 1981 Greece became the tenth member, and in 1986 Spain and Portugal signed the Treaty of Rome as the eleventh and twelfth members (Figs 16.1 and 16.2). Norway, Sweden, Austria and Turkey are in the queue.

Fig. 16.1 The European Community at a glance

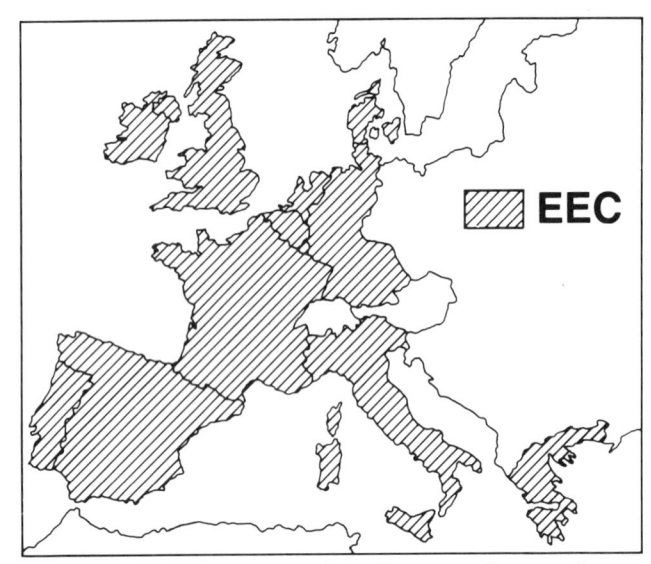

Fig. 16.2 Member nations of the European Community

Advantages of membership

Britain needs a large market for its finished goods. The present Community forms the largest trading bloc in the world (see Fig. 16.3), having a population of 320 million and a domestic market larger than the USA or the USSR. One-sixth of all our exports go to Europe, upon which 2½ million jobs depend. A person from Britain may now work freely in any country in the Community.

Developing economic and political union will make it less likely that the countries involved will engage in another war. A strong, united Europe can lessen tension, while encouraging co-operation between the superpowers.

Britain has received financial help from the Community for training and employment schemes, handicapped people, industry in Northern Ireland and protection of the environment, particularly fish stocks around the coast.

Disadvantages of membership

Community regulations oblige Britain to accept all the rules of membership. Decisions taken in Brussels (headquarters of the European Commission) affect Britain's overseas trade, regional planning, fisheries, association with non-Community countries and immigration policy. These decisions do not always favour British interests.

Britain's annual contribution to the Community's budget amounts to many millions of pounds. Contributions are used to finance European projects, of which we receive a share.

Britain has had to agree to conditions concerning trade with Commonwealth countries, from whom we received much of our food, often at advantageous prices. These countries cannot be expected to treat Britain as favourably as before if a change of Community policy affects their exports to this country.

The European Community tends to be inward looking and unaware of the real needs of the poorer nations. The *Common Agricultural Policy* (see below) has threatened to bankrupt Community finances. Some changes in agricultural support policy are essential.

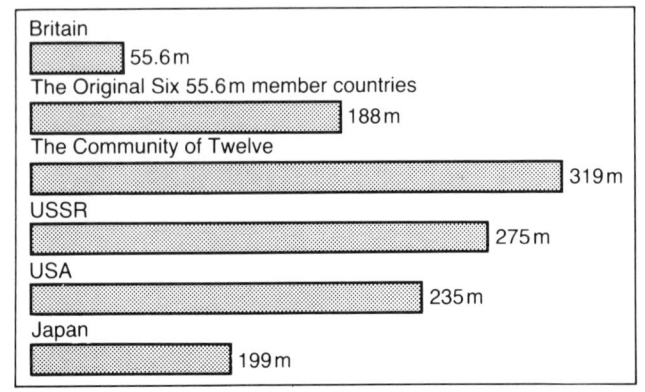

Britain 55.6m
The Original Six 55.6m member countries 188m
The Community of Twelve 319m
USSR 275m
USA 235m
Japan 199m

Fig. 16.3 Comparison of population sizes

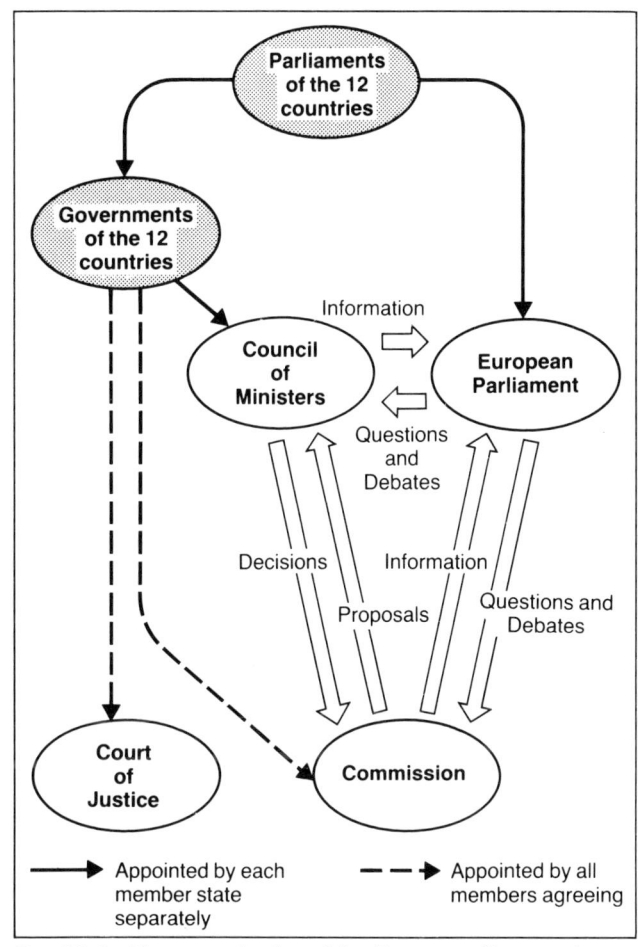

Fig. 16.4 The organisation of the European Community

Machinery of the Community

There are four institutions of the European Community: (see Fig. 16.4):

Council of Ministers This includes one member of the government from each of the twelve member states, each state in turn providing the President of the Council.

The Commission Britain is represented by two commissioners, who join similar representatives from other member countries. Each commissioner assumes responsibility for a section of Community business – agriculture, fisheries, iron and steel, etc.

Court of Justice Judges from each member country are given the task of deciding differences between member states, or between firms and individuals within them.

European Parliament 518 Members of the European Parliament (MEPs), are elected by member countries (Britain elects 81). MEPs debate Community policy and ask questions of the Commission or the Council. This body meets in Strasbourg and Luxembourg.

The Common Agricultural Policy (CAP)

The CAP's annual review of food prices is an artificial way of fixing farm prices. The review assures a reasonable return on food production, guarantees markets and restricts imports from non-Community countries.

This policy has at times gone seriously wrong and Community countries have started to look for alternatives to the large sums of money spent subsidising farmers to grow produce that nobody wants.

The Green Pound

The Green Pound is an artificial rate of exchange, favourable to Britain, which reduces the normal price of dairy produce and vegetables imported from Europe. This protects Britain from the full impact of the Common Agricultural Policy, but leaves British farmers complaining that they are receiving less for home-produced food than they could get by selling (say) beef in Belgium.

The European Monetary System (EMS)

Sometimes called *the Snake*, Britain is not yet a member of the EMS. All the other Community countries have agreed that their currencies will have values which rise and fall *together*. In theory all Community currencies (e.g. the franc, Deutschmark, guilder and lira) can then protect each other against market forces. Britain's pound is said to *float*; sometimes its value rises against other currencies and sometimes it falls, in tune with world-wide demand.

●SOURCES OF INFORMATION

1 Commissioner of the European Communities, 8 Storey's Gate, London SW1P 3AT, or Rue de la Loi 200, B1049 Brussels, Belgium, or Community member's embassy in Britain.
2 Council for Education in World Citizenship, 19–21 Tudor Street, London EC4Y 0DJ

●QUESTIONS

1 Study Fig. 16.1. Suggest why membership of the European Community is important to the economic welfare of Britain. Why is 1992 so important?
2 From Fig. 16.2, identify where each country of the European Community is. Which countries are shown unshaded? Suggest possible reasons why they are not also members of the Community.
3 From Fig. 16.3, calculate Britain's population as a percentage of the total population in the European Community.
4 Use Fig. 16.4 as a guide and research the following: (a) How many ministers serve on the Council of Ministers, and who is the current President? (b) Who are the commissioners currently representing Britain? For what are they responsible? (c) Where does the Court of Justice meet? (d) When is the next election for MEPs?

●THINGS TO DO

Write a polite letter asking your MEP to visit your group.

UNIT 16.2
Imports and Exports

Imports

Imports are all those goods and services which originate abroad and are 'consumed' in Britain.

Imported goods include raw materials (copper, nickel, etc.), food, manufactured goods (cars, electrical equipment, etc.) and wines.

Imported services include: shipping, British people's holidays abroad and dividends paid on foreign investments in Britain.

Exports

Exports are all those goods and services which originate in Britain and are 'consumed' by people abroad.

Exported goods include: manufactured goods (steel, computers, scientific instruments, aircraft and satellites), raw materials (coal, china clay, etc.) and food and drink products (e.g. whisky).

Exported services include: banking, insurance, income from tourists and dividends received from investments abroad.

Re-exports

Re-exports are goods and raw materials brought to Britain from abroad to be graded, blended, packed, etc. and then re-exported. Such goods, never intended for 'consumption' in Britain, are part of the *entrepôt trade* (see Unit 13, section 13.3, on Freeports).

Visible and invisible trade

All *goods*, imported and exported, are part of Britain's *visible* trade. All *services*, imported and exported, form Britain's *invisible* trade.

Any country importing more *goods* than it exports is said to have an adverse *balance of trade*. Britain is in this category. By comparison, Japan has a favourable balance, because it exports more goods than it imports. Britain has a deficit, Japan a surplus, on visible trade. However, Britain is able to export far more *services* than it imports, so it has a surplus of invisible trade. Adding together both visible and invisible trade gives the *balance of payments*.

Balance of payments

Before the North Sea oil boom began in the 1970s, Britain's deficit on visible trade was usually larger than its surplus on invisibles. Adding the two together produced a *balance of payments deficit*. That is, the total value of imports was larger than the total value of exports. Britain was paying out in £ sterling more than it received in foreign currency.

Then, during the boom years of North Sea oil (until the mid-1980s), Britain was able to export large amounts of oil. This improved the country's visible trade balance, and so produced a *balance of payments surplus*.

Now, in the late 1980s, Britain's oil exports are falling. Once again the balance of visible trade is firmly in deficit, and this means an overall balance of payments deficit of worrying proportions.

Imports and exports of visible goods and invisible services make up the *current account* in the calculation of the balance of payments (Fig. 16.5). In addition, all countries invest capital abroad. For example, the Japanese companies Sony and Nissan built factories in England and Wales to produce electrical goods and cars; these are *capital* investments. Britain makes similar investments overseas, and there is a balance of capital-type trade, which does not feature in the calculations involving balance of trade, balance of payments or the current account.

The City and invisible exports

Banking institutions, the stock market, the money market, commodity exchanges, the Bank of England, the Baltic Exchange and Lloyd's are all part of *the City* (see Units 9–12). These institutions do a geat deal of business for foreign governments, multinational corporations registered in Britain and abroad, shipping companies plying their trade and manufacturing/extractive industries conducting business world-wide. For these international services the city is paid in yen, francs, drachmas, dollars, rupees, etc. – in fact, in every currency and from every region of the world. The income from such services is an important part of Britain's invisible earnings.

Payment for international trade

Britain's imports have to be paid for in the currency of the country in which the goods and services originated. Wheat from the United States is paid for in dollars and electrical goods from Japan in yen. Sometimes, however, goods are priced in US dollars. For instance, crude oil, whether it comes from the North Sea, Saudia Arabia or Texas is always priced in dollars. All Britain's exports must be paid for in pounds. Dollars, francs, yen and pounds can be bought and sold on the *money markets* of the world (see Unit 10, section 10.1).

You will see from Fig. 16.6, that the number of dollars, francs and Deutschmarks you can get for £1 varies. For example, in 1976 you could buy just over 6 Swiss francs for £1. In 1986 £1 would buy only 2.29 Swiss francs. The pound bought nearly four times the number of Portuguese escudos in 1986 than it did in 1976. What are the current ratios?

Value of the £

To maintain Britain's share of overseas trade, the pound is not allowed to rise too much in value relative to other currencies. If this were to happen, Britain's exports would become too expensive for customers abroad, and our overseas trade would diminish. At the same time, imports would become cheaper and sell more readily in Britain. The balance of trade (and possibly the balance of payments) would slip 'into the red'. If the situation did not improve, Britain would become poorer compared with those countries which are able to maintain a trade surplus.

On the other hand, if the value of the pound was allowed to fall too far, this could also damage Britain's economy and trade. Imports would become so expensive that manufacturing industry would not be able to pay for the essential raw materials that it needs to buy in from abroad.

British Overseas Trade Board (BOTB)

Every government knows that selling abroad is not the easiest way of making profits. For this reason, the Department of Trade and Industry gives steady support to exporting firms. It supplies information on overseas markets, organises trade fairs and, through embassies and high commissions, helps build up a climate of trust which eases the task of marketing British goods abroad. The Board can arrange finance for an overseas order; in particular, it provides insurance for those risks that the City will not cover for a reasonable premium. In other words, the BOTB exists to smooth away problems connected with exporting, to help with paperwork and to offer business advice services overseas.

Export Credits Guarantee Department (ECGD)

This is a government agency which helps exporters with their trade. Exporters want to collect their money as quickly as possible after despatching goods but importers are unwilling to pay until the goods have actually arrived. The ECGD runs a banking system which eases these problems and assesses the credit worthiness of customers.

General Agreement on Tariffs and Trade (GATT)

In general, international free trade benefits everybody. Unfortunately some countries protect their own (domestic) industry, and exports to that country are almost impossible. This restricts the flow of trade between countries. Such countries restrict trade either by denying entry to competing goods or by applying customs duties (*tariffs*) so heavy that the goods involved become too expensive and sell badly.

GATT is an international agreement signed by 23 countries with the aim of reducing tariffs and persuading signatories to be more generous when deciding their policies on imported goods. There has been a series of international conferences to reduce tariffs and almost abolish quotas. GATT members now account for about 80% of international trade.

Methods of exporting

An export order may come from any of the following sources:

1 A long-standing association between firms.
2 Trade fairs and exhibitions in Britain and abroad.

Fig. 16.5 The balance of payments current account

3 An invitation to *tender* (quote a price) for plant, e.g. a dam, a power-station or an oil tanker.
4 Agencies abroad, as in the motor-car industry, where dealers are given a franchise to sell and maintain certain makes of cars.
5 Inquiries originating from abroad, sometimes on the recommendation of an existing customer.
6 Speculative selling abroad through agents using samples.
7 Manufacturing under licence, which arises through an agreement to set up abroad plant to manufacture goods (e.g. cars) where royalties are payable.
8 Trade delegations, often at government level, making visits abroad to arrange commercial treaties for the exchange of goods to the mutual advantage of both countries.
9 The sale of British television programmes abroad (e.g. *East Enders* and *The Benny Hill Show*).
10 Selling 'technical know-how', e.g. computer software.

●SOURCES OF INFORMATION

1 British Overseas Trade Board, Friars Bank, 52 Horseferry Road, London SW1P 2AG
2 Export Credits Guarantee Department, Aldermanbury House, Aldermanbury, London EC2P 2EL
3 Department of Trade and Industry, 1–19 Victoria Street, London SW1H 0ET
4 British Export Houses Association, 69 Cannon Street, London EC4N 5AB
5 Yellow Pages – see under 'import and export merchants'.
6 Eikis International Ltd, 3 Johnson's Court, Fleet Street, London EC4A 3EA

●THINGS TO DO

1 On your next visit to a supermarket, make a list of the countries of origin of some of the goods displayed. Look at a world map to find the position of the countries involved and trace the routes (land, sea, air) by which you think the goods reached Britain.
2 Research the reference section in your local library to discover the type of goods Britain imports from the following countries: (a) Brazil, (b) Zambia, (c) India and Pakistan, (d) Jamaica and Trinidad, (e) Sweden, (f) Japan, (g) France, (h) the USA, (i) Australia.
3 Write to a large firm in your area and ask if they export any of their manufactured goods. Or send a questionnaire to a number of local firms asking about their exports. With which countries do(es) the firm(s) involved transact business?
4 Make a survey of a local car-park. What proportion of cars are likely to have been imported and what proportion manufactured in Britain? From which country does Britain import most cars?
5 Copy out the table in Fig. 16.6. Then complete the table by filling in the *current rate* column with the current rates of exchange for the pound. Get your information from national newspapers or a local bank branch.
   Next draw a chart to illustrate the movement of the pound against any three currencies shown in the table.
6 Using Fig. 16.5, explain the *current account* and the importance of *visible* and *invisible* trade to Britain's *balance of payments*.

Foreign exchange rates since 1976	1976	1978	1980	1982	1984	1986	1988
French franc	9.71	8.28	10.56	11.96	11.90	9.21	10.60
Swiss franc	6.01	3.44	4.11	3.67	3.18	2.29	2.61
Belgian franc	82.70	58.75	73.25	83.40	79.00	57.70	65.35
Dutch guilder	5.69	4.03	4.93	4.69	4.41	3.12	3.51
Swedish kronar	9.33	8.36	10.25	12.54	11.64	9.81	10.93
Austrian Schilling	39.60	26.75	31.75	29.60	27.60	19.40	21.80
West German Deutschmarks	5.50	3.76	4.56	4.30	3.94	2.76	3.10
Italian lira	14.88	15.40	21.62	23.86	23.20	19.64	23.20
Spanish peseta	132.40	142.00	183.00	195.00	216.00	189.25	202.50
Portuguese escudo	57.80	80.00	122.00	148.00	176.00	207.00	258.00
US dollar	2.35	1.82	2.35	1.70	1.51	1.48	1.80
Greek drachma	71.14	65.50	121.00	118.00	126.00	218.00	262.00

Fig. 16.6 Value of the £ against major foreign currencies

UNIT 16.3
The Balance of Trade

In section 16.2 we saw that all those goods and services that Britain imports must be paid for with money earned from those goods and services we export to our customers abroad. Ideally, a country's trade with the rest of the world should balance or produce a small surplus (i.e. profit). Fig. 16.7 illustrates the results of Britain's trading during a period when there was a small deficit on visible trade and a smaller deficit overall once invisibles had been added.

Not every month or year is the same. During the North Sea oil boom years, Britain's trade figures improved, and the balance of payments was favourable.

Oil revenues

The big change in Britain's fortunes (as mentioned in section 16.2) was the discovery of oil in the North Sea. This transformed our export trade during the 1970s and early 1980s. World demand for oil is high, and North Sea oil is of good quality. Unfortunately, the quantity of oil recoverable from the North Sea has proved limited. Plenty is left, but extraction is becoming more difficult and costly. The benefits of oil revenues for Britain's balance of trade are starting to fall.

The terms of trade

Britain sells its exports in order to pay for the goods it needs to import: aircraft (like jumbo jets), raw materials (for manufacturing industries), fruit and vegetables (to supplement home-grown varieties), and so on. All goods have an international value, and we must ensure that our own exports compete in terms of quality and price or we will lose orders to foreign competitors. The prices we can charge for the goods we manufacture for export and the services we sell overseas are limited by *competition* from foreign suppliers.

Some of the goods Britain imports (e.g. cotton, foodstuffs, rubber and wool) are *seasonal* crops. They are affected by all the problems of weather, lack of water, fire and pests. If the coffee crop suffers from frost, the price of coffee soars. A poor rubber or cotton harvest leaves so little for sale that the price shoots up. In these circumstances the *terms of trade* have moved against the importing country, because the cost of imports has increased relative to the price that can be charged for exports. The balance of trade moves 'into the red'.

However, Britain's problem today is not that raw materials are expensive. It is rather that we import more manufactured goods than we export. Our trade with the poor countries of the world is favourable, but our trade with other rich industrialised countries, particularly within the EC, is not so successful.

The debt crisis Raw materials are mostly cheap for an industrialised country like Britain to buy. This is because these commodities are produced by poor countries in larger amounts than the rich countries want them – so the price falls. This is one of the main causes of the *debt crisis* of the poor countries. *They* are the ones that suffer from unfavourable terms of trade when they want to buy expensive machinery from Europe or the USA. They have to borrow in order to exist, and struggle to repay.

Multinational corporations

See also Unit 1, section 1.3. Decisions made by these giant corporations on where to expand manufacturing or where to cease manufacturing have an enormous effect on a country's balance of trade. Ford makes gear-boxes in South Wales and exports these to car plants all over Europe thus helping our balance of payments. When Chrysler (now Peugeot) stopped making cars at Linwood, near Glasgow, this had a very bad effect on local employment and on the balance of trade.

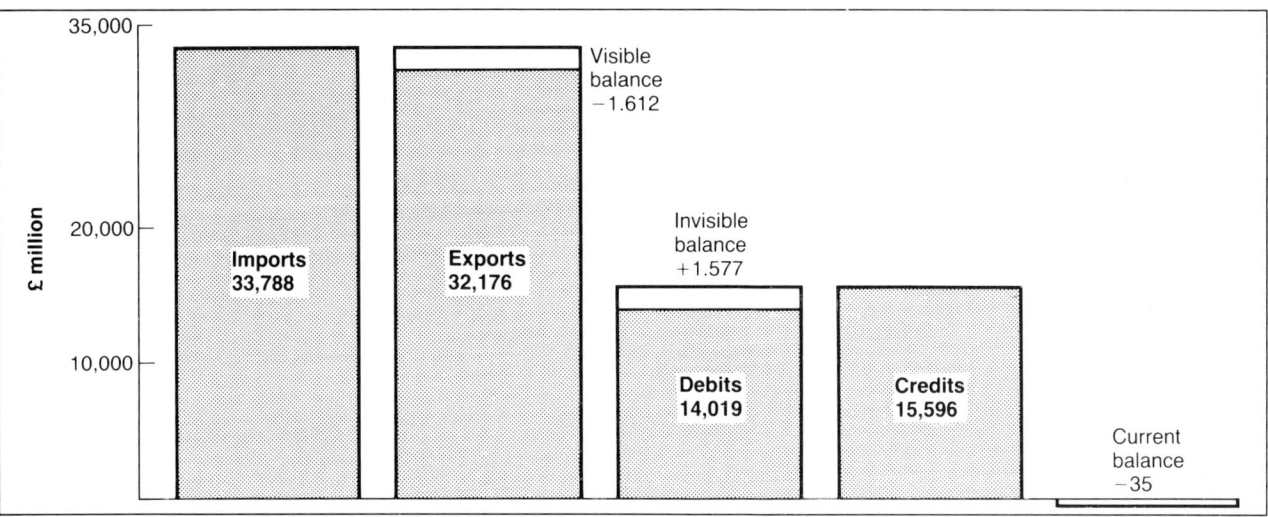

Fig. 16.7 An example of Britain's current account during one period of trading

Imports 33,788
Exports 32,176
Visible balance −1.612
Invisible balance +1.577
Debits 14,019
Credits 15,596
Current balance −35

Specialisation and diversification

Britain is basically a manufacturing country, but also has a strong agricultural industry. The City of London is one of the world's leading centres, providing invisible earnings from shipping, banking and insurance. The tourist trade is also a major earner of foreign currency. We are said to have a *diversified economy*, because we do not rely on any one industry for overseas earnings.

All countries produce what they are best at with the resources they have. Some countries are largely agricultural, producing dairy goods, fruit and vegetables, meat, animal hides and wool. Others – mostly the poorest countries – rely upon a single, usually primary, industry, like copper, sugar, rubber or cocoa. These countries are said to have *specialised economies*. The wealthier industrialised countries like Britain, with a diversified economy, have a distinct economic advantage, particularly with the terms of trade.

Government statistics

The figures to calculate the balance of trade and the balance of payments are collected from returns made to the Department of Trade and Industry. The *statistics* (figures) that are available from ports and airports give the values of goods imported and exported. The City makes separate returns of commercial services done for overseas customers and the invisible earnings which result. Figures are published monthly by the government, and the annual figures give an overall indication of a year's trading.

Gold and foreign reserves

The government has a reserve of gold and foreign currency in the vaults of the Bank of England. If we have a balance of payments deficit, then gold and foreign reserves will diminish as we pay our debts abroad. But a surplus will mean that gold and foreign currency will flow into Britain to the value of the surplus, and our reserves will increase.

●SOURCES OF INFORMATION

1. Department of Trade and Industry, 1–19 Victoria Street, London SW1H 0ET
2. BP Exploration Ltd, Britannic House, Moor Lane, London EC2Y 9BU
3. BP Educational Service, Britannic House, Moor Lane, London EC2Y 9BU
4. Crown Agents, 4 Millbank, London SW1P 3JD

●THINGS TO DO

1. Research the countries of origin of goods in a discount warehouse. Is there any pattern to your findings?
2. Write to BP (British Petroleum) to inquire about oil exploration, particularly in the North Sea. Make a chart of the existing oil rigs. Which other companies are involved?

●QUESTIONS

Answer the following questions using Fig. 16.7:

1. Why did Britain have an adverse balance of trade during the period in question? What was the amount of that deficit?
2. Was the *invisible* balance a surplus or a deficit?
3. What was the position on the balance of *payments* over the period in question? Was Britain in deficit or surplus?
4. If the current balance shown were repeated over each month of that year, what would the deficit on the balance of payments amount to at the end of the year?
5. How would that deficit be covered?

UNIT 16·4
Documentation

Sending goods half-way across the world requires care. The paperwork is complicated and consists of the following:

1. *Bill of lading* (usually prepared in sets of four)   This is the contract between the exporter and the shipowner for the carriage of goods by sea or air. One copy is kept by the exporter, another copy goes to the shipper, and two copies are sent to the customer so that he or she can claim the cargo at destination (Fig. 16.9).
2. *The manifest*   This is a list of the total cargo carried by any one ship or aircraft and is a summary of all the bills of lading.
3. *Consular invoices*   Some countries require special invoices to be certified by their embassy for customs or health purposes.
4. *Certificate of insurance*   This is a policy (usually prepared at Lloyd's) to cover the cargo in transit by sea or air.
5. *Certificate of origin*   This describes the goods and their country of manufacture or origin.
6. *Customs declaration*   Goods imported into a country are usually subject to customs and/or excise duties. This document details the goods and quotes their value.
7. *Import licence*   This may be needed for dangerous substances or goods restricted by regulation.
8. *Bill of exchange*   This is a promise to pay a given sum when presented (Fig. 16.8; see also Unit 10, section 10.1, on *acceptance houses*).

An exporter normally uses an *insurance broker* to arrange the policy of insurance, and a *shipping agent* to book the necessary transport and prepare the paperwork. A bank will arrange a suitable method of payment.

Method of payment

No exporter will dispatch goods without being satisfied about payment. The third copy of the bill of lading is the document used to prove *title* (ownership) of the consignment of goods, and the goods on board ship will not be handed over to the importer until he or she produces that bill. The exporter will not release the bill until he or she has been paid or agreement is reached about finance.

Payment may be arranged through a bank with overseas branches. The important bill of lading can be sent airmail, together with other necessary documents, while the consignment is at sea. The bank will then arrange to release the bill of lading only when payment is made. With the bill the importer can claim the goods, and the transaction is complete.

Banks may agree to finance an export/import transaction just as they may extend credit to any other business deal. Governments also guarantee payment in approved cases (e.g. via the Export Credits Guarantee Department).

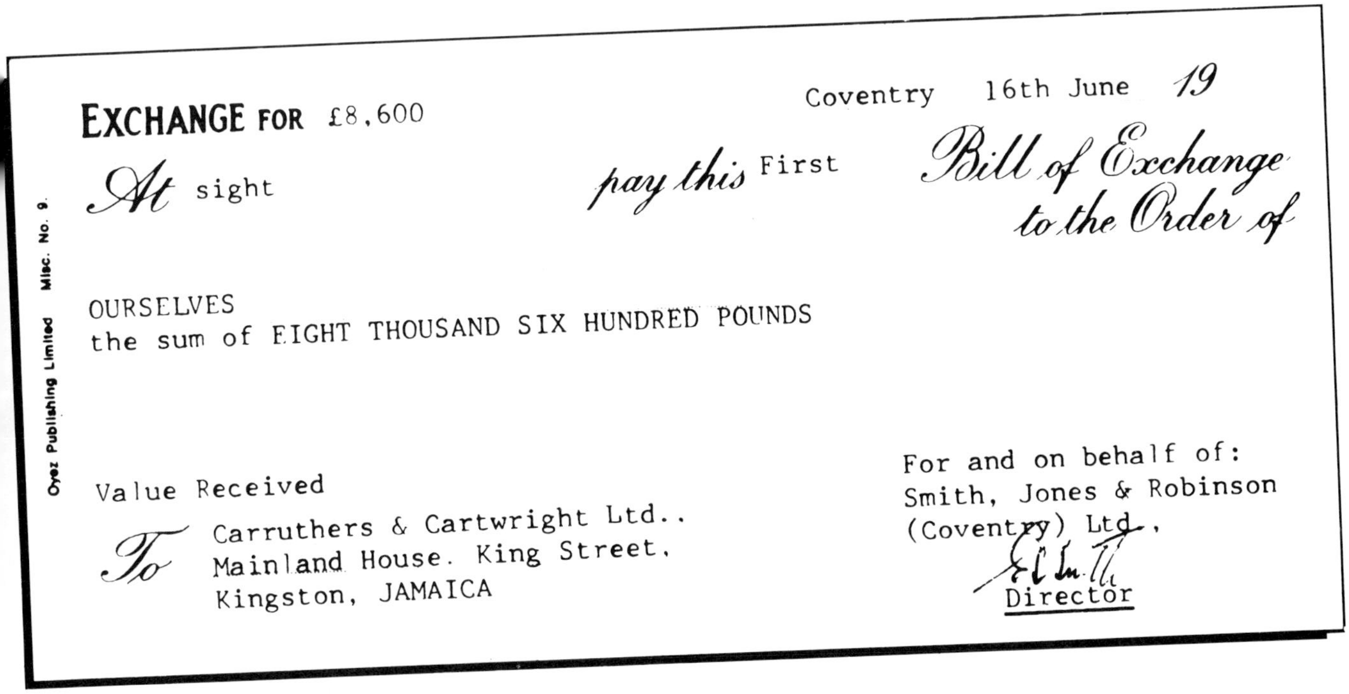

EXCHANGE FOR £8,600   Coventry   16th June   19

At sight   pay this First   Bill of Exchange
                                                    to the Order of

OURSELVES
the sum of EIGHT THOUSAND SIX HUNDRED POUNDS

Value Received   For and on behalf of:
                                              Smith, Jones & Robinson
    To   Carruthers & Cartwright Ltd.,   (Coventry) Ltd.,
         Mainland House, King Street,
         Kingston, JAMAICA
                                                      Director

Fig. 16.8   A Bill of Exchange

B/L No.

Shippers Ref.

F Agent's Ref.

HARRISON LINE

TRANS-ATLANTIC WEST BOUND

Shipper
SMITH, JONES & ROBINSON (COVENTRY) LTD
RESIN WORKS,
MARKET STREET,
COVENTRY.

Consignee (If "Order" state Notify Party) ORDER Notify:
CARRUTHERS & CARTWRIGHT LTD.,
MAINLAND HOUSE,
KINGS STREET,
KINSTON, JAMAICA.

†Notify Party (ONLY if not stated above: otherwise leave blank)

*Local vessel	*From (Local port of Loading)			
Ocean vessel: EXPLORER	Port of Loading: LIVERPOOL		Number of Bs/L signed: ONE	
Port of Discharge: KINGSTON	*Final destination (if on-carriage)	Freight payable at: LIVERPOOL		

Marks and Numbers	Number and kind of packages; description of goods	Gross weight	Measurement
C C 1234 KINGSTON 1-100 MADE IN U.K.	100 DRUMS SYNTHETIC RESIN	23,500k	30.900
	30.900 @ £25.50	£ 787.95	
	- 9¾%	76.83	
		£ 711.12	
	BUNKER ADJUSTMENT @ £2.50	77.25	
FREIGHT PAID	JAMAICA STEVEDORING @ 80p	24.72	
	LIVERPOOL HANDLING @ 50p	15.45	
		£ 828.54	

ABOVE PARTICULARS DECLARED BY SHIPPER

RECEIVED in apparent good order and condition (unless otherwise stated herein) for shipment on board (the Local vessel subject to clause 19 hereof, if such a vessel be named above, but otherwise on board) the Ocean vessel, or other vessel employed by the Carrier, at the Port of loading thereof, the pieces and/or packages said to contain goods (herein called "the goods") above specified, warranted lawful merchandise at the Port of loading, throughout the voyage, and at the Port of discharge and Final destination, to be carried by the Ocean vessel from the Port of loading thereof bound on a voyage, as described and agreed by clauses 8, 9, 10, 11 and 12 hereof, and/or to be forwarded by any other vessel or vessels and/or other method or methods of conveyance as agreed under clause 20 hereof, and to be delivered (such carriage and delivery being subject to the exceptions, limitation, conditions and liberties herein agreed) in the like order and condition at the Port of discharge or Final destination (as the case may be) named above or so near thereto as the carrying vessel may safely get always afloat unto the Consignee or his or their assigns.

IN WITNESS whereof the Master or Agent of the ocean vessel has signed the number of Bills of Lading stated above, all of this tenor and date, one of which being accomplished, the others shall stand void.

Number of Pieces or Packages (in words)
ONE HUNDRED.

SINCE SHIPPED
T. & J. H. LTD.

FOR BILLS OF LADING ONLY
THOS. & JAS. HARRISON LTD 13 JUN 19
PER

Dated in LIVERPOOL ______ 19 ____

SEE CONDITIONS OF CARRIAGE AND OTHER CONDITIONS ON REVERSE

Printed in England by Rockliff Brothers Ltd., 2 Rumford Street, Liverpool, 2.

†No claim shall under any cirmcustances be attached to the vessel or her owners by reason of the absence of notification.
*Applicable only when document used as a Through B/L

Fig. 16.9 A Bill of Lading

Letter of credit

This is the most common form of payment for export goods. The importer arranges for his bank to instruct a bank in the exporter's country to make payment on receipt of the bill of lading. (Read Unit 10, section 10.1 about *bills of exchange*.)

Terms in overseas trade

When quoting for an overseas order, exporter and importer need to know what the price covers, as additional costs like transport and insurance can be very high. The following terms are used:

Ex-works: price is the cost of the goods as they stand in the factory (or *works*); all transport and insurance charges are the responsibility of the buyer.

FOR Free on rail: price includes delivery to the station nearest to the manufacturer.

FAS Free alongside ship: price includes delivery to the dockside.

FOB Free on board or *full on board*: price includes delivery into the hold and ready to sail.

CF Cost and freight: price includes all transport to the port of destination.

CIF Cost, insurance and freight: the same as *CF* but including insurance whilst in transit.

In bond All transport charges to a named bonded warehouse (see below).

Franco or *free* The price is the cost of goods and *all* charges to the customer's own premises, door to door.

So a written quote which stated £50000 CIF would be understood to include the cost of the goods themselves plus insurance plus freight charges to the port of destination. All costs from that point would be the responsibility of the importer.

Customs and Excise and bonded warehouses

Once docked, cargoes are unloaded and are subject to customs clearance. At this point an import duty or *tariff* may be applied. This may be a *specific duty* (calculated according to bulk, e.g. a litre of wine or a tonne of tobacco). Or it may be an *ad valorum duty* (calculated according to value, e.g. jewellery or cars).

Customs officers are also required to prevent certain goods being imported at all (e.g. drugs) and to see that quotas are observed. *Quotas* restrict entry to a given quantity of any goods decided by government regulations.

Bonded warehouses exist at all ports where dutiable goods can be stored (but see Unit 13, section 13.3 on *Freeports*). Duty is not paid until imports are withdrawn from bond.

● SOURCES OF INFORMATION

1 Yellow Pages – see under 'Export agents', 'shipping and forwarding agents', 'shipbrokers' and 'consular agents'.
2 Telephone directory – HM Customs and Excise.
3 Any bank, for details of *aids to exporters*.
4 If you live near a port or airport, the larger insurance brokers should be able to offer advice on insurance cover for exporters.
5 SITPRO (Simplification of International Trade Procedures), Almack House, 26–28 King Street, London SW1Y 6QW (or Freepost, London SW1Y 6BR)

● THINGS TO DO

1 As a group, discuss *why* it may be necessary to assist a small firm to sell its goods overseas. What help will be needed? Who, or what organisation, is likely to help?
2 Write a polite letter to a whisky distillery in Scotland and ask for information on excise duties, re-exports and whisky in bond.
3 Research the sale of a consignment of pottery from Stoke to Chicago. Make notes on the transport arrangements, the documents that may be necessary and the available methods of payment.

● QUESTIONS

Answer the following questions using Figs. 16.8 and 16.9:

1 Which three firms are involved in the transaction? Name the exporter and the importer.
2 Which shipping line is involved? Which vessel is to be used? Where will the ship sail from, and what is its destination?
3 What was the total cost of transport and port-handling charges?
4 What was the total cost of cargo and charges?
5 When is the bill of exchange payable?

17 THE GOVERNMENT AND ECONOMIC ACTIVITY

●UNIT 17.1
'Great Britain Ltd'

The public sector

The state supplies some goods and services to its citizens free of charge. The health service, education, roads and defence are 'free goods'; they are services we all consume at one time or another in our lives, and for which no *direct* payment is expected. (As taxpayers, of course, we pay for them indirectly.)

Both national government and local government also provide goods and services for which we have to pay directly. British Rail charges fares, and British Coal sells its products. Local authorities provide policing, parks, gardens, libraries and many museums free; but they also run leisure centres, theatres, swimming pools, car-parks and public transport, for which a charge is made.

All these goods and services provided by central and local government make up the *public sector* of the economy (see Unit 7, section 7.2).

Employment

Most of the goods and services in this public sector are *labour intensive*, that is, they depend upon the employment of large numbers of people: civil servants, local government officers, doctors, nurses, teachers, train drivers, miners, engineers, architects, lawyers, cooks, technicians, librarians, mechanics and every type of craft worker.

There is no kind of enterprise, from the extractive industries through to final distribution, in which the state is not involved. The number of people employed by 'Great Britain Ltd' (the public sector) runs into millions.

Fig. 17.1 Children playing in a municipal playground

Fig. 17.2 A British stand at an International Trade Fair

Government contracts

The public services also need to buy goods and services from the private sector (private firms). The National Health Service needs buildings, furniture, linen, drugs, dressings and instruments. Defence requires ships, aircraft, armaments, food and uniforms. Both national and local government activities rely on industry and commerce to supply their many wants. Together they are the largest customers in *any* country.

Many businesses flourish on government contracts, which can be worth billions of pounds annually. Such consumption of goods and services keeps many people in employment, both in Britain and abroad. There is no sector of industry or commerce which does not benefit, directly or indirectly, from the commercial activity of government.

Foreign policy

Britain is a manufacturing country which has to sell goods and services overseas to pay for imports. This international trade is both helped and hindered by the relationship Britain has with other countries. Britain's popularity, or lack of popularity, as a trading nation can be influenced by the attitude the British government adopts abroad, agreements signed with foreign governments and our treatment of foreign nationals.

Our membership of the European Community requires us to adopt certain policies in countries that previously relied heavily on trade with Britain. For example, Australia and New Zealand no longer receive *Imperial preference* – a trade advantage they formerly enjoyed due to their close ties with Britain as members of the Commonwealth; their exports of meat, dairy produce and fruit to Britain declined as a result. Similarly, the Caribbean countries (e.g. Jamaica) have suffered losses in their sugar industries.

British relationships with Spain and Argentina are not as good as they would be if we gave up possession of Gibraltar and the Falkland Islands respectively. However, long-standing close political, economic and cultural links with North America mean that British trade is welcomed on that subcontinent.

Generally, where we are liked and our policies are approved, our goods sell well. Where we are not liked, our international sales staff have a hard time.

Overseas aid

As part of its foreign policy Britian makes available large sums to aid underdeveloped, Third World countries. Where possible, grants are arranged *in kind* (rather than in cash), e.g. assistance with an irrigation project, farm equipment like tractors and bulldozers, seed to re-establish farming in an area damaged by locusts or plant to manufacture household goods. Such assistance is usually accompanied by specialist help. It may be 'one-off' or a project which extends over a long period. Foreign students are often assisted to study or research in Britain.

Britain is not alone in offering overseas aid. The United States and the USSR, Canada and the countries of Western Europe and Scandinavia are all major aid-givers. Most developed countries, particularly those in Europe (the old colonial powers), feel a responsibility to assist those countries they once exploited. It is also good business, since the governments involved tend to offer commercial favours in return.

However there is a great deal of debate about aid. Pressure groups and agencies like Oxfam and War on Want argue that rich countries don't give nearly enough help to poorer ones, and that we all suffer as a result.

Embassies and High Commissions

Britain, like every other country in the world, maintains formal relationships overseas through an *Embassy* (and an *Ambassador*) or a *High Commission* (and a *Commissioner*). In all Commonwealth countries we maintain a High Commission. In most of the rest we have an Embassy; both are staffed by diplomats responsible for (say) trade or cultural matters.

These diplomatic establishments monitor the well-being of British subjects living and working abroad and our trading links with the country involved. The staff concerned work hard to develop an interest in British goods and to promote London as a centre offering commercial services like banking and insurance.

●SOURCES OF INFORMATION

1. SITPRO (Simplification of International Trade Procedures), Almack House, 26–28 King Street, London SW1Y 6QW (or Freepost, London SW1Y 6BR)
2. British Overseas Trade Board, Friars Bank, 52 Horseferry Road, London SW1P 2AG
3. HM Treasury, Information Division, Parliament Street, London SW1P 3AG
4. Department of Trade and Industry, Education Unit, 89 Eccleston Square, London SW1V 1PT
5. Hansard Society, 16 Gower Street, London WC1E 6DP
6. Oxfam, Youth and Education Department, 274 Banbury Road, Oxford OX2 7DZ

●QUESTIONS

1. What do you understand by the term 'free goods'? Can you name some? In your view why are 'free goods' essential to each individual? Are there any advantages to industry and commerce?
2. Why do you think that local authorities are prepared to maintain free libraries but charge a fee for using their swimming-pools? Is this fair?
3. Explain why Britain is like a giant trading company. Give examples of its trading activities.
4. What is a 'foreign policy'? Who determines foreign policy and what effects does this have on commercial activity?
5. Which parts of the world are likely to receive British overseas aid? Will such aid promote commercial activity? Why are such countries termed *underdeveloped*?

Fig. 17.3 An irrigation scheme in Mali

UNIT 17.2
National Policies

The post-war change

All governments play some part in the management of their country's economy. A stable and growing economy is essential to maintain standards of living and the provision of 'free goods'. Before the Second World War, Britain followed a policy of *laissez-faire* ('leave well alone'). As a consequence, between 1918 and 1939 we suffered from depression. The results were wide areas of poverty in Scotland, the North of England and Wales, and a collapse of major industries such as shipbuilding, iron and steel and coalmining. Many people blamed government policies. The economy was rescued by the need to boost production during the Second World War.

Following that war the Labour government in 1945 adopted a programme of more government involvement in the economy. The nationalisation of industry was coupled with a policy of financial aid to regions most needing assistance. They aimed to revive industrial and commercial interests and create employment. From then until the election of the Conservative government in 1979, each British government followed much the same policies but with varying success.

New Towns

Housing was a major need and *New Towns* were developed around London. Hemel Hempstead, Stevenage, Welwyn Garden City and Crawley were enlarged. Industries were offered financial help to move to the new areas of population. The second wave of New Towns included Peterborough, East Kilbride, Cumbernauld, Milton Keynes, Peterlee, Warrington and Skelmersdale which have also offered subsidies to new industries relocating in these areas. The availability of housing to rent has attracted a skilled workforce to serve those industries.

Direct intervention

The Conservative government since 1979 has believed less in *direct intervention* (government involvement) in the economy than previous governments. Earlier post-war governments, as we have seen, nationalised many industries and companies. Some of the companies nationalised, like Rolls-Royce (the aero-engine section, not the cars) and British Leyland (Austin Rover), were brought into public ownership in the mid-1970s because they were in financial difficulties. It was thought that they could not be allowed to go bankrupt. Rolls-Royce and Jaguar Cars (part of Austin Rover) have been sold back to shareholders.

Other areas of the economy – coal, steel, gas, electricity and oil – were thought to need government involvement because they were so large and important. The government has now sold its interest in British Petroleum after years of holding many thousands of shares in that company. Exploration for oil in the North Sea is controlled by government agencies. Various companies interested in exploration have paid commissions and taxes, producing a very good income and helping the balance of payments.

Legislation

A great many Acts of Parliament cover the way in which businesses can be conducted. The legislation includes the Companies Acts, Consumer Protection Acts, Consumer Credit Acts, Health and Safety at Work Act, Public Health Acts, Employment Acts, Trade Union Acts, Sex Discrimination Act and Race Discrimination Act. The government also issues regulations (like the Dangerous Substances Regulations) which have the force of law.

All these laws regulate and control how firms and individuals behave in the world of business. There are stiff penalites when the law is broken. In general, the law is aimed at protecting the weak from being harmed by the strong in all matters of trade, employment and commerce.

Local authorities control *planning permission* in their districts. This means they can regulate new building and the use to which premises can be put. They can withhold permission if the development of a particular trade or retail outlet, for example, is considered harmful to a residential area.

Business growth and the Monopolies Commission

Business growth   Businesses can grow by amalgamating with other firms (*mergers*) or by buying others (*take-overs*). Mergers often take place between companies in the same kind of business (see. Fig. 17.4). Or a firm may try to reduce its costs by obtaining a larger building from which to operate related trades.

In the example in Fig. 17.5, the minicab/car-hire firm acquires a petrol forecourt, a counter service for spares, car servicing bays and a franchise for new and second-hand cars. All of this enlarges the scope of the original merger of firms A and B, cuts the costs of servicing and maintaining the company's fleet and provides a launch pad for setting up other identical outlets elsewhere.

Fig. 17.4   Mergers

Fig. 17.5 Expansion into other areas of business

The firm is now large, with numerous forecourts. As a dealer in cars it purchases its own vehicles much more cheaply than before; it supplies its own petrol, oil and spares, and services its own vehicles. The opportunities seem endless: a wedding and funeral service, coaches for outings and foreign holidays and a travel agency with associated hotels.

The Monopolies Commission There comes a time when a very large company begins to dominate its industry. If there are any further mergers or take-overs, competition by price or quality of service might cease to exist. What may be good for individual companies is not necessarily good for the consumer or the country as a whole.

At this point the government can exercise its power, through the *Monopolies Commission*, to examine any proposal for further amalgamation. If the Commission reports that this will be against the public interest, the government has the power to prevent the monopolistic growth of a large company.

A recent example was British Airways. The Monopolies Commission agreed to let BA take over British Caledonian, but only if other small British airlines could compete on local British air routes.

● SOURCES OF INFORMATION

1. Monopolies and Mergers Commission, New Court, 48 Carey Street, London WC2A 2JT
2. Commission for the New Towns, Glen House, Stag Place, London SW1E 5AJ
3. Corby Industrial Development Centre, Douglas House, Queens Square, Corby, Northants
4. Development Corporation, PO Box 49, Warrington, Cheshire WA1 2LF

● THINGS TO DO

1. There will probably be a New Town in your area. Write politely to the Commission for New Towns, asking for details of the industrial and commercial companies which have relocated in the area. Investigate any evidence of growth in population and in employment opportunities which have resulted.
2. Marks & Spencer PLC is now a very large corporation. Discuss what firms (if any) provide competition, either in part or in all of the stock sold by M&S. In what circumstances do you feel the Monopolies Commission might become interested if M&S plans further growth?
3. Your school or college, currently sited in old and run-down buildings in the middle of a housing estate, is due to move to new buildings. A developer wants to take over the site, pull down the buildings and build a DIY warehouse and food hypermarket. Think about the attitude and possible reactions of your local authority, who are discussing an application for planning permission. What might their objections be?

UNIT 17.3
Enterprise Zones and Development Areas

The location of industry

Figs. 17.6 and 17.7 show those areas specially chosen for government assistance. With the exception of the London Docklands, the South-East, being mostly well off, is not included. The Docklands are now being developed with new industries, housing and leisure complexes.

Enterprise Zones and *Development Areas* are located in the regions of highest unemployment. Here traditional employment opportunities have declined, and the workforce already possesses industrial skills. Most of the regions designated for government assistance are well placed in terms of transport links. New industries such as computers and electronics are established to set up in these areas, and existing industries are encouraged to *relocate* (move) to them. Freeports have been established in places like Liverpool and Cardiff as a further boost to trade in those areas.

Inner-city decay

The nature of the problem As towns expanded they spread outwards from the centre. Poorly maintained housing together with decaying industrial sites were abandoned as firms moved to larger premises or the goods manufactured and services offered were no longer required. Most of the towns closely associated with the Industrial Revolution (e.g. Sheffield, Leeds, Manchester), together with areas like Merseyside and Tyneside, were left with an embarrassment of nineteenth century development no longer required and rapidly becoming both an eyesore and a financial burden of huge proportions.

Enterprise Zone

* Rates (local tax) Free until 1991.
* No industrial training board levies.
* 100% of building costs available for initial depreciation allowance.
* No development land tax.
* Eased customs warehousing facilities.
* Simplified planning procedures.

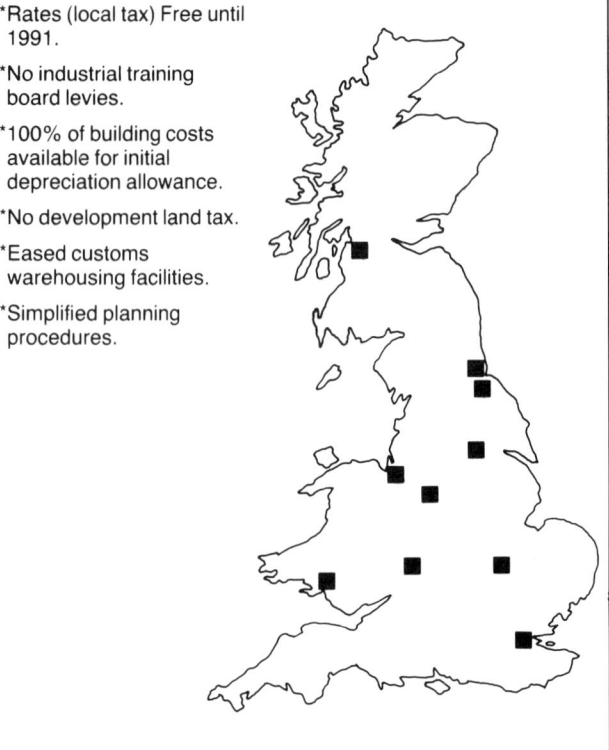

Fig. 17.6 Enterprise Zones

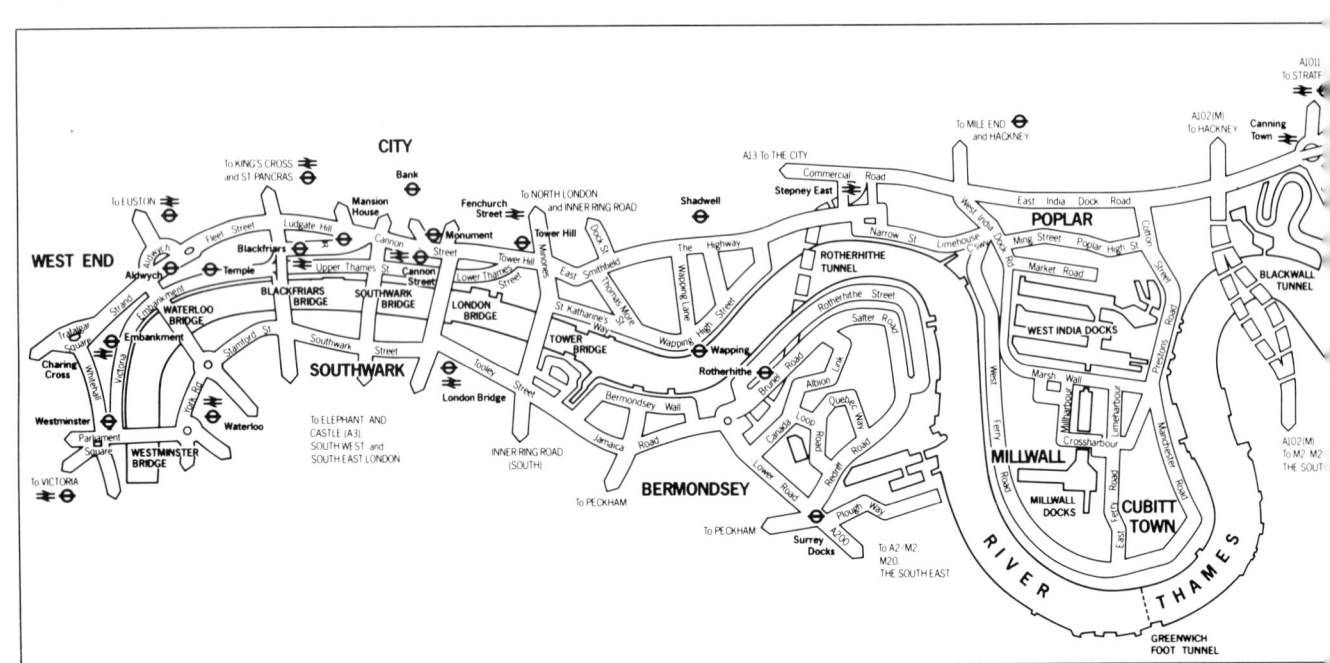

Fig. 17.8 London Docklands – a new business community

Development Area

* 15% grant on new buildings. Rent free periods if building leased.
* 15% grant on new plant machinery and equipment.
* Training cost assistance.
* 100% of plant machinery & equipment for initial depreciation allowance.
* 75% of building costs available for initial depreciation allowance
* Selective assistance to projects if they would not locate in development area without assistance and/or if project improves UK economy.

Fig. 17.7 Development Areas

These decaying areas stand on prime land, right in the centre of cities where people could easily live and work rather than travelling long distances from the outer suburbs and adjoining villages. The problem was, how to revitalise these areas, how to attract new businesses providing new jobs, how to replenish the existing housing stock or to provide new homes where a simple 'face-lift' was not sufficient. The question above all was, 'Who is to provide the capital necessary, nationwide, to redevelop our inner-city areas?'

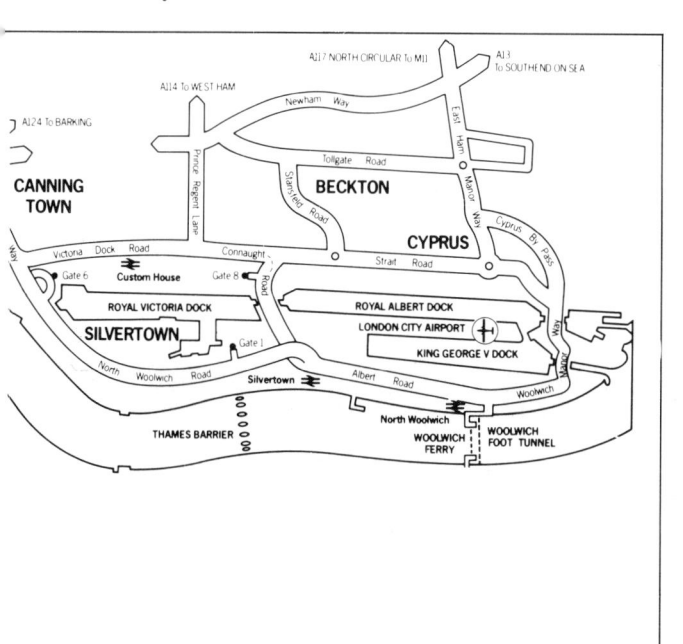

An example – London Docklands

The area is vast (see Fig. 17.8) stretching from Tower Bridge in the West to Woolwich in the East: approximately 8 miles of river frontage together with the associated warehouses, docks, commercial premises and housing, occupying both banks of the Thames. With the development of larger ships London Docks, no longer able to cope or provide the necessary services, became a watery monument to nineteenth-century technology. Jobs in London Docklands disappeared, so local families (most of whom had worked in the docks for generations) living in historically famous areas like the Isle of Dogs, Silvertown, Bermondsey and Wapping, were forced to seek new opportunities for employment, often in other parts of the country.

Fig. 17.9 London City Airport

Housing developments have been of two kinds. Many of the older houses, situated in once leafy squares, were seen as elegant and desirable by affluent incomers, who worked not very far away in the City. They bought relatively cheaply, spent money on improvements and a new breed of East-Enders emerged. The former slums were pulled down and blocks of flats erected in their place, providing high-rise accommodation for a community which preferred the old streets and companionable living.

The solution – the London Docklands Development Corporation

The LDDC was born in January, 1981 and acquired power to develop Docklands under the Local Government Planning and Land Act, 1980. The necessary capital has been obtained partly from public funds, from private companies prepared to invest in property development and from individual businesses (like News International) which decided to leave Fleet Street and relocate in Docklands.

In addition to newspaper interests, the LDDC has developed 12 000 new homes, a vast shopping centre, a scenic park, a cinema/leisure complex, a sports stadium, communication networks (see below), a marina, an airport, a banking and financial centre, a training scheme (Skillnet) and a completely new system of river transport, roads and railways to service this vast area which links with motorways, ports and British Rail. To date, 2000 firms have relocated in Docklands attracting grants, loans and tax benefits, 10 000 new jobs have been created and people are beginning to move into attractive waterside homes within walking distance of potential employment.

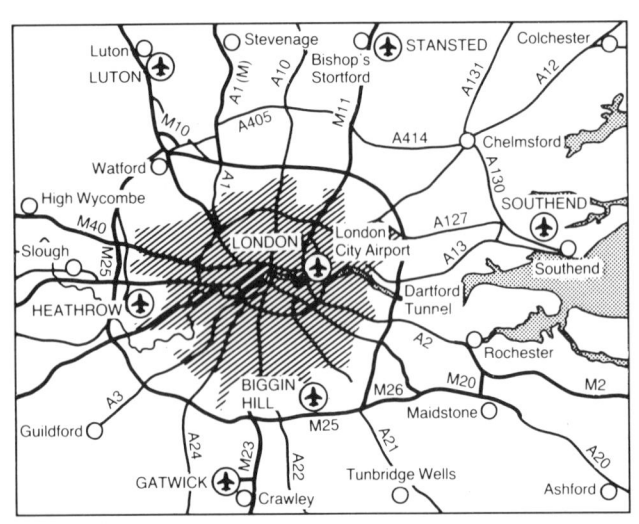

Fig. 17.10 London City Airport links with the motorway system

Fig. 17.12 The new DLR station at Island Gardens, Isle of Dogs

Transport Three unique transportation projects have made Docklands Development into a model scheme for the rest of the UK. These include the London City Airport, the extension of the M11 motorway (allied to a proposed East London river crossing) and the Docklands Light Railway (Figs. 17.9–17.13). The Docklands Light Railway, (DLR) completely controlled by computer (there are no drivers), links the City with Greenwich and Stratford Station (B.R. and Central Line – London Transport) (Fig. 17.14). The route stations (with names like West Indian Quay, Crossharbour and Mudchute) are unmanned and without barriers, the whole system being automatic. A proposed extension will link the DLR with the City Airport. The whole development is destined to be a major tourist attraction.

Fig. 17.11 The Docklands Light Railway

Fig. 17.13 The new riverbus on the Thames

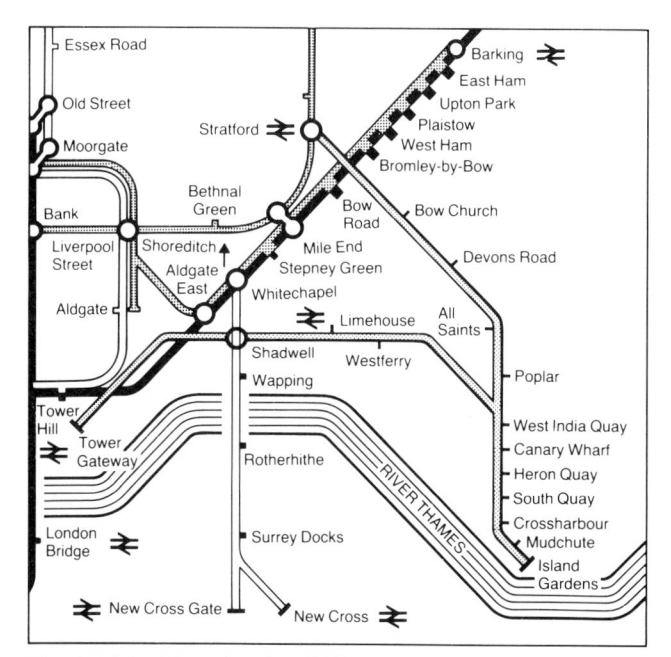

Fig. 17.14 Map showing DLR's links with London's Underground and BR stations

The London City Airport, using special short take-off and landing aircraft (hence the term STOLPORT), is situated between the Royal Albert and King George Docks. Aircraft fly daily services to all parts of Britain and across the Channel.

Communications Much of the new development in Docklands is 'high-tech': National Telephone Systems, British Telecom and Mercury have all established satellite communication systems along the banks of the Thames. Such advanced technology is supported by computer software organisations like Dockview (a computer database for use by local industry). Such enterprises have come to be known as the 'Sunrise Industries' which will transform commercial activity in the 21st century.

The pattern extended

The developments in Docklands provide a model for similar redevelopment elsewhere (e.g. Liverpool). As our former 'heavy' industries decline, 'high-tech' projects will take their place. It would be foolish to extend our major cities further and further away from the centres, when redevelopment can provide new industries, new jobs and new homes on derelict sites.

●SOURCES OF INFORMATION

1 London Docklands Development Corporation, West Indian House, Millwall Docks, London E14 9TJ
2 Any town hall for details of redevelopment projects in your area.
3 'Transport for a New City', *Esso Magazine*, Autumn 1987 – or any similar articles in newspapers or magazines.
4 Department of Trade and Industry, 1–19 Victoria Street, London SW1H 0ET for details of Development Grants.

●THINGS TO DO

1 If you are located in the London area, Docklands Development provides many opportunities for research. Choose from: (a) communications; (b) transport; (c) community activity; (d) housing, or (e) leisure industries. Write to the agencies involved and plot growth and development on one of the many maps available. Arrange a visit.
2 If you are located outside London, then there will be redevelopment projects in your area (e.g. the new shopping centre in Basildon promoted and financed by Norwich Union). Contact your town hall for details and research these developments.
3 Examine how your city or town is tackling inner-city decay. Evaluate: (a) shopping; (b) housing; (c) transport; (d) leisure projects. To what extent do you think that such developments meet the needs of *your* area and *your* age group?

UNIT 17.4
Economic Intervention

In this section we will discuss the investment of government money in individual enterprise, training and the development of new businesses.

Enterprise Allowance Scheme

Organised by the Department of Employment, this scheme offers government grants to those who wish to start up in business on their own. The *Small Firms Service* provides advice on taxation, employment, finance and marketing for people in business on their own. The *Business Advisory Centres* guide potential self-employed individuals towards a successful launch of their own business. There are now 1.6 million small businesses and 2.7 million self-employed people in Britain.

Regional Development Grants

Once a business is started and is doing well, the proprietor(s) can apply for Regional Development Grants, as long as the firm is in a Development Area (see Fig. 17.7 in section 17.3).

Other sources of business assistance

In addition to government sponsorship, privately funded schemes exist to aid new businesses in specified areas:

1 *The 3i's scheme,* sponsored by Investors in Industry plc, exists to help small and medium-sized businesses grow, providing venture capital. Anita Roddick's *Body Shop* was one of the ideas developed with cash from 3i's (Fig. 17.15)

2 Most banks operate a *loan guarantee scheme* in association with the Department of Employment. Finance can then be found for risky or unusual projects.
3 *The Manchester Business Venture,* sponsored by Shell (UK), Citibank and the Royal Bank of Scotland, provides start-up resources for business schemes which are not fundable by any national scheme.
4 Many *Chambers of Commerce* provide funds for commercial ventures. The Manchester Chamber of Commerce resourced a vegetarian restaurant set up by a women's co-operative, the 100th start-up scheme backed by the Manchester Chamber.

Training schemes

Controlled by the Department of Employment, the programmes include the *Youth Training Scheme,* and *Employment Training.* Each of these includes a period of skill training, approved placements with employers using the skills acquired and a job search programme towards the end of the training period. The trainees receive a training allowance and expenses to cover travelling and subsistence.

Other schemes sponsored by government departments include *PICKUP* (Professional, Industrial and Commercial Updating). Employers are encouraged to release staff into approved training programmes. Grants are paid to cover the cost of release, the wages involved and any other expenses.

Pay policies

Governments do not usually admit to a policy designed to keep down annual increases in wages and salaries. However, it is recognised that high wage and salary awards lead to a large increase in the cost of manufacture. This in turn makes British exports more expensive than similar goods produced by foreign competitors. If British goods cannot be sold overseas, the result will be inflation and a balance of payments deficit.

The government cannot negotiate salary scales in the private sector. But employees within the public sector – nurses, teachers, police and local government officers – are all paid more or less what the government thinks is right. The level of pay increases in the public sector influences those offered in the private sector, while constant government warnings about the dangers of *inflation* (see below) have had a calming effect upon the level of wage demands.

The rate of inflation

A country's economy is said to be suffering from *inflation* when prices are rising uncontrollably. During the 1970s, Britain had high inflation rates – prices were rising at sometimes 25 per cent each year.

Fig. 17.15 Anita Roddick, founder of Body Shop

Satisfaction with the levels of wage and salary increases depends partly on a government's ability to keep inflation under control. The *rate of inflation* (the annual increase in price levels) was about 6 per cent at the time of writing. Most wage increases were in excess of that figure, and the average standard of living in Britain was rising steadily as a result.

In these circumstances wage and salary earners are reasonably happy, though we all feel that a little more would be welcome. If inflation were to get out of hand, as happened in the 1970s, wage demands would increase to match, leading to greater inflation, and we would be locked in what is called a '*wages spiral*'.

Taxation and benefits

Governments can change the economic situation by reducing or increasing the levels of taxation. This increases or decreases the amount of money in the pockets of the general public to spend as it wishes. Any move from direct to indirect taxes shifts the burden of taxation on to the poorly paid and those (like the retired population) who exist on fixed incomes.

Benefits are the financial help given by the nation to the unemployed, to the sick, to the retired, to the handicapped and to those looking after children. The levels of such benefits are adjusted from time to time, but because of the number of individuals in receipt of benefits, any large increase would push the economy towards inflation.

Fig. 17.16 Alan Sugar and Amstrad

Free goods

All of us enjoy 'free goods' like education and the health service, the benefit from which is part of our total income. Think of the consequences if such services were *not* free. Decisions by any government to increase or decrease national spending on free goods will affect most people's income and standard of living.

If you are ill, a decision to increase the charge for medical prescriptions means that you have less to spend on other things.

Fig. 17.17 The birth of Marks & Spencer

●SOURCES OF INFORMATION

1. Small Firms Service, Freepost, London SW20 8TA
2. Public libraries, for details of training schemes like YTS
3. MOD Small Firms Advisory Division, Room G179, St Christopher House, Southwark Street, London SE1 0TD
4. NatWest Small Business Service, Freepost, Hounslow, Middx TW4 5DR
5. Any major bank, for Small Firms Loan Guarantee Scheme.
6. Your telephone directory, for the local Chamber of Commerce.
7. Department of Employment (Training Division), Moorfoot, Sheffield, Yorks SI 4PQ
8. Small Business Bureau, 32 Smith Square, London, SW1P 3HH

●THINGS TO DO

1. Write to the Training Division for details of their aid to new businesses and small firms. Discuss in your group what opportunities are available to start and run your own business. Agree a particular business and decide what will be necessary to launch your project successfully.
2. Ask a representative of the Banking Information Service (see Unit 9, section 9.2, *sources of information*) to come and talk to you about the services offered by a bank which might assist the launch you discussed in 1. How much capital would you need, and what is the annual cost of borrowing that amount?
3. Ask a YTS student, with his or her managing agent, to come and talk to you on the advantages and disadvantages of the scheme.
4. Write to your MP. Ask what, in his or her view, the present government has done since the last general election that is of general benefit to: (a) business firms in your area; (b) individuals living and working in your area. Assess his or her replies to see if you agree with them.
5. To what extent does your group feel that it is still possible to start like Jack Cohen (Tesco), Anita Roddick (Body Shop), Alan Sugar (Amstrad: Fig. 17.16) or Simon Marks (M & S: Fig. 17.17) and finish as a millionaire?

UNIT 17.5
Taxation and the Community Charge

There are two forms of taxation: *income tax*, a system of direct taxation and *indirect taxation*, a tax on spending.

Income tax

Most people pay income tax through a system known as *Pay as you earn (PAYE)*. The wage and salary earner receives income *net*, that is, after income tax has been deducted. The employer then accounts for the total tax deducted from all employees and sends the amount collected to the Inland Revenue.

People who are self-employed also have to pay income tax and National Insurance. Each self-employed individual must declare income to the Inland Revenue, which then assesses liability for tax.

Limited companies, owned by shareholders, are assessed for *corporation tax*, a kind of income tax on the amount of profit declared in any one year.

Income tax supplies governments with much of the money they need to run the country (see Fig. 17.18) and is said to be a direct tax because it is raised directly from people and companies. The more you earn, the more you will be expected to pay in tax.

Indirect taxes

The second major form of raising revenue is by indirect taxation, a tax (or taxes) on spending. *Customs duty* is included on goods like tobacco and spirits. When you buy such goods that are subject to a customs duty, the cost includes the tax. Few people realise just how much they are paying for the goods and how much is actually tax. Cigarettes, whisky, gin and petrol are taxed to such an extent that most of the cost of these goods is an indirect tax.

Value Added Tax

When it was introduced in April 1973 *value added tax (VAT)* was applied on a wide range of goods and services. Some goods like newspapers, books and magazines, and some services like house improvements, were *zero-rated*, that is, they carried a 0 per cent of tax. Other goods and services (notably food, insurance, bank charges and dentistry) were exempt. This means that they were entirely removed from the provisions of VAT.

Since 1973 we have had rates of 8, 10, 15 and 25 per cent, as well as the zero rate mentioned above. The present rate of 15 per cent VAT is used in the following example.

An example Suppose a firm manufactures stainless-steel cutlery. It buys £1000 worth of steel, on which 15 per cent VAT is charged. Total bill = £1000 + £150 = £1150.

The goods are manufactured and sold to retailers for £3000, plus 15 per cent VAT. Total = £3450.

The manufacturer has paid £150 in VAT and has received £450. It must remit the difference (£300) to the Customs and Excise authorities, who are responsible for collecting VAT.

The goods are now with the retailer, who sells them for £5000, plus VAT at 15 per cent. Total = £5750.

The retailer has paid £450 in VAT and has received £750. He or she must remit the difference (£300) to the Customs and Excise, who have now received £150 from the steel producer, £300 from the manufacturer and £300 from the retailer, a total of £750. This is 15 per cent of £5000, the retail price of the goods.

VAT paid to a supplier is called an *input tax*, while VAT received as a result of a sale is called an *output tax*. Returns of both are made to the Customs and Excise.

Licences and duties

Other indirect taxes, paid by both businesses and individuals, include motor vehicle *road fund licences*, *customs duties* on imported goods, *stamp duty* on the sale and transfer of land and buildings and the *National Insurance* contribution. There are also licence fees, like those for television and *betting tax*, which finance particular services.

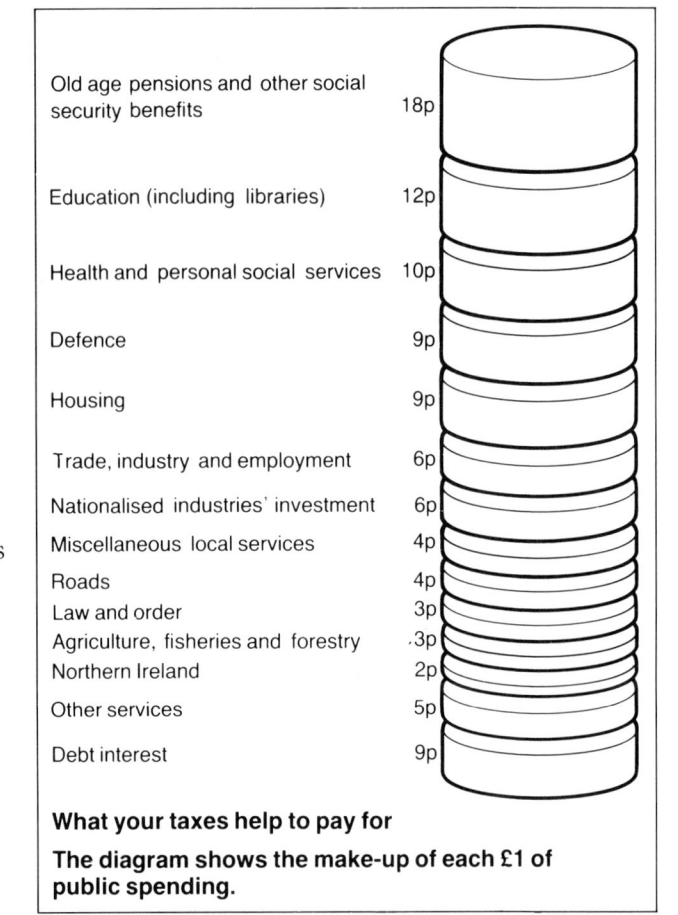

Old age pensions and other social security benefits	18p
Education (including libraries)	12p
Health and personal social services	10p
Defence	9p
Housing	9p
Trade, industry and employment	6p
Nationalised industries' investment	6p
Miscellaneous local services	4p
Roads	4p
Law and order	3p
Agriculture, fisheries and forestry	3p
Northern Ireland	2p
Other services	5p
Debt interest	9p

What your taxes help to pay for

The diagram shows the make-up of each £1 of public spending.

Fig. 17.18 Taxes and public spending

Government spending

Every government collects taxes and duties in order to pay for public spending. But the money raised from taxation does not cover every need, and the rest must be borrowed. If you own savings certificates or Premium Bonds, such loans to the government help to finance projects like the building of schools and hospitals. Much larger sums are raised from business, both here and abroad, upon which the government pays interest.

Fig. 17.18 shows the various ways in which the government spends taxpayers' money. Note that the values indicated are examples only, and are not necessarily exact for any one year.

Rates and local authority services

Local authorities, for example Leeds Borough Council, Hertfordshire County Council and Epping Forest District Council, all provide services such as swimming-pools, parks and leisure facilities, road repairs, housing and refuse collection. Some of the costs are covered by entrance fees, rents and charges. But the majority of local authority income comes from government grants, rates and borrowing. *Rates* are levied on householders, industries, shops and offices according to size and location.

An example of local authority spending is illustrated in Fig. 17.19.

Community charge (poll tax)

In 1987 the government announced its intention to introduce a *community charge* or *poll tax* (i.e. tax per person or 'head'). Starting in Scotland in 1989 it will then come into force in England and Wales. This charge will replace the rates as the main source of local authority income. Each adult will be required to meet a standard charge, unlike rating where the charge was levied on the occupier of property only.

●SOURCES OF INFORMATION

1 DHSS Leaflet Unit, PO Box 21, Stanmore, HA7 1AY
2 Inland Revenue Education Service, PO Box 10, Wetherby, West Yorks LS23 7EH
3 Your local telephone directory – see under Customs and Excise.
4 Commission for Local Administration in England, 21 Queen Anne's Gate, London SW1H 9BU
5 Any town hall, civic centre or public library, for details of local authority services.
6 HM Treasury, Parliament Street, London SW1P 3AQ

●QUESTIONS

1 If you pay £1400 a year in income tax, estimate from Fig. 17.18 the amount of your personal tax contribution for education.
2 Using Fig. 17.19, if I own a house with a rateable value of £550 p.a., calculate what I should pay in rates if the rate in the pound (£) is 218p for this year. What part of that amount will be spent on education?

●THINGS TO DO

1 Write politely to your local town hall. Ask for details of services and amenities provided by the local authority. List all the main services and amenities and 'flag' them on a map of the area. Are there any gaps which would benefit the community if they were filled?
2 The cost of many goods purchased and services received contains an element of VAT. See if you can find any old bills at home where VAT is shown as an *addition* to the total due. How are the purchase and VAT shown?
3 Visit a Crown post office in your area to collect a leaflet on *government securities*. Calculate what I could expect to receive in interest for an investment of £1000? What would I have to pay (eventually) in income tax on the interest received?
4 Arrange the example given earlier in this section of the application of VAT in the form of a sum. Start with the £1000 worth of stock and finish with £5000, the retail value of the goods.

PAYING FOR SERVICES

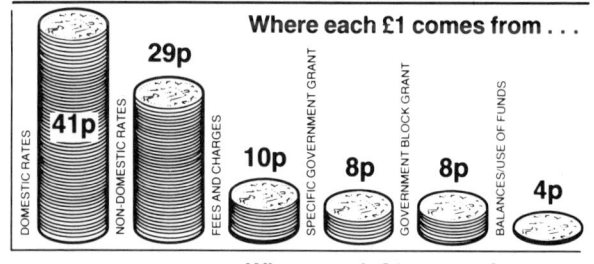

Where each £1 comes from...

- DOMESTIC RATES: 41p
- NON-DOMESTIC RATES: 29p
- FEES AND CHARGES: 10p
- SPECIFIC GOVERNMENT GRANT: 8p
- GOVERNMENT BLOCK GRANT: 8p
- BALANCES/USE OF FUNDS: 4p

Where each £1 comes from...

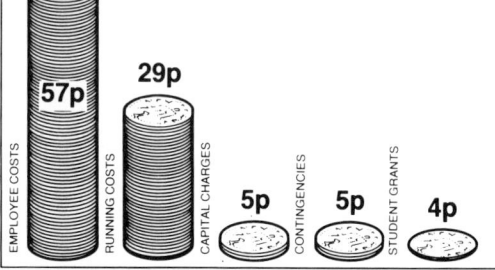

- EMPLOYEE COSTS: 57p
- RUNNING COSTS: 29p
- CAPITAL CHARGES: 5p
- CONTINGENCIES: 5p
- STUDENT GRANTS: 4p

WHO WORKS FOR THE COUNTY COUNCIL?

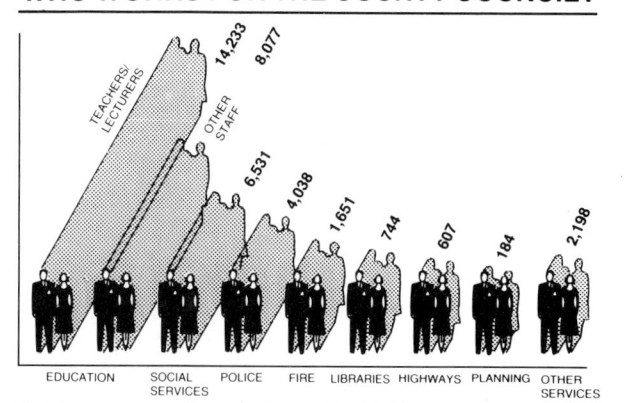

- TEACHERS/LECTURERS: 14,233
- OTHER STAFF: 8,077
- EDUCATION: 6,531
- SOCIAL SERVICES: 4,038
- POLICE: 1,651
- FIRE: 744
- LIBRARIES: 607
- HIGHWAYS: 184
- PLANNING: —
- OTHER SERVICES: 2,198

Part-time posts are included as parts of full-time posts.

Fig. 17.19 Local authority income and spending

18 ASSIGNMENTS

UNIT 18.1
Paying in at the Bank

Cheque crossings

Crossings on a cheque are of two kinds: (1) a *general* crossing and (2) a *special* crossing.

Fig. 18.1 is a general crossing. Cash cannot be obtained over the counter; the cheque *must* be paid into a bank account.

Fig. 18.2: this crossing has the effect that the cheque can only be paid into a bank account of the named payee, but at any bank.

Fig. 18.3: this special crossing is more restrictive, and the cheque can only be paid through the payee's account at National Westminster, Bromford.

Fig. 18.4: again, a special crossing, which is a protection against loss or theft. If a cheque so crossed is mislaid or stolen, no one can benefit by fraudulently presenting the cheque for payment. A *not negotiable* crossing is really a warning: 'Be careful from whom you take this cheque.'

A crossing may be drawn in ink, or your bank may print the cheque with a crossing before it issues it to you. Banks prefer to issue pre-crossed cheques as a protection to their customers, but open cheque forms can be obtained if preferred.

Instances where payment may be refused

1. The drawer may have forgotten to sign a cheque, in which case it will be sent back through the system for a signature to be added.
2. The amount shown in words and the amount shown in figures may disagree. In which case the paying bank may agree to meet the lower of the two amounts.
3. The cheque may not be dated. In which case the holder is entitled to add a date of his or her choice.
4. The cheque may be *out of date*, i.e. bearing a date over six months previously. Such cheques will be returned to the payee.
5. A cheque may be *post-dated*, i.e. bearing a date in the future. Such cheques will not be paid until the date shown.
6. A cheque may be issued for a greater amount than the balance outstanding on the account involved. In which case the manager of the branch concerned has discretion to meet the cheque, if he or she is prepared to allow the customer to overdraw, otherwise the cheque will be returned.
7. A cheque may be *stopped*, i.e. by the drawer issuing instructions to the bank not to meet a particular cheque, in which case it will be returned to the payee.
8. A cheque may appear to have been altered; all alterations should be initialled by the drawer. If the bank is not satisfied it will return the cheque to the payee.

Any cheque returned through the clearing system will be marked *R/D* (refer to drawer). Usually a reason is given for the return, e.g. 'out of date' or 'words and figures do not agree'.

Fig 18.1

Fig 18.2

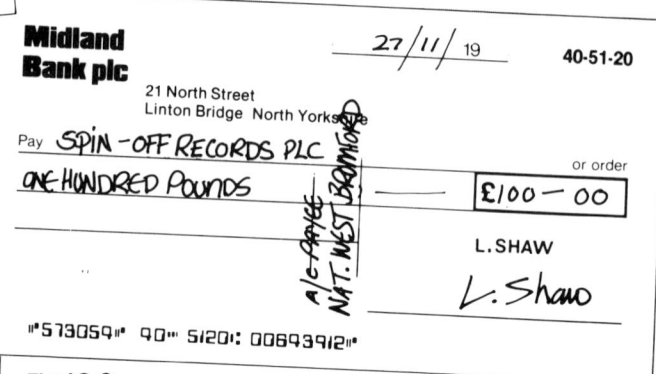

Fig 18.3

Endorsement

Endorsement is the signing of the payee's name on the *back* of a cheque. In theory this allows a cheque to be passed on to another person, who can then deposit the endorsed cheque into a bank account.

In the past, when fewer people had bank accounts, endorsement was useful for those who didn't have a bank account. They could then cash the cheque with a shopkeeper or some other person who knew them.

Nowadays, about the only time you will be asked to endorse a cheque is when you are using a cheque card at a strange bank. They will check your (endorsed) signature with that on your cheque card as a means of identification.

● THINGS TO DO

You are the proprietor of Spin-Off Records PLC and are about to pay your takings into the bank. You have received:

(a) The cheques shown in Figs. 18.1 to 18.4.
(b) One £50 note.
(c) 8 × £20 notes.
(d) 21 × £10 notes.
(e) 143 × £5 notes.
(f) 110 × £1 coins.
(g) 59 × 50p coins.
(h) £20 in other silver.
(i) £10 in bronze coins.

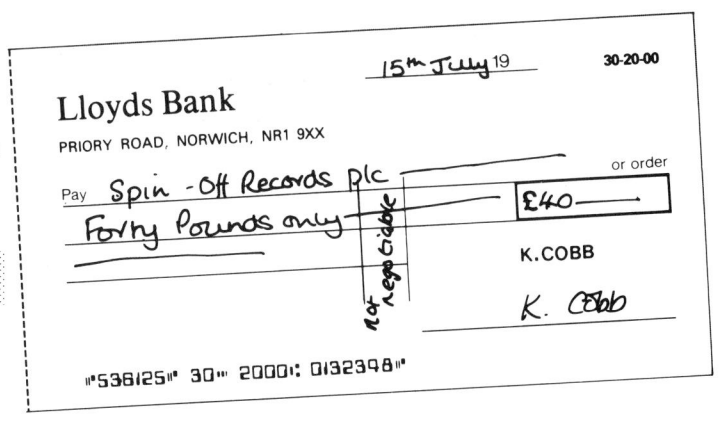

Fig 18.4

Obtain from a bank a *bank giro credit slip* and counterfoil (Fig. 18.5). Complete the bank giro credit and counterfoil as an in-payment into your National Westminster account in Bromford (bank code 08 30 41, account code 0800727). Your address is 23 South Street, Bromford. Use today's date.

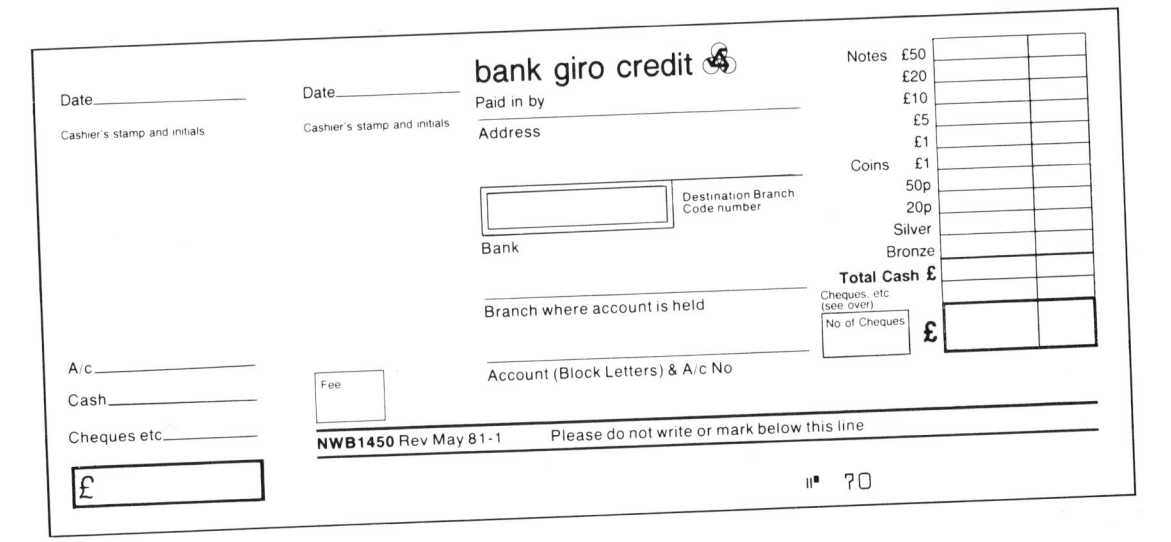

Fig 18.5 Bank giro credit form

●UNIT 18.2
Insuring Your Property

●THINGS TO DO

For this assignment it is a good idea to work in pairs. First of all, write to an insurance company, or visit an insurance broker, to obtain a *proposal form* like the one shown in Fig. 18.6. Then work through the following:

1 Read *all* the instructions on the proposal form *before* you start.
2 Discuss and make sure you understand the various questions shown on the form.

Eagle Star
Home 'All-in' Insurance
Proposal Form

Please complete all details on this page.
Please write in BLOCK LETTERS and tick ☑ correct answer boxes.
You should keep a record (including copies of letters) of all information supplied to us in connection with this insurance. We will provide you with a copy of the completed proposal form on request.

Office use only
Policy number
Branch/Agent

General details

1 **Date you require insurance from**
Day Month Year

2 **Full names of proposer(s)**
State: Mr, Mrs, Miss, Ms or other title
Forenames
Surname
State: Mr, Mrs, Miss, Ms or other title
Forenames
Surname

3 **Occupation** *(If Company Director, Manager or similar, state nature of business.)*
Proposer
Wife or husband

4 **Full postal address**
Postcode

5 **Daytime telephone number**

6 **Address of property where insurance is required if different from 4**
Postcode

7 **Is the home:**
a owner-occupied? Yes☐ No☐
b rented unfurnished? Yes☐ No☐
c rented furnished? Yes☐ No☐
If you have ticked a shaded ☐ box, is the home also self-contained with no shared facilities (such as kitchen, bathroom etc) and with its own lockable entrance door? Yes☐ No☐

8 **Is the home:**
a or any part of the building or grounds used for any trade or business purpose? Yes☐ No☐
b a weekend or holiday home? Yes☐ No☐
c occupied by anyone except your family? Yes☐ No☐
d in an area that has a history of flooding, subsidence, ground heave or landslip? Yes☐ No☐
e showing signs of damage by subsidence, ground heave or landslip? Yes☐ No☐

8 **(cont.) Is the home:**
f built of brick, stone or concrete and roofed with slates, tiles, metal or concrete? Yes☐ No☐
g in good repair and will it be so maintained? Yes☐ No☐
If you have ticked a shaded ☐ box please give full details on the back

9 **How many people occupy the home?** Adults ____ Children ____

10 **How many bedrooms are in the home?** Number

11 **Does each sum insured represent the full replacement cost of the property to be insured** (except for wear and tear, if appropriate) **and will they continue to do so while the policy remains in force?** Yes☐ No☐

12 **Have you been insured before for any of the risks proposed?** Yes☐ No☐
If Yes, who was your insurer?

13 **Have you or anybody who normally lives with you ever:**
a had any insurance refused, subjected to special terms or been asked to take extra precautions? Yes☐ No☐
b been convicted of, or been charged with but not yet tried for, arson or any offence involving dishonesty of any kind such as fraud, robbery, theft, or handling stolen goods? Yes☐ No☐
c sustained loss or damage by any of the risks or liabilities you now wish to insure? Yes☐ No☐
If you have ticked a shaded ☐ box please give full details on the back

14 **Do you wish to pay the premium by instalments?** Yes☐ No☐

15 **Declaration and signature**
I declare that to the best of my knowledge and belief the information on this form is true in every respect.
I also declare that if anything on this form was written by another person, he or she acted as my agent for this purpose.
I agree that this proposal and declaration will be the basis of the contract between me and the company.

Signature of all proposers
Date
Date

The company reserves the right to refuse any proposal.

Please continue overleaf

section
A Buildings

16 **Do you require cover under this section?** Yes☐ No☐
If Yes, please give the total floor area of your home in square feet ____ sq. ft.

What amount do you wish to insure?
The guide in the information booklet may help you work out the figure
The lowest we accept is £25,000 £ ____ A

Do you require accidental damage cover?
(not available if any part of the home is lent, let or sub-let) Yes☐ No☐ Y

Is the legal interest of a mortgagee, freeholder or similar to be recorded on the policy? Yes☐ No☐ Y
If Yes, please give name, address and type of interest here or on the back.

section
B Contents

17 **Do you require cover under this section?** Yes☐ No☐
If Yes, what amount do you wish to insure?
This guide in the information booklet may help you work out the figure
Your attention is drawn to the minimum premiums shown in the information booklet. £ ____ B

Does the proposed sum insured include valuable property (as defined in the information booklet):
a worth more than one third of the proposed sum insured? Yes☐ No☐
b over £1,000 for any one article, set or collection? Yes☐ No☐
If you have ticked a shaded ☐ box please give details and values below and continue on the back if necessary.
(Do not include any property that is to be insured under Section C 'All Risks'.)
Please attach a valuation or sales receipt for any item worth more than £1,000.

Do you require accidental damage cover?
(not available if any part of the home is lent, let or sub-let) Yes☐ No☐ Y

section
C 'All Risks'

18 **Do you require cover under this section?** Yes☐ No☐
If Yes, do you wish the sums insured to be index-linked (not applicable to pedal cycles)? Yes☐ No☐

Item 1a. Unspecified personal possessions

19 **Do you require cover under this item?** Yes☐ No☐
If Yes, what amount do you wish to insure?
See information booklet for details before stating the amount you wish to insure
The lowest we accept is £500 £ ____ CA

Item 1b. Clothing (including furs up to 20% of the amount insured or £500 whichever is less)

20 **Do you require cover under this item?** Yes☐ No☐
If Yes, what amount do you wish to insure?
The lowest we accept is £500 £ ____ CB

Fig 18.6 Insurance proposal form

3 Complete the form as far as you are able.
4 Assume that: (a) your home is an owner-occupied house worth £60000; (b) the contents are worth £15000; (c) you live in cost area A (see Fig. 18.7).
5 You can use your own family as a model, or an imaginary family, when answering the questions.
6 Decide if you wish to include *all risks* (read the information in Fig. 18.7 carefully).
7 Consider *accidental damage* cover. Is it too expensive? What *extra* cover is offered?
8 Calculate the *total* premium for: (a) buildings insurance; (b) contents insurance; (c) all risks and accidental damage (if you have decided to include this).
9 Add all the premiums together. Then make a copy of the cheque in Fig. 18.8 and complete it in payment. Don't forget the counterfoil.
10 Using a calculator, calculate the cost per day of insuring your house and contents. Is insurance cover 'value for money'?

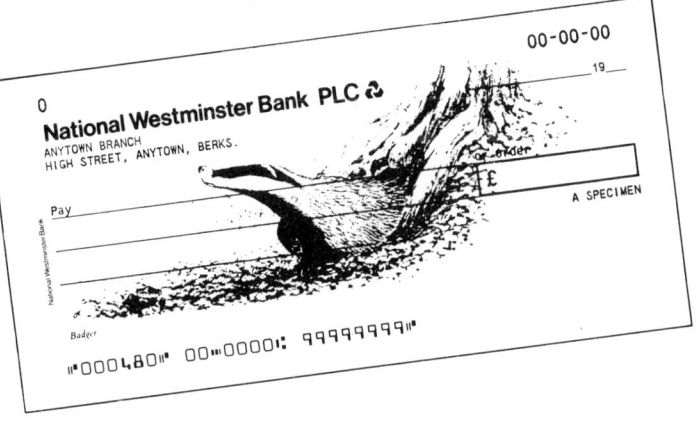

Fig 18.8 Your cheque for payment

Choose the insurance you need from the wide range of cover. These two pages give a guide to the normal costs. Some of the costs shown depend on the area you live in.

section

A Buildings

Covers the buildings of your home.
Cost per £1,000 insured is £1.80 or £2.10 if you include accidental damage cover.

The lowest sum insured we accept is £25,000

section

B Contents

Covers household goods, personal belongings, money and valuable property.

Cost area	Cost per £1,000 insured	Minimum cost
A	£14.00	£140.00
B	£12.50	£125.00
C	£11.00	£110.00
D	£ 9.50	£ 95.00
E	£ 8.00	£ 80.00
F	£ 7.00	£ 70.00
G	£ 5.50	£ 49.50
H	£ 4.50	£ 40.50
I	£ 3.50	£ 31.50

Extra cost for accidental damage cover is £1.70 per £1,000 insured for all costs areas.
Cost for rented furnished and non self-contained accommodation will be quoted on request.

section

C 'All Risks'

Covers valuables and special items against loss or damage anywhere in the world.
High value items may be subject to special terms.

Item 1 Unspecified personal possessions, clothing and named items.

Cost per £100 insured is:
Areas A-C   Area D: £2.50   Area E: £2.20
£3.00   Area G: £1.80   Area H: £1.50
Area F: £2.00
Area I: £1.20

Fig 18.7 Information booklet for domestic insurance

UNIT 18.3
Buying a Motor Vehicle on Credit

Credit and Motor Insurance

Pat, who is 17, wants to go on holiday with a group of friends, all of whom have motor cycles. Pat is attracted by an entry in the local paper (Fig. 18.9).

GRAND PRIX 'CYCLES

GET ON THE ROAD THIS SUMMER

100's of Beautiful Reliable Bikes
Fully Reconditioned – 12 Months Warranty
No Deposit Terms – Lowest Credit Charges
Ride Away Prices – Best in Town
Part Exchanges – Insurance Arranged

FULL M.O.T. INCLUDED

Fig 18.9 The advert Pat found in his local paper

THINGS TO DO

1. Pat needs advice. Discuss with Pat the following phrases used in the local pages advert:
   (a) No deposit terms.
   (b) Lowest credit charges.
   (c) Part exchanges welcomed.
   (d) Insurance arranged.
   (e) Full MOT included.
   (f) 12 months' warranty.

2. The dealer advertises 'Ride Away Prices'. What in your view should be included in this offer: (a) for a new motor cycle, and (b) for a second-hand machine?

3. Pat would have to provide a provisional licence.
   (a) What does the word *provisional* mean?
   (b) Where would Pat obtain such a licence?
   (c) How will Pat's learner status be displayed on the scooter?
   (d) What does Pat need to do to obtain a *full* licence?

4. Discuss with Pat the need for insurance and the implications of the following:
   (a) Cover note.
   (b) Third party, fire and theft.
   (c) Fully comprehensive insurance.
   (d) No-claim bonus.
   (e) MOT.

The credit sale

Pat visits the dealer's showroom and is offered a second-hand machine at £500, on credit terms (hire purchase), if Pat can provide a guarantor to the hire purchase agreement. Pat's father says that hire purchase is expensive and offers to obtain a personal loan from his bank. Pat's mother suggests they use her credit card instead. The following table shows the various forms of finance available to Pat, who wants to spread the loan over two years.

	Monthly payment	No. of Payments	Credit charge/rate of interest	APR
Credit sale agreement	£28.33	24	18% per annum	36.4%
Personal loan	£25.42	24	11% per annum	22.9%
Credit card	£26.50	24	2% per month	26.8%

●THINGS TO DO

1. Calculate the *total* cost of the purchase in each case.

2. What part of that total cost has been charged for credit terms?

3. If Pat chooses to finance the purchase by means of a hire purchase agreement, who could act as a guarantor? Why does a young person of 17 need a guarantor when signing a contract of hire purchase?

4. Imagine you are the motor-cycle dealer. Before Pat signs the hire purchase agreement, what points would you emphasise?

5. Pat finally signs the agreement with Grand Prix Cycles and takes home the new motor bike. But after only a few days, the bike begins to give trouble. A mechanic friend of Pats suspects a transmission fault, suggesting that the machine should never have been allowed on the road in that condition. Advise Pat what to do next.

UNIT 18.4
How Will You Get to Work?

You are very happy to receive a letter from the National Westminster Bank appointing you to a full-time cashier's job at a branch about ten miles from your home. You are also happy to find that there is a frequent bus service (almost door to door) and that the train service (a short walk at each end) is also convenient and fast. Both of your parents also commute (travel to work). They suggest that you buy a small moped, because this may be a cheaper and better way of travelling than by bus or train.

THINGS TO DO

The class should now split into four groups. Each group should investigate *one* of the following:

1 *Travel by bus* (Fig. 18.10) The group should work out the cost of a typical ten-mile journey by your local bus services. Is a daily fare cheapest or are there season tickets to cut costs? What are the problems of season tickets, and is insurance advisable in case of loss? Can a season be used on only one route? Is it available for use at weekends? What is the *annual* cost of the cheapest ticket?

2 *Travel by train* (Fig. 18.11) This group should find out the cost of a daily ticket or a season over a typical ten-mile journey. Much the same questions arise as above, and your inquiries should seek to resolve any problems. How frequent is the service? Are the trains comfortable or are they packed at rush hours? What is the *annual* cost of the cheapest ticket?

Fig 18.11 Travel by train

3 *Travel by moped* (Fig. 18.12) This group should consider the cost of purchase and the possible life of the moped. New or second-hand? Cost of petrol, oil, maintenance, insurance, road fund licence? Is safe parking available? Use at weekends? Alternatives in case of breakdown? What is the *annual* cost of your moped to and from work?

Fig 18.10 Travel by bus

Fig 18.12 Personal transport – by moped

4 *Other alternatives* You own a bicycle. Is this a realistic alternative, considering your job? Some athletes run to work, and many others cycle. Once started, you may discover a colleague who will give you a lift on three days a week. What are the chances of sharing a flat over the bank? Is this realistic from a financial point of view?

You may find the following table of use in your research. You will need to collect or calculate the following:

Each group should make a verbal presentation of its findings to the class (5 minutes each group). A vote should then be taken on: (a) the best presentation, and (b) the most convincing case for the method of travel involved.

Finally, suppose your take-home pay (i.e. the amount remaining after all deductions) is £87. What percentage of that amount will be spent on travel to and from work by the method you studied? And what *amount* will remain for other purposes?

In your calculations, remember that it is usual to have four weeks' annual holiday, and banks do not open on bank holidays. Otherwise assume a five-day week.

Bus and train	*Moped*
• Bus or train timetable showing frequency of service and times for journey. • Cost of single/return fares each day. • Availability of season tickets and cost of weekly, monthly, annual season. • Possible cost of insurance on (say) annual returns. NB The bank will probably lend you the money for an annual season and charge 5% interest on the loan. The total will then be repaid by a weekly deduction from pay. • Does a season ticket entitle you to travel in the evenings or at weekends? Is this an advantage? • Is a season ticket transferable to another person or to another route?	• Brochure of machine showing miles per gallon, etc. • Cost of gear, licences and insurance. • A calculation of the amount of petrol/oil to be used. • Possible cost of servicing/repairs on annual basis. • Parking charges, if any, plus incidentals like a driving test. NB The bank will probably lend you the money required for a new moped and charge 5%, the total repayable over two years. • What *value* do you place upon having your own transport in the evenings and at weekends? Assume that, once you have passed your test, you can carry passengers.

UNIT 18·5
Doing Market Research

Subject: Gravy thickeners/seasoners: (a) Oxo Cubes; (b) Bovril Cubes; (c) Bisto Granules (Fig. 18.13). The object of the survey is to test market response to advertising and to determine consumer preferences.

Method
First of all, ask permission from the manager to set up a table or stall in the area of a supermarket on a Friday evening or Saturday morning (the peak shopping times). Wear identification badges with your name and/or have a small stand with the school or college name clearly shown.

It is essential to ask the questions exactly as written and mark the relevant boxes when the answers are given. Approach people on their way into the shop, and remember to be polite. You could say, 'Do you mind answering a few questions? It will only take a moment.' Your clients will probably mostly be female, but try to spot some male cooks too. If some people refuse to co-operate, don't worry – even professional researchers experience lack of interest sometimes.

Manner
It is a good idea to do some practice interviews on your family. Take the interview calmly. Don't rush the person. Be bright and cheerful. Above all, thank the person warmly when the interview is complete.

Equipment
Compile your own questionnaire based on the one provided in Fig. 18.14. You will need multiple copies – use a fresh sheet for each interview. Try to use a proper interviewer's clip-board. Have more than one pencil handy. Don't forget that you need examples of the products, or at least the boxes as visual aids.

Conclusions
Aim for 100 or so completed questionnaires. Then analyse these replies so as to answer the following questions:

1. Is one of the products more popular than the other two?
2. Do you feel that there is a reason for this preference?
3. How many of your clients had tried the alternative products only to return to their preferred thickener/seasoner?
4. Does your survey give any indication of the reason for any preference?
5. Was the preferred product advertised regularly on TV?
6. Did your clients feel that advertising had influenced their choice?

Finally
1. Test product preferences and the result of your survey by asking the supermarket manager to identify the best-sellers. He or she will respond if your approach is polite.
2. This kind of research can be used for soap powders/detergents, coffee/tea, breakfast cereals and other products. Adapt the questionnaire to suit another range of products.

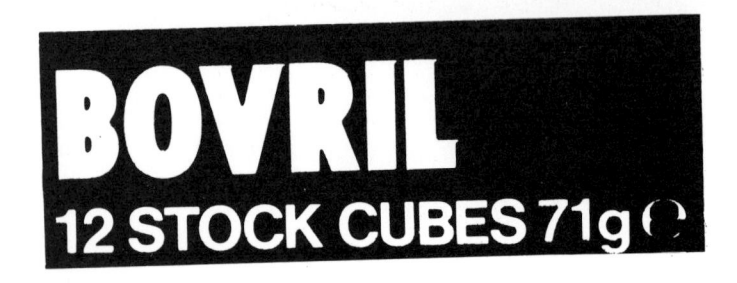

Fig 18.13 Doing market research

```
┌─────────────────────────────────────────────────────────────────────┐
│                    MARKET RESEARCH QUESTIONNAIRE                    │
│                                                                     │
│                 SUBJECT : GRAVY THICKENERS/SEASONERS                │
│                                                                     │
│           (a) OXO CUBES    (b) BOVRIL CUBES    (c) BISTO GRANULES   │
│                                                                     │
│   NB: It is essential to display examples of each to obtain         │
│       realistic results.                                            │
└─────────────────────────────────────────────────────────────────────┘
```

(i)   Do you ever use any of these products?
      (point to examples).   YES ☐   NO ☐

(ii) If you get a 'NO' answer - say - 'What product to you use to
      thicken and season your gravy ?'

      (a) Write answer.
      (b) If none, say: 'Thank you for your help'.

(iii) Assuming a 'YES' answer - say, 'Which of the three products do
      you prefer ?'

              (a) OXO CUBES   ☐
              (b) BOVRIL CUBES   ☐   NB: (Tick one box only)
              (c) BISTO GRANULES   ☐

(iv) Have you ever used either of the other products?

              (a) OXO CUBES   ☐
              (b) BOVRIL CUBES   ☐   NB: (Tick no more than
              (c) BISTO GRANULES   ☐   two boxes)

(v)   Do you feel that your preferred thickener is superior to the
      other two?

              YES ☐   NO ☐   NB: (Tick one box only)

(vi) Is that preference due to:

                      PRICE ☐   TASTE   ☐
                      HABIT ☐   CONVENIENCE ☐

(vii) Have you ever seen your preferred
      product advertised on TV?   YES ☐   NO ☐

      Regularly?   YES ☐   NO ☐

(viii) Do you feel that advertising generally influences your shopping
       habits?

                                                   YES ☐   NO ☐

At the end, say: 'Thank you for your help - enjoy your weekend.'

Fig 18.14   Example questionnaire

● UNIT 18.6
Using Graphics and Illustrations

Information can be presented in many different ways. Pictures, diagrams or charts (all known as *graphics* or *illustration*) can usually be understood more quickly and more effectively than words. Illustrations can make dull facts and figures eye-catching and of interest. This assignment asks you to interpret different types of graphics and then to construct some of your own.

Graphs

Graphs provide an easy way of showing the changes in something over a given period of time The graph in Fig. 18.15 shows the percentage rate of inflation over 18 years. Look at it carefully and then answer the following questions:

1. Is the rate of inflation rising or falling?
2. In which year did inflation reach 25 per cent?
3. Write a sentence describing the pattern of inflation during the years in question.
4. How could this graph be improved to make its message clearer?
5. Research the current rate of inflation. Extend your graph.

Bar charts

Bar charts are used to show the comparison between things at different times or in different places. The bar chart in Fig. 18.16 shows the number of passengers using different stations in the rush-hour. Look at the bar chart and then answer the following questions:

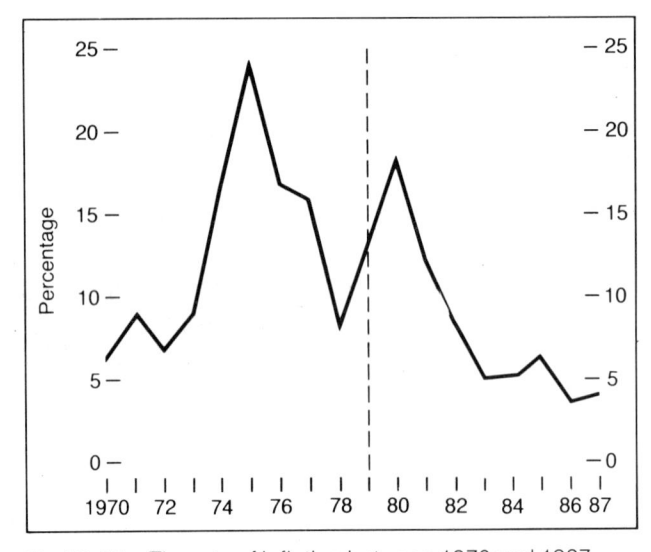

Fig 18.15 The rate of inflation between 1970 and 1987, shown as a graph

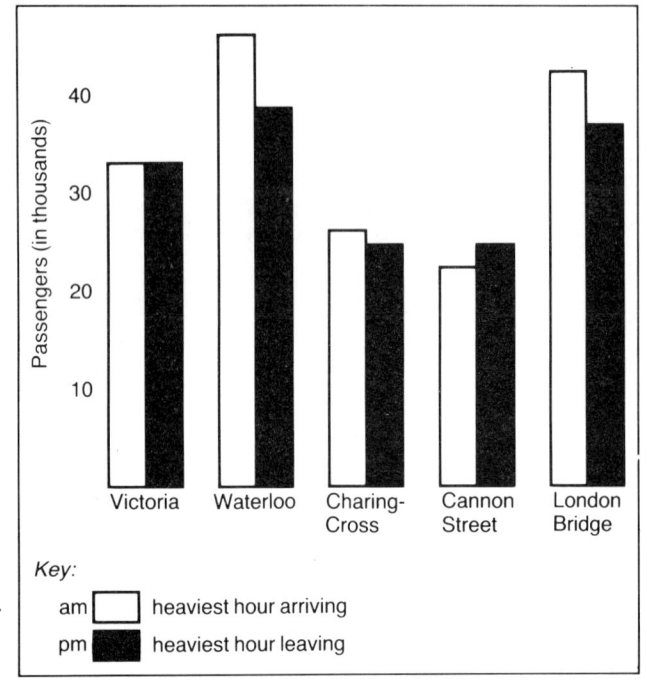

Fig 18.16 The number of rush-hour passengers at different stations, shown as a bar chart

1. Which station has the greatest number of passengers in the morning?
2. Which station has exactly the same number of passengers both in the morning and in the evening?
3. At which station is there the greatest difference between the number of people arriving and leaving?
4. Draw a *table* to show the number of passengers using each station both in the morning and in the evening. Is the table more or less useful than the bar chart?
5. What might the information given by this bar chart be used for?

Pictograms

Pictograms can use small drawings known as *symbols*. In the example in Fig. 18.17 we can see how many telephone calls are received by one person in one week. To make it simpler to interpret, each telephone symbol stands for 5 telephone calls. Small parts of the telephone symbols are used to show less than 5 calls received.

1. Study the pictogram and then copy out and complete the table below.

	Monday	Tuesday	Wednesday	Thursday	Friday
Number of calls received					

● 148

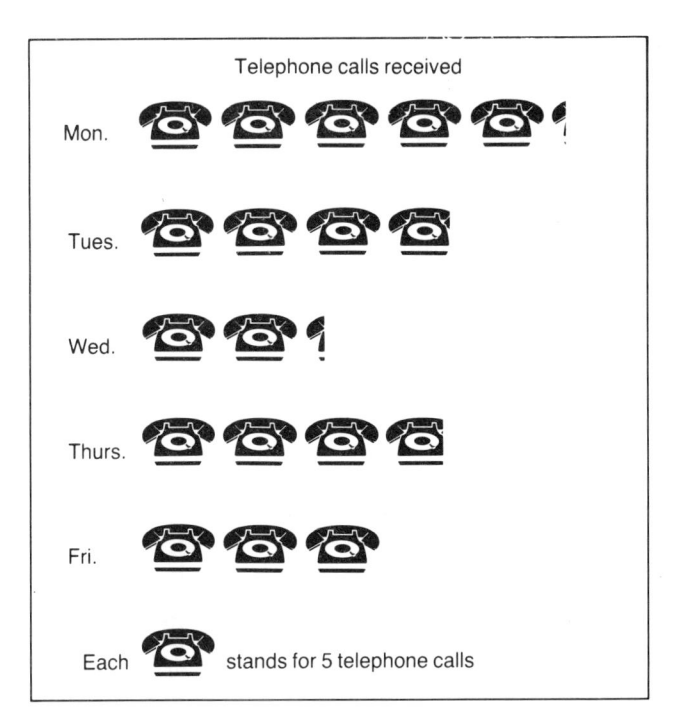

Fig 18.17 One person's incoming telephone calls during one week, shown as a pictogram

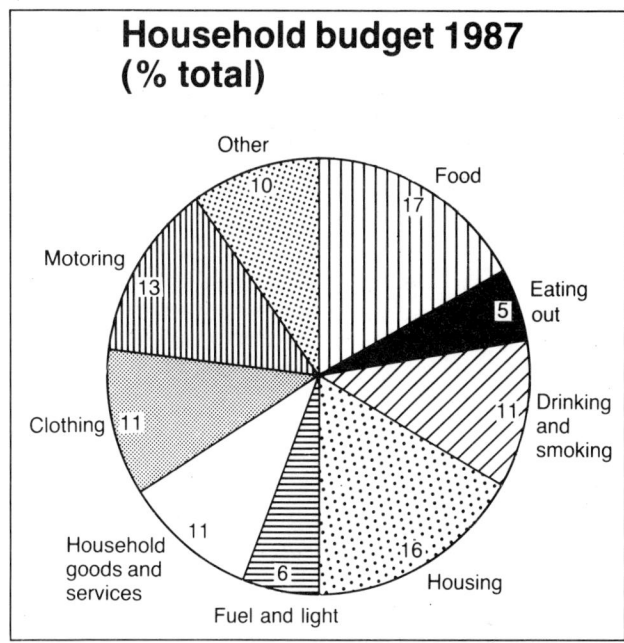

Fig 18.18 An average household's budget spending, shown as a pie chart

2 Keep a record of the number of phone calls received in your home over a week. Use a pictogram to illustrate this information.
3 This information could have been given in a bar chart. What advantage does the pictogram have over the bar chart method?
4 Suggest different symbols to represent: (a) money spent; (b) records bought; (c) books read; (d) canned drink drunk; (e) sweets eaten.
5 Think of a subject to survey. Illustrate the results using pictogram symbols of your own choice.

Pie charts

Pie charts are used to show how something is divided up. In the example in Fig. 18.18 we can see what percentage of an average household budget is spent on different household items. Look at the pie chart before answering the questions:

1 Which expense takes up the highest percentage of the household budget?
2 Food, eating out, drinking and smoking and housing each make up what proportion of this household's budget?
3 Write out the information given in Fig. 18.18 in the form of a list. Put the items of expenditure in order – highest at the top. Is this list as useful at giving the breakdown of the household budget as the pie chart? Give reasons.
4 If the household's monthly income is £1200, how much is spent on rent/mortgage payments?
5 Discuss where the money goes with your family. Try to draw up a pie chart to show your family's outgoings in a similar way (your teacher will explain how to measure the segments).

●THINGS TO DO

1 Choose the best method of showing the following to interest your readers. You may need to do some survey work first.
   (a) The total number of hours spent watching TV on each day of the week in your home.
   (b) The ways in which you spend your allowance or pocket-money.
   (c) The different ways in which you and your classmates travel to school or college.
2 Start a collection of graphs, bar charts, pictograms and pie charts from newspapers and magazines. For each example write a brief explanation of what is being shown. Mount a wall chart.
3 Fig. 18.19 is a variation on a pictogram. Using your own local authority, show their income and expenditure in a suitable way.

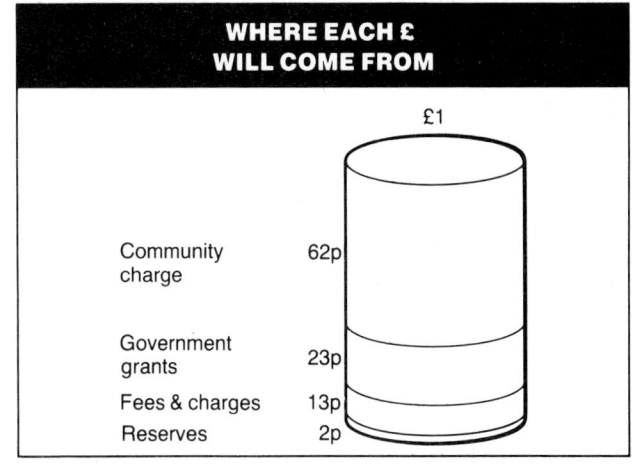

Fig 18.19 Local authority budget, shown in graphic form

149

Index

A1 at Lloyd's, 91
acceptance house, 74–5
Access card, 21
account period, 80
acknowledgement of order, 38
Acts of Parliament
   Bank of England (1946), 72
   Consumer Credit (1974), 79
   Fair Trading (1973), 78
   Food and Drugs (1955), 111
   Partnership (1890), 49
   Sale of Goods (1893), 111
   Sale of Goods (1979), 111
   Sunday Trading (1987), 26
   Supply of Goods (Implied Terms) (1973), 111
   Supply of Goods and Services (1982), 111
   Trade Descriptions (1968–72), 111
actuaries, 88
ad valorum duty, 125
adding value, 96
advertising, 44–7
   codes of practice, 44, 110–11
   consumer, 44–5
   image-building through brand names, 46
   market research, 46–7
   media, 44
   promotional, 47
   trade, 44
Advertising Standards Authority, 44, 45(fig), 78
advice note, 38
agency services, Post Office, 104
agents
   insurance, 87
   shipping, 123
agents of production, 8
agreed price, 82
Agricultural Revolution (1750–1800), 9
air charter, 83
air mail, 104, 105(fig)
air traffic control, 103
air transport, 102–3
airlines
   independent, 102
   state, 102
Ambassador, 127
American Express charge card, 21
Annual Percentage Rate (APR), 78
annuity, 84
appreciation/depreciation, *see under* capital
arbitration service, 83
assessor (loss adjuster), 84
assets, 58
Association of British Travel Agents, 114
Association of Estate Agents, 113
Association of Mail Order Publishers, 44
assurance policies, 85

at the price agreed, 80
automatic vending machine, 29
automation, 13

bad debts, 66
balance of payments, deficit/surplus, 118
balance sheet, 58–9
Baltic Exchange, 82, 83
bank(s) (banking), 64–7
   building societies compared, 70
   computer use, 12
   credit, 42
   High Street, 64
   joint stock, 64
   merchant, 74–5, 76(fig)
   statement, 65
   types of account, 64
Bank of England, 72–3
Bankers' Automated Clearing Ltd (BACS), 69
Bankers' Clearing House, 68–9
banking, international, 74
barter, 41
bear, 80
benefits, state, 135
betterment, 84
betting tax, 137
bid-offer spread, 80
bill of exchange, 74–5, 123(fig)
   endorsed, 74
   discounted, 75
bill of lading, 123, 124(fig)
black box, 103
'bleep', 108
board, public corporation, 50
board of directors, 48
bonded warehouse, 125
borrowing, 20–1; *see also* credit
brand
   awareness (product identification), 46
      leaders, 26, 44
   names, 46
branded goods, 110
British Coal, 50
British Overseas Trade Board (BOTB), 117
British Standards Institute (BSI), 113
British Telecom, 102, 108
British Toy Manufacturers' Association, 114
broker
   commodity, 82
   insurance, 87
budget account, 64
budgeting, 16–17
building societies, 52, 70
bull, 80

Business Advisory Centres, 134
business growth, 128–9
business insurance, 87–8
business interruption, 87
business organisations
    private sector, 48–9, 54
    public sector, 50–1, 54
buyer, chain store, 32

call bird, 26
call option, 82
canals, 98
capital
    authorised (registered), 58
    growth (appreciation/depreciation), 18
    investment, 62, 118
    issued, 58
    start-up, 56
    sum (principal), 21
    working (employed), 59(fig)
capitalist economy, 54
cash, 41
    card, 64
    transfer, 66
cash and carry, 24–5
cash flow, 60
'cash on the nail', 41
caveat emptor, 111
Ceefax, 108
Central Bankers' Clearing House, 68
certificate of insurance, 123
certificate of origin, 123
chain store buyers, 32
chain stores, 31
    arising from mergers, 33
    voluntary, 30
chairman/person, 50
Chambers of Commerce, 134
Chancellor of the Exchequer, 72
Channel Tunnel, 93, 94(fig)
charge cards, 21, 42, 43(fig)
charities, 54
chartering, 83
cheque, 27, 39, 42 (fig), 64(fig)
cheque
    book, 41, 64
    clearing, 68; *see also* Bankers' Clearing House
    fraud, 27
cheque, personal, 64, 104
cheque guarantee card, 27
choice, definition, 62
Citizens' Advice Bureau (CAB), 113
City, 91, 118
city centre shopping, 36
Civil Aviation Authority (CAA), 103
Clearing House Automated Payment System (CHAPS), 69
coastal routes, 98
code of fair practice, 110
codes of conduct, trade, 115(fig)
collateral, 21, 72

commercial
    documents, 38–9
    jargon, 38–9
commercial services, 23
commission, public corporation, 50
Commission, 117
Commissioner, 127
commodity
    grading, 82
    sampling, 82
commodity broker, 82
commodity market, 82
Common Agricultural Policy (CAP), 55, 117
Common Market *see* European Community
communications
    London Docklands, 108(fig), 133
    Post Office, 194–6
    technological advances, 12
    Telecommunications, 107–9
communist economy, 54
Community Charge (poll tax), 137
company
    holding (parent)/conglomerate, 49
    private limited, 48
    public limited (PLC), 49
company law, 48
competition
    advertising use, 46
    exclusivity, 26
    pricing/non-pricing, 26
computer use
    banks (banking), 12, 68
    debt settling, 43
    Post Office, 104
    retail trade, 12–13, 33, 34
    Stock Exchange, 80
conglomerate, 49
connect card, 42
consequential loss, 87
construction industries, 22
consular invoice, 123
consumer advertising, 44–5
consumer advice centres, 113
consumer protection, 78, 110–11
    advertising codes of practice, 44, 110–11
    enforcement, 113–15
    legislation, 111
    mass media, 113
    professional/trade organisations, 114
Consumers' Association, 113
containerisation, 93
contingent risks, 87
continuous credit (reducing account), 78
contract note, 80, 81(fig)
cooling off period, 78
co-operative, 33, 53, 54
Co-operative Bank, 33
Co-operative Development Agency, 53
Co-opcrative Insurance Service, 33
co-operative movement, 52–3
Co-operative Wholesale Society, 53

corner shop, 36
corporation
    multinational (transnational), 49
    public *see* nationalised industries
corporation tax, 136
copywriter, advertising, 44
Council of Ministers, 117
Court of Justice, 117
credit
    account, 38, 39, 64–5
    card, 21, 42, 43(fig); *see also* Electronic Funds Transfer
    facilities, 20, 62, 77; *see also* cooling off period
    letter, 125
    note, 39
    rating, 79
    reference agencies, 78–9
    sale calculation, 78
    trading, 27, 38; *see also* mail order
    transfer, 69
credit, bank, 42
credit, continuous, 78
Crown post offices, 70, 104
cum divi – ex divi, 80
current account, 64
Customs and Excise, 125
customs declaration, 123
customs duty (tariff), 119, 125, 136

dangerous substances, 111
Datapost, 194
debenture, 56; *see also* yield
debt, bad, 66
debt crisis, 121
debt settling, computerised, 43
delivery note, 38
demand, 8, 54–5, 55(figs), 63
Department of Trade and Industry, 119
department stores, 33
deposit, 64
    bank use of, 65
deposit (savings) account, 16, 64
depression, economic, 128
designer, advertising, 44
de-skilled crafts, 10
developed ability, 7
development areas, 130–3
Diners Club charge card, 21
direct
    buying, 25, 34
    selling, 28
direct debit, 42, 43, 66
direct intervention, 128
Director General of Fair Trading, 78, 79, 113
discount store, 34
discounted bill of exchange, 75
distribution, chain of, 22–3; *see also* transport
distributive trade, 28
diversified economy, 122
dividend, 18, 56, 59
    cum divi – ex divi, 80

    warrant, 80, 81(fig)
door-to-door selling, 29
drawings, 60
duties, 137
    customs, 119, 125, 136

economic activity, level of, 7
economy
    capitalist, 54
    communist, 54
    diversified, 122
    government intervention in, 134–5
    market, 54
    mixed, 54
    planned, 54
    specialised, 9, 122
    state-owned sector *see* public sector
    voluntary sector, 54
education, 135
Electricity Consultative Council, 114
Electronic Funds Transfer at Point of Sale (EFTPOS), 43
electronic point of sale, 34
embassy, 127
employment levels, 13
Employment Training (ET), 134
endorsement, bill of exchange, 74
endowment policy, 19, 85
English Civil War (1642–6), 90
Enterprise Allowance Scheme, 134
enterprise zones, 130–3
entrepôt trade, 100
entrepreneur, 8
equal opportunities, 10, 11(fig)
errors and omissions excepted, 39
estimate, 39
European Community (Common Market), 55, 111, 116–17
European Monetary System (EMS/the Snake), 117
European Parliament, 117
excise duties, 100–1
export(s), 118–20
Export Credits Guarantee Department (ECGD), 119
exported goods, 118
exported services, 118
exporting methods, 119–20

'face lift', 131
factoring service, 66
factors of production, 54
fair trading, 78, 113
ferries, 95–6
    roll-on/roll-off, 100
finance
    business, 56–61
    personal, 14–21
finance houses, 77
financial planning, 16
Financial Times (FT) Index, 80
finished goods, 7

fire insurance, 87
First World War (1914–18), 102
fixed amount, 66
float, Britain's pound, 117
floor, 80
food tasting, 34
foreign currency reserve, 122
foreign exchange market, 74
foreign policy, British, 126–7
franchise, 30
free (franco), 125
'free goods', 128, 135
Freeports, 100–1
Freepost, 104
freight ferries, 95–6
freight (goods) transportation, 92
Friendly Societies, 52
future price, 82
futures market, 82

General Agreement on Tariffs and Trade (GATT), 119
general public, 110
gilt-edged stocks/gilts, 73
Girobank, National, 70–1
global village, 12
gold reserve, 122
goods (freight) transportation, 92
government bonds (gilt-edged stocks/gilts), 73
government services, 54
government spending, 137
grading, commodity, 82
Great Britain
   domestic/national policy, 128–9
   foreign policy, 126–7
Great Fire of London (1666), 87
Green Pound, 117
guarantee, 111

harbours, 98–100
'hard sell' advertising, 45
'have now, pay later', 38, 62; *see also* hire purchase
head post office, 104
health service, 135
heavy industry, decline, 133
hedging, 82
'high and dry', 98
High Commission, 127
'high tech', 10, 133
hire purchase, 20, 77–8; *see also* 'have now, pay later'
hiring (leasing), 78, 79(fig)
holding (parent) company (conglomerate), 49
housing association, 53
hypermarket (superstore), 34, 36

3 i's scheme, 134
Imperial preference, 126–7
import(s), 118–20

import licence, 123
imported goods, 118
imported services, 118
impulse buying, 34
in kind, 127
income, 14
income tax, 15, 136
incorporation, 48
indemnity, 84
independent airline, 102
Independent Broadcasting Authority, 114
indirect taxation, 136
industrial changes, 10
Industrial Common Ownership Movement (ICOM), 53
Industrial Revolution, 7, 9, 98
industries
   high-tech, 10, 133
   nationalised (public corporations), 50
industry, location, 10–11, 130
industry sectors
   primary, 8
   secondary, 9
   tertiary, 9
inertia selling, 28
inflation rate, 134–5
inner-city decay, 130
insurable interest, 84
insurance
   agents, 86
   certificate of, 123
   claims, 84
   companies, 87, 88
      investment, 88
   policy, 84
   premium, 84, 87
   proposal form, 84
insurance, business, 87–8
insurance, personal, 84–5
Intelpost, 104
intercontinental travel, 102
interdependence, town/country, 7
interest, 16
interest rates, 72
international banking, 74
international co-operation, 7
international subscriber dialling (ISD), 107
international television links, 107
international trade, 116–25
   documentation, 123–5
   exports, 118–20
   imports, 118–20
   see also overseas trade
international trade balance, 121–2
international waterways, 98
'in/into the red', 119
investment, 18–19, 62
invisible earnings, 83, 91(fig)
invisible exports, 91, 118
invisible trade, 91, 118
invoice, 39
   consular, 123

itinerant trader, definition, 28
itinerant trading, 28–9

joint stock banks, 104
junk mail, 28

Kellogg's advertising campaign, 44
kite mark, British Standards Institute, 113

labour intensive, 126
laissez-faire, 128
leasing (hiring), 78, 79(fig)
'leave well alone', 128
legal tender, 41
legislation
   business, 128
   consumer, 78, 111
'let the buyer beware' (*caveat emptor*), 111
letter(s), 104
letter of enquiry, 38
level of economic activity, 7
liabilities, 58
liability
   limited, 48
   public, 87
   claims, 88
   unlimited, 90
licences, 137
life assurance, 85
limited liability, 48
liner, 83
liquidity, 60
Lloyd's Coffee House, 90
Lloyd's List, 91
Lloyd's Log, 91
Lloyd's of London, 90
   agents, 91
   members (names), 90
   Register of Shipping, 91
loan(s)
   business, 56
   personal, 20–1
   security, 21
loan guarantee scheme, 134
local government services, 54, 137
logo, 44
Lombards, 87
London City Airport, 131(fig), 132
London Docklands, 130–2
London Docklands Development Corporation (LDDC), 131–2
London Metal Exchange, 82
long-distance haulage, 96
loss adjuster (assessor), 84
loss leader, 26

mail order, 28

Mail Order Protection Scheme, 113
Mail Order Publishers' Authority, 44
Mail Order Traders' Association, 44
Manchester Business Venture, 134
manifest, 123
manufacturer's label, 110
manufacturing industries, 22
marine insurance, 87
market(s)
   Baltic Exchange (ships/aircraft), 83
   commodity, 80–3
      futures, 82
   foreign exchange, 74
   money, 75, 118
   produce, 24, 28(fig), 29, 36
   share, 80–1
   stocks, 80–1
   wholesale, 24
market-maker, 80
market economy, 54
market rate of exchange, 72
market research, 46–7
mass media consumer protection, 113
material facts, 84
measures/weights, 111
media advertising, 44
   buyers, 45
Memorandum and Articles of Association, 48
merchant banks, 74–5, 76(fig)
Mercury Communications, 108
merger, 75, 128
micro-electronics, 12–13
miniaturisation, 13
mixed economy, 54
money market, 75, 118
money values, 63
Monopolies Commission, 128–9
monopoly, 107
mortgage, 21
multinational influence, 11
multinational (transnational) corporation, 49, 121

names, 90
National Debt, 72–3
National Debt Commissioners, 73
National Girobank, 70–1
National Insurance (NI) contributions, 15, 137
national savings, 71
National Telephone Systems, 133
nationalised industries (public corporations), 50–1, 54
needs, 8
New Covent Garden Market, 24
new towns, 128
non-pricing competition, 26
North Sea oil/gas, 11
North-South divide, 10

occupational change, 10, 11(fig)
Office of Fair Trading, 113

oil revenues, 121
ombudsman, definition, 113
    banking, 66–7
one-trip shopping (out-of-town centres), 36
open 'all hours', 26, 36
options, commodity dealing, 82
Oracle, 108
order of goods, 38
ordinary shares, 56
out-of-town centre (one-trip shopping), 36
overdraft, 21, 56
overtime, 14
Owen, Robert (1771–1858), 53
own-brand products, 24
overseas aid, 127
overseas trade, 66
    competition limitations, 121
    jargon, 125
    re-exporting, 101, 118
    see also international trade

page, teletext, 108
parcels, 104
part charter, 83
partnership, 48
Pay As You Earn (PAYE), 15, 136
pay policies, 134
pay slip, 14–15
personal identification number (PIN), 64–5
personal insurance, 84–5
petrol station, 29
photographer, advertising, 44
planned economy, 54
plastic money (credit cards), 21, 42, 43(fig)
poll tax (Community Charge), 137
pooling of risk, 85
    business, 87
ports, 98–101
postcodes, 104, 106
Post Office, 104–6
    agency services, 104
    banking services, 70–1
Post Office (PO Box) number, 104
Post Office Users' National Council (POUNC), 106
preference shares, 56
Premium Bonds, 16, 71
prepacked food, 111
Prestel, 108
price, 63, 82
pricing competition, 26
principal (capital sum), 21
private firms, 54
privatisation, 50
product identification (brand awareness), 46
production agents, 8
Professional, Industrial and Commercial Updating (PICKUP), 134
profit, gross/net, 60
proposal form, insurance, 84
prospectus, 56

public corporation *see* nationalised industries
Public Health Department, 113
public liability insurance, 87
    claims, 88
public sector, 50–1, 126

quota, 125
quotation, 38

railways, 92–3, 94(fig)
rates, 137
raw materials, 7
recorded delivery, 104
reducing account, 78
re-exporting, 101, 118
Regional Development Grants, 134
registered post, 104
Registrar of Joint Stock Companies, 48, 56, 58
reinsurance, 87–8
relocate, 130
Retail Standards Authority, 114
retail trade, 23
    atomsphere selling aid, 36
    buying from manufacturer, 25, 34
    changing patterns, 36
    computer use, 33, 34
    large-scale, 32–5
    location, 36
    pilfering prevention, 34
    small-scale, 30–1
reward, 8
risks
    business, 87
    personal, 84
    pooling of, 85, 87
    uninsurable, 84
risk-takers (entrepreneurs) 87
riverbus, 132(fig)
rivers, 98
road(s)
    distribution of goods, 95
    passenger traffic, 95
road fund licence, 137
Robinson Crusoe, living like, 6
Rochdale Pioneers, 52
roll-on/roll-off (RORO) ferries, 100
Room, the, 90
'round the clock' retailing, 28
Royal Charter 1694, 72
Royal Mail, 104, 105(fig)

safe-deposit, 66
salaries/wages, 14–15
sales promotion, 26
sampling
    commodity, 82
    market research, 47

satellites, 107
Save As You Earn, 16
saving, 16–17, 18–19, 20(fig)
savings (deposit) account, 16, 64
savings stamps, 71
sea transport, 100
seasonal crops, 121
Second World War (1939–45), 73, 90, 102, 128
Secretary of State for Trade and Industry, 51
security
    against loans, 21
    collateral, 21
self-insurance, 88
'sell by' date stamp, 110
selling party, 28
settlement days, 80
share market, 80–1
share(s), 18, 80,
    certificate, 80, 81(fig)
    face value, 56
    issue, 56, 58, 75
    offer for sale (prospectus), 56
    preference/ordinary, 56
shipping agent, 123
Shipping Index, 9
shopping centre, 36
shopping mall, 36
shopping precinct, 36
small businesses, 19
small claims court, 14
Small Firms Service, 134
Smiles, Samuel (1812–1904), 52
Smithfield Meat Market, 24
Snake, the 117
society of underwriters, 90
'soft sell' advertising, 45, 47
sole proprietor (trader), 48, 49(fig)
Sony Walkman, 13
sort code, 68
special delivery, 104
special offer (call bird/loss leader), 26, 30
special short take off and landing aircraft (STOLPORT), 133
specialist, 6
    retailer, 30
specialist economy, 9, 122
specific duty, 125
specimen signature, 64
spending choice, 62
spending worth, 62
spot price, 82
stag, 80
stamp duty, 137
standing order, 42, 43, 66
state airline, 102
state benefits, 135
statement of account, 39
statistics, 122
sterling value, 118–19
    floating, 117
stock, 60

turnover, 60–1
Stock Exchange (floor), 80
stockmarket jargon, 80
stocks, 80–1
    gilt-edged/gilts, 73
    undated, 73
storage, 22
sub-post office, 104
subscriber trunk dialling (STD), 107
subsidies, state, 51
Sunday trading, 26
Sunrise Industries, 133
supermarket, 34
superstore (hypermarket), 34, 36
supply and demand, 8, 54–5, 55(figs)

take over, 75, 128
tariff *see under* duties
tariff houses, 85
taxation, 135, 136–7
technological changes, 12–13
Telecom Tower, 107(fig)
telecommunications, 107
telephones, 107
    cellular, 12
    commercial radio link, 108
teletext, 108
television licence 137
tender, 39, 120
    legal, 41
term policy, 85
terms of trade, 121
3 i's scheme, 134
time charter, 83
title (ownership), 125
tolls, 95
town centre shopping, 36
town hall, 113
trade, entrepôt, 100
trade, international, 116–25
trade balance, 121–2
trade unions, 52
trading standards officers, 79
training schemes, 134
tramp steamer, 83
transnational (multinational) corporation, 49
transport
    air, 102–3
    chain of distribution, 22–3
    freight ferries, 95–6
    railway, 92–3, 94(fig)
    roads, 95
    technological advances, 12
    waterways, 98–101
Transport International Routier (TIR), 96
Transport Users' Consultative Council, 114
travelling (itinerant) sales, 28–9
travelling shops, 28
Treasury bill sale, 73

Treaty of Rome (1957), 116
turnover, stock, 60–1

updated government stocks, 73
underwriting, 75, 87
   society of, 90
Underwriting Room (the Room), 90
uninsurable risks, 84–5
unit trusts, 80
units of labour, 9
unlimited liability, 90
'utmost good faith', 91

value/'value for money', 63
Value Added Tax (VAT), 39, 136
value of £ *see* sterling value
varying amount, 66
vending machine, automatic, 29
Visa card, 21
visible trade, 118
voluntary protection, 110
voluntary sector, 54
voyage charger, 83

wages/salaries, 14–15
'wages spiral', 135
wants, 8, 62
warehousing, 22
warranties, 111
watchdogs, 113, 114
water transport, 98–101
waterways, international, 98
weights/measures, 111
Which magazine, 113, 114(fig)
'white goods', 34
whole life policy, 8
wholesale market, 24
wholesale trade, 24–5
William III, king (d 1702), 72
withdrawal, 64–5
working aircraft, 102–3
working (employed) capital, 59(fig)

yield, 57
Youth Training Scheme (YTS), 134

zero-rated goods/services, 136